Elizabeth P. Quintero

Critical Literacy in Early Childhood Education

Artful Story and the Integrated Curriculum

PETER LANG
New York • Washington, D.C./Baltimore • Bern
Frankfurt am Main • Berlin • Brussels • Vienna • Oxford

Library of Congress Cataloging-in-Publication Data

Quintero, Elizabeth P.
Critical literacy in early childhood education:
artful story and the integrated curriculum / Elizabeth P. Quintero.
p. cm. — (Rethinking childhood; v. 44)
Includes bibliographical references.
1. Language arts (Early childhood) 2. Literacy—Social aspects.
3. Critical pedagogy. 4. Storytelling. I. Title.
LB1139.5.L35Q55   372.6—dc22   2009007196
ISBN 978-1-4331-0613-2 (hardcover)
ISBN 978-1-4331-0612-5 (paperback)
ISSN 1086-7155

Bibliographic information published by **Die Deutsche Bibliothek**.
Die Deutsche Bibliothek lists this publication in the "Deutsche
Nationalbibliografie"; detailed bibliographic data is available
on the Internet at http://dnb.ddb.de/.

The paper in this book meets the guidelines for permanence and durability
of the Committee on Production Guidelines for Book Longevity
of the Council of Library Resources.

© 2009 Elizabeth P. Quintero
Peter Lang Publishing, Inc., New York
29 Broadway, 18th floor, New York, NY 10006
www.peterlang.com

Printed in the United States of America

Critical Literacy in
Early Childhood Education

Rethinking Childhood

Joe L. Kincheloe and Gaile Cannella
General Editors

Vol. 44

PETER LANG
New York • Washington, D.C./Baltimore • Bern
Frankfurt am Main • Berlin • Brussels • Vienna • Oxford

To

Guillermo R. Quintero
Alejandro D. Quintero
Rafael R. Quintero

My three sons, who continually remind me of the importance of critical, personal story, and keep me focused on what really matters.

CONTENTS

ACKNOWLEDGMENTS

I first want to thank dear friends and mentors, Joe Kincheloe and Shirley Steinberg who have supported me, and so many critical pedagogists, over the years.

I am indebted to early childhood teacher education students and teachers in New York City, Minnesota, and Southern California for inspiration and for their work in critical pedagogy with young learners. A special thanks to Jacqueline Brechbill, Deanna Ochoa, Danielle Rivera, Julie Raplere, and Anna Izaguirre. I also thank Mary Kay Rummel, dear friend and poet of problem-posing, and Mary and Tom Gallant, advisors in many things.

CHAPTER ONE
Introduction

We live today with multiple representations, some we call science, some we call art, precise, abstract, vivid, and evocative, each one proposing new connections...Human beings construct meanings as spiders make webs—or as appropriate enzymes make proteins. This is how we survive...(Bateson, 1997, p. 52)

Multiple Representations—Why Story?
Telling our own stories is intricately related to survival. Surviving is a complex task. There is physical survival. There is emotional survival. And, of course, there is historical and cultural survival. It may be that one of the best ways to delve into survival is through personal story. In many ways, we are all responsible for being what Romo (2005) calls microhistorians. We are equally responsible to pay attention to the microhistories of others. Romo (2005) says,

> We all have our biases and limited viewpoints. It all depends on where we stand. Microhistorians, I think, are just a little more honest about it. We tend to believe that there is no such thing as a definitive History—only a series of microhistories. (p. 18)

Children, in my experience, are natural microhistorians. Children are the consummate communicators, questioners, and listeners. They weave their webs of connection to others in their families, communities, and worlds. They don't live or grow in a bubble, and they don't sit in school and "study" to be adults, with their attention only on what "will be" when they are adults. They are experts at being "in the moment." All children, from all backgrounds and histories, learn through their stories while engaging in play and in other daily activities. They experience development in multiple domains and engage in multidimensional learning when given the opportunity and encouragement.

Novelists, artists, and visionaries have relied on the importance of story for centuries. Rymes (1991) documents her "field work in educational borderlands" (p. 12) and acknowledges that storytelling saves many an educational activity. I believe that story makes the connection between the identity and the history of participants and the educational programs of study. Sfard and Prusak (2005) say, "We believe that the notion of identity is a perfect candidate for the role of 'the missing link' in the researchers' story of the complex dialect between learning and its sociocultural context" (p. 15).

Story is a way to make language and culture visible through multicultural literacy events. This is crucial for all learners and especially for immigrant students of all ages in school. To belong is to be recognized as a full participant in the practices that shape knowledge, identities, and action. Yet, to learn is to draw upon one's own and others' knowledge sources, to transform these, and to formulate conceptual frames for future learning. Both urban and rural neighborhoods and schools have increasing numbers of people representing ethnic, racial, and religious diversity. Many students today in schools around our country have exquisitely complex stories of going and coming. They have gone from a home country for a myriad of reasons, and they have come to their new country with a multitude of experiences. The experts in our newest refugee and immigrant neighborhoods have much to teach other students, other families, and us educators. Teachers and students can use multicultural story and critical literacy as a way to enter neighborhoods and begin to learn from other stories of the various groups of people. Furthermore, the study of our students' histories must be ongoing and a part of literacy education. What does history mean when studying literacy curriculum and learning? Critical literacy is a process of both reading history (the world) and creating history (what do you believe is important?). Thus, my research questions based on critical literacy were Whose stories are important and in what ways? What ways can we learn from the stories? Whose background knowledge will we respect and include and in what ways? Whose and which knowledge is power and in what ways? What ways can we use literacy for specific transformative action?

I work with groups of student teachers in urban and rural schools. We support students' multiple languages and recognize ways that multiple knowledge sources, identities, and language forms can contribute to the formation of new relationships and meanings in all aspects of learning. As a community of scholars in a wide variety of classrooms, we respect the children's backgrounds, plan carefully for their current experiences in school, and prepare them for the future challenges of standardized testing, competitive learning programs, and a variety of future journeys. Our work uses critical literacy as a framework. We define critical literacy as a *process of constructing and critically using language (oral and written) as a means of expression, interpretation, and/or transformation of our lives and the lives of those around us.*

Our work uses critical literacy as a framework for integrated curriculum that includes all the traditional content areas of study, the arts, and new forms of cross-disciplinary ways of knowing. By using a problem-posing, critical literacy approach with multicultural children's literature and the words of many community members who are not currently "heard," this environment of possibility is optimized for students. Even the complex issues of a world in conflict and confusion can be addressed in an ongoing dialogue. Large sweeps of history take meaning from the small stories.

This approach of critical literacy lends itself to ongoing scholarly research of teaching and learning. Teachers can and should join the culture of researchers if a new level of educational rigor and quality is ever to be achieved. In such a culture, teacher scholars will begin to understand the power implications of technical standards. In this context they gain heightened awareness of how they can contribute to the research on education. Indeed, they realize that they have access to understandings that go far beyond what the expert researchers have produced. Likewise, educational researchers and curriculum developers who have never been in a classroom must be exposed to the day-to-day synchrony of activities, strengths, and perspectives of possibility that children bring to the learning events. This book is for all of us—teacher researchers, teachers, teacher educators, educational researchers, curriculum developers, and all interested in story and learning.

We researchers and teachers create the context for learners to pose questions and encourage the consideration of the strengths of students and their families and the consideration of the barriers they face daily. This process, combined with the mutual respect that becomes generative in this context, provides support for transformative action on the part of parents, children, teachers, and community members.

Design and Methods

The research presented here is a qualitative study over a period of five years that documents various groups of teacher education students' work as they have journeyed through their own teacher development process in literacy and curriculum development work. The participants are teachers, student teachers, and their pupils (pre-K through grade 3).

In critical theory, the underlying elements are participation by all, respect for multiple sources of knowledge, and the responsibility of transformative action. I have found over the years of working with teacher education students, children, and community participants that this framework, combined with qualitative research methods, provides a mechanism for addressing complex, critical issues, among multiple participants, in an honest and collaborative way. Although no research and teaching methodology can be a panacea and should never be a recipe, the combination of qualitative methods and critical theory gives all participants ways to collaborate and learn from each other.

For example, in my mind, an admittedly over-simplified model of the important components of critical theory might look like:

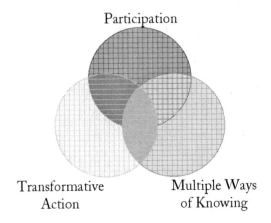

And a model using qualitative methods to support investigating critical theory in an organized, purposeful, and recursive way might look like:

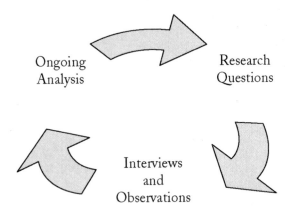

In other words, I use the methodology to structure research in ways that the theory keeps at the forefront the underlying question of research "What is really going on here?" for the community participants—that is, children and their families—and for us as qualitative researchers.

Theoretical Framework

The theoretical framework for this research is critical theory. Some current scholars label critical theory as critical social theory (Leonardo, 2004). They believe that through critical social theory classroom discourse broadens students' horizon of possibility and expands their sense of a larger humanity (Leonardo, 2004). The multidisciplinary knowledge base of critical social theory affirms the role of criticism and rejects the radical differentiation between theory and practice as two separate poles of a dualism. Critical social theory encourages the production and application of theory as a part of the overall search for transformative knowledge. Of course, critical social theory is not a unified field and contains debates. Critical social theory was popularized by the late Paulo Freire, who emphasized participation through personal histories, sharing of multiple ways of knowing, and transformative action.

According to Freire (1997), freedom can occur only when the oppressed reject the image of oppression "and replace it with autonomy and responsibility" (p. 29). Those who adopt Freire's pedagogy need to be aware that it is not made up of techniques to save the world. Instead, he felt that "the progressive educator must always be moving out on his or her own, continually reinventing me and reinventing what it means to be democratic in his or her own specific cultural and historical context" (Freire, 1997, p. 308). Freire's work has given education a language that neglects neither the effect of oppression on people nor their ability to intervene on their own behalf, nor the terrorizing and structure consequences of capitalism and other systems. Freire's (1985) ideas about conscientization, defined as "the process by which human beings participate in a transforming act" (p. 106), form the focus of this book.

Freire was able to draw upon and amalgamate several ideas and practices of educational thinking from the philosophers and teachers of the past and present.

Freire argued for informed action and therefore provided another perspective countering educators in the late 20th century who wanted to diminish the use of theory in educational practice. Freire's approach is curriculum-based, in spite of the emphasis on participatory knowledge sharing and dialogue. It is the relating of curriculum-specified information to the knowledge and strengths of the learners that accounts for its brilliance.

And there is much misunderstanding about Freire's work. Some of these misunderstandings are addressed throughout the book.

For example, in Freire's work, both research and pedagogy, there is sharing of knowledge—both personal and not personal—and there is transformative action. It is the totality that is praxis. Some interpretations (Bartlett, 2005) of Freire's intention and use of "knowledge" are simply incorrect. "Knowledge" in the Freirean sense is both personal/communal knowledge and knowledge of various canons that all learners must have if they are going to undertake transformative action.

I use Freire's (1973) approach based on critical theory in my teaching, research, and writing. The pedagogical method, often called problem-posing, leads students of any age, experience, or ability level to base new learning on personal experience in a way that encourages critical reflection. All activities focus on active participation. This method has not been widely used with younger learners, but lends itself well to integrated literacy development and curriculum activities. Problem-posing combines reflective thinking, information gathering, collaborative decision making, and personal learning choices. I encourage students to choose and examine voices in literature through poetry, fiction, academic research reports, and memory, focusing on authenticity of multiple experiences in multiple contexts. This combination of story, literature, and critical theory allows readers to use autobiography to move beyond a neutral conception of culture (Willis, 1995). All problem-posing begins with self-reflection; therefore, the stories generated by participants become sources of autobiographical narrative (Rogers, 1993).

This self-reflection is also, as explained in auto-ethnography, an attempt to explain self to other and an explanation of how one is "othered." This is more than a simple self-narrative in isolation. Through problem-posing, a pattern of events, beliefs, or behaviors can be traced through a series of reflections (Reed-Danahay, 1997).

Previously, I defined critical literacy as a process of constructing and critically using language (oral and written) as a means of expression, interpretation, and/or transformation of our lives and the lives of those around us. Critical literacy and a critical approach to teaching and learning are powerful because they situate the participants as the activists in the dance between lived experience and new information. Critical literacy and critical learning encourages a natural movement from reflection toward action.

The various groups of teacher education students and practicing teachers studied, designed, and implemented curricula based on critical literacy. The methods involved participant observation, interviews, teacher journals, and a collection of learners' work samples. Data were then analyzed by categories that emerged, particularly as they relate to the theoretical perspective of critical theory.

As a teacher researcher, I believe that we must consistently reflect on our work and our convictions. This constant clarification of our own values and action in all areas of pluralistic work with students is the ongoing aim of education. Freire (1985) addresses this clarification when he defines conscientization (based on the Brazilian *conscientizaçao*) as "the process by which human beings participate critically in a transforming act" (p. 106). I make the case throughout this research that critical theory as a framework for study and analysis combined with qualitative research methodology is an effective way to learn more about the importance of children and teachers using critical literacy in their learning.

In addition to the activist work and philosophy of Paulo Freire (1973, 1997), this particular research study is also informed by the writings of Benjamin (1987) and Bakhtin (1988). According to Benjamin (1987), history should not be seen as "what has happened," but rather as something that is "to be done," a possible action. Time is not considered to be fixed. Benjamin argues that people do not believe in an unalterable past, an unalterable present, and an unalterable future. The critical theory of culture and modernity (Freire & Macedo, 1985; Kincheloe & Steinberg, 1997) reconfigures this question. Considering the link between theory and methodology, the intention of this research is not to sacrifice either authenticity or significance, but to provide opportunity for the participants to speak out for themselves (Benjamin, 1984).

People's own histories are the contexts for developing identity, learning cultural information, and learning all new information—from academic English to the most complex of mathematical functions. Life histories—which are often explored through various forms of story—are considered to be a collective memory of the past, a critical awareness of the present, and an operational premise for the future (Kramer, 2001). According to Benjamin (1987), to escape what he calls barbarity and isolation, it is necessary to establish alternative relationships with tradition and culture, and this underlines the importance of memories. Reviewing the past enables one to view the present in a critical way and to effect changes in the future. Thus, history is no longer understood in a chronological way, but rather as a process in which meanings are recreated. Life histories and literacy histories supply major theoretical-methodological support. Once participants—both adult and child learners—start remembering, they see new meaning in their own lives and begin to see possibilities for change as well. Therefore, to recall is at the same time to reenact, reconstruct, and rethink past experiences, a process that involves a relationship with both history and culture. Every person's personal memories are linked in some way to the collective memory, so they are bound together by collective ties. Furthermore, since the participants relive and reenact their experiences by telling, they create language and at the same time be created by it. Rereading one's history and reviewing past and present experiences autobiographically entail rewriting that history, and lending new meaning to it. For the purposes of analysis, this contribution from Benjamin adds depth to all three aspects of critical theory delineated here.

According to Bakhtin (1988), the production and reception of meaning is what truly establishes language. Language has a dialogical and ideological dimension that is historically determined and built. Comprehension implies not only the identification of the formal and normative aspects and signs of language but also the sub-texts, the intentions that are not explicit. Discourse always has a live meaning and direction. At the same time, meaning and communication imply community. One always addresses someone, and that someone does not assume a purely passive role; the interlocutor participates in the formation of the meaning of the utterance, just as the other elements of speech do. Bakhtin (1988) says that language is constitutively intersubjective and social. It is not experience that organizes expression. Again, this structure helps in the connection of critical theory to critical literacy.

In addition to critical theory, current scholarly work by Lee (2008) in cognitive research and cultural research has influenced the analysis of this research. As Lee (2008) points out, "The cognitively oriented studies of how people learn are not in dialogue with those that focus on culture and cognition (Bransford, Brown, & Cocking, 1999); the multiculturalists are not in dialogue with the culture and cognition researchers (Banks & Banks, 1995); cognitively oriented research and the world of human development have little to do with each other ..." (p. 268). Although there clearly are differences among these paradigms, they share a number of fundamental propositions: (1) Context matters—contexts help shape people, and people shape contexts; (2) Routine practices count; and (3) The cognitive, social, physical, and biological dimensions of both individuals and contexts interact in important ways (Lee, 2008, p. 268).

The processes through which human beings learn in and from their environments and adapt to them always entail risks. Spencer's research and her Phenomenological Variant of Ecological Systems Theory (Spencer, 2006) argue that to be human is to be placed at risk, "... understanding the nature of risks faced by individuals and communities, how people actually experience those risks, and the nature of the supports that are or are not available to them, is necessary for understanding the range of variation in developmental pathways" (Lee, 2008, p. 273).

Analysis of this five-year study has been a long and dynamic process. Analysis and interpretation worked together to construct meaning. Interpretation pointed to patterns, themes, and issues in the data, and findings were seen in relation to one another and against larger theoretical perspectives as well as evolving emergent views not found in the "the literature." As the observation logs, teacher journals, student work in the form of planning, implementation, and evaluation of learning activities, and analytic memos provided bits and pieces of the information, the whole story of the research was kept in sight. This main story relates to the purpose (Wolcott, 1990) of the research.

In the writing of the research it is important to do what Geertz (1988) advises: "to convince our readers that we have actually penetrated (or been penetrated by) another form of life, of having, one way or another truly 'been there'" (pp. 4–5). It is important for readers to see—especially in these early childhood learning settings—that these findings are part of the real lives of real people.

Thus, as this research and the resulting implications revolved around participatory, learner-driven curriculum, I have taken advice from Pinar (2004) as I think about the presentation of the findings. Pinar (2004) advises:

> The complicated conversation that is the curriculum requires interdisciplinary intellectuality, erudition, and self-reflexivity. This is not a recipe for high test scores, but a common faith in the possibility of self-realization and democratization, twin projects of social subjective reconstruction. (p. 8)

So, whereas the data have fallen into categories of emerging themes that overlap, and thus are presented in the separate chapters, each chapter begins with what I call, thanks to Pinar, *Complicated Conversations* relating to the particular theme that has emerged. These conversations come from the qualitative study. Some information comes from participants' discussions of literature in the field, some comes from the wisdom of informants through their interviews, and some comes from the observations during the five-year period. Then, following the *Complicated Conversations* section, excerpts from case studies are included to illustrate not only the themes as they emerged in the early childhood classrooms, but also the aspects of critical theory—participant histories, multiple forms of knowledge, and transformative action. As Bruner (1990) reminds us, one way adults learn is through their own and other people's stories to understand cultures and build relationships. These case study excerpts show some of the interactions in various classrooms when this curriculum based on critical literacy was implemented.

Personalizing Stories and Young Children's Learning

Centuries ago, Middle Eastern poet Rumi asked, "Of these two thousand 'I' and 'we' people, which am I"? (Rumi, 1995, p. 12). Contemporary poet Francisco X. Alarcón asks us whether we can "hear the voices between these lines?" (Alarcón, 1997, p. 28). I believe that the personal voices of teachers, of students, of friends in our communities around the world are the voices we hear between the lines in all literacy events. For this reason, when I speak of literacy, all literacy is—or should be—critical literacy. This constructing of personal and communal meaning and taking action according to the meaning is the most authentic way to personalize literacy. Our cultural, human roots that we pass on to children are no longer neatly contained within borders. According to Clandinin and Connelly (1996), stories are the nearest we can get to experience as we tell of our experiences. They say that the act of our telling our stories seems "inextricably linked with the act of making meaning, an inevitable part of life in a . . . postmodern world" and only becomes problematic "when its influence on thinking and perception goes unnoticed" or is ignored (Goldstein, 1997, p. 147).

As I reflect upon the many children I have known over the years as they interact with their friends, using their imagination and their stories, I realize that they create as if their lives depend on it, and they act as if the lives of others depend on it. We have a lot to learn from children while at the same time, as early childhood educators, we have a huge responsibility to provide reinterpreted, updated information for them as they grow and develop.

In Faith Ringgold's *Tar Beach* (1996) and *Aunt Harriet's Underground Railroad in the Sky* (1995), the character Cassie uses her imagination and her stories that nourish her to overcome oppression and limitations. Children, through their play, especially when immersed in an environment of literature and art, can provide us with voices and perspectives of possibility. For example, a student teacher was just beginning to study the ways that critical literacy are exemplified by young children. She wrote in a reflective journal assignment:

> I observed a child and his father riding the subway together. The train was very crowded and there was only enough room for the child to sit down, so the father stood in front of him. He put the child in the seat and gave him some paper and pen to draw with. The child looked around for a while and then finally began drawing. After some time, the father asked the child what he was drawing. The boy said he was drawing the father riding the subway. The father replied, "But I'm standing, not sitting down." The child then said, "Not on this train, the train in my drawing has seats for everyone to sit down." (Quintero, 2009, p. 3)

This child has used some very important critical literacy through his imagination and his art.

Children's literature author Lunge-Larsen (1999) reminds us of the importance of literature in children's lives in the introduction to one of her children's literature books:

> Children, like the heroes and heroines in these stories (folk tales), perceive their lives to be constantly threatened. Will I lose a tooth? Will I be invited to play? Will I learn to read? By living a life immersed in great stories and themes, children will see that they have the resources needed to solve life's struggles. And, while listening to these stories, children can rest for a while in a world that mirrors their

own, full of magic and the possibility of greatness that lies within the human heart. (p. 11)

Teaching with critical literacy using problem-posing and children's literature nourishes an integrated curriculum that supports young children's meaningful learning. This method encourages integrated learning that is both developmentally and culturally meaningful through interacting with story, reading literature, and participating in related learning activities. Problem-posing method was developed by Paulo Freire (1973) and critical pedagogists with roots going back to the Frankfurt School of Critical Theory in the 1920s, initially for use with adult literacy students. This method leads students of any age, experience, or ability level to base new learning on personal experience in a way that encourages critical reflection. All activities focus on active participation.

Simply defined, the problem-posing method is comprised of several components: Listening, Dialogue, and Action. Participants listen to each others' stories, discuss issues of power that shaped their identities, and present ways in which action, or transformation, can take place in their own lives. These discussions ultimately lead to students' creating a complex form of autobiographical narrative. This combined use of literature and the arts pushes participants to use their autobiography as a means of understanding how their learning was not "neutral," and that the relationship between schools and families must be a move toward a more well-defined conception of culture that reflects our pluralistic, multicultural society (Willis, 1995).

As explained earlier, the teacher education students participated in a variety of problem-posing activities in teacher education courses before they began planning and implementing similar activities for the children they work with. The autobiographical narrative and qualitative research began at the outset of their participation and continued throughout the use of problem-posing critical literacy with young learners in their classrooms.

Problem-Posing and Curriculum

The word "curriculum" comes from a Latin word that means to run a race. Now, in contemporary educational circles, people generally think of the curriculum as "the course to be run," which suggests that it is not the actual running, but the plan for the race. Others (Ely, 2003) argue that curriculum is not the plan or the recipe for the plan, but is, in fact, what transpires in the teaching and learning context for learners individually and as a part of the classroom community (Quintero, 2004). Besides worrying about the definition, we educators struggle with how curriculum is developed. Especially in times of expensive, one-size-fits-all, "named" curriculum kits promoted by corporate publishing companies and high stakes testing, teachers who want to be the intellectuals (Giroux, 1988) they have studied for years to become find that the task of creating learner-focused curriculum becomes crucial.

Teacher education programs are attempting to respond to the push by state boards of teaching and other credentialing bodies for "more content-area" knowledge in each of the teaching fields—including Early Childhood and Elementary Education. However, those of us who have spent years in early childhood classrooms participating with preschoolers and elementary students, and those of us who continue to review both the new research and the wisdom of our predecessors, worry. We worry that children's and families' cultures will be dismissed; we worry that play will not be valued; we worry that the policy makers and curriculum developers who haven't studied and worked with young children will push inappropriate, isolated content on the young ones. At the same time, we want young children to have the benefits of exposure to people, places, and ideas that enrich their worlds and stimulate their potential. And yet, most of all, we want to ensure that the children know that their family, their communities, and their schools support their learning (Quintero, 2004).

For decades early childhood educators have worked toward an understanding of supporting development by a commitment to the recognition that cognitive development, social development, emotional development, and physical development are integrated in unique ways in each individual child influenced by both nature and context. We know the importance of viewing childhood as inquiry rather than as a prescription to encourage a broader, less linear view of development and, therefore, more inclusive strategies of care and education (Mallory & New, 1994). And, as global societies have become more and more interwoven, we early care and education professionals promote pluralistic programming. We also work continually to better understand how early childhood programs can support the sociocultural knowledge and experiences children bring to our early care and education programs while we provide instructional experiences that prepare children for success in school and life in the cultural context of the United States of America.

Current research in many states in the United States is investigating quality indicators for early childhood and programming for younger learners. Large, well-known corporations such as the Rand Corporation have sponsored much of the research. One study done in early childhood contexts in the state of California is vocal about one of their findings that correlates quality programs with what they call "research-based curricula" and "named curricula." These named curricula are almost entirely prepackaged, expensive curriculum plans offered by publishing corporations. The implicit message, furthermore, is that the only curricula that are research-based are those that fall into the "named" category published by well-known and well-funded companies. Thus, unspoken further implications are that if programs that use these "named" curricula are representative of "quality," then programs that use teacher/participant-developed curricula are not research-based, therefore, not quality programs.

Many of us believe that this is a dangerous perpetuation of the notion that teachers are not capable of designing and implementing curricula; they are mere technicians, not intellectuals. Throughout my many years of working with early childhood teacher education in community college programs, university bachelor's programs, and graduate programs, I can say unequivocally that all teachers in early care and education who have studied and completed a teacher education program do create curricula that is research-based. And without question, participants who happen to be children, or multilingual, or from cultural histories from around the world, can be counted on to contribute to curriculum design.

In my work with immigrant and refugee families, I remember discussions with Hmong women describing their own "childhoods" in refugee camps in Thailand and Somali women describing family life in East Africa during the past decades. I would say that the "childhood" experience of these families is very different from that of many families in the United States, Western Europe, and many other countries. Brooker (2006) reports that Bangladeshi families in south London construct childhood in different ways from those of native British families. Cannella (1997) believes that the knowledge base used to ground the field of early childhood education actually serves to support the status quo, reinforces prejudices and stereotypes, and ignores the real lives of children. Cannella's (1997) work raises questions in terms of social justice and early education. Her questions include: How do we eliminate the two-tiered system? Does the curriculum respect the multiple knowledge and life experiences of younger human beings from diverse backgrounds? Sadly, we still are unsure how to effectively answer Canella's questions.

What we are sure of is that because of the changing needs of families and the persistence of Western intellectual, psychological, and cultural perspectives, changes must continue to be made. Family childrearing practices must be supported and built upon to enhance social, emotional, cognitive, and physical development. Educators and parents must collaborate to determine appropriate early childhood programming that recognizes that the school's goals may be different from those of families and cultural groups with generations of different life experiences. Educational programs can build rapport through an informal, non-threatening environment, in which staff help parents to feel welcomed and comfortable so that they share the important sociocultural meaning in their lives. A problem-posing curriculum emphasizing family and cultural story and children's literature, especially multicultural children's literature, encourages collaboration and enhances multidirectional participatory learning. In other words, in this context, not only is learning transmitted from teacher to students, but teachers learn from students, and students from each other. We must "search for intelligence where one has previously seen only deficiency" (Kincheloe, 2000, p. 81).

I maintain that with the help of the children, families, and community members, learners of all ages can reflect upon issues and concepts in a profound way. James, Jenks, and Prout (1998) challenge teachers and researchers to pay attention to children's experiences and to what situations might mean for children, not for the purposes of evaluating them in accordance with adult goals, but for the ways they inform us about how our practices contribute to children's unequal status. These authors also criticize the emphasis that current models of education put on reading and interrogating childhood as a text. They call for inquiries that combine a focus on critically examining childhood with attention to children's lived experiences. My research doesn't push for an imposed interpretation of individual stories for the students, but the Listening, Dialogue, and Action framework of problem-posing based on critical theory and critical literacy support the conviction that learners are individuals who are members of families and communities.

Personal, Family, and Community Histories

Many researchers, most notably Vivian Gussin Paley (2000, 1993, 1986), have shown that children through their play, especially when immersed in an environment of literature, art, and story, can provide us with small voices and perspectives of possibility. In my work with students and their families, I have found that the multidirectional learning that happens through multicultural story, in its many forms, is generative. In some of the cultural groups who have recently come to the United States, such as the Hmong people, storytelling and art through embroidery or weaving has been the means to pass along history over many generations. Other groups use cultural artifacts to provide the visual and the concrete learning for young children, and others use stories, proverbs, and poetry to educate their young children.

Reporting life experiences by way of storytelling, autobiographies, and memories is, therefore, part of the process of making history. My teacher education students and I believe that learning develops among particularities, among persons and objects in families and communities. Tolkien (1977) has said that a legend or a story that has been handed down for generations lives on the brink of history. Anaya (2004) says,

> I believe there is inherent power in the stories of our ancestors. Folk tales began in the imagination eons ago, and they nurture our creativity today. We recognize the values and concerns of the people in the folktales ... Understanding and respect for other cultures can begin by learning their stories. (p. 201)

In a novel Anaya (2006) wrote for young adult readers, he spoke about a project implemented by the protagonist, a writing teacher who worked with community youth. She asked the young people to collect oral histories from their parents and grandparents.

Anaya (2006) reported through the narrator,

> They quickly learned from these stories of hard work and survival that their parents had performed heroic deeds. The struggle to immigrate to a new country produced heroes. The hero acted for the good of the family and the community. The hero actually embodied the culture.
>
> The kids looked closely at their own lives and saw the challenges they faced. They developed strategies to deal with problems. As one young man said during the early part of the workshop; "Hey, we poor Mexicans have heroes? Wow!"
>
> Someone added: "Yeah, Jesus, Cesar Chavez, Corky Gonzalez, Martin Luther, and the guy Odee-sus."
>
> "And la Virgin de Guadalupe, la Llorona, Selena, Frida Kahlo."
>
> "And Pedro Infante. I read ..."
>
> A girl added: "Our parents are heroes." (pp. 97–98)

Historically, much of humankind's most profound reflections have emerged in the form of story. Children benefit from the opportunity to react to multicultural ideas through various activities such as reading picture books, drawing, journal writing, and storytelling. Story is the way people learn with all the complexities of related issues in teaching, as in life, intact.

Author's Personal Story

Story has been important to me since I was a child. I remember arguing with my sister all summer long—every summer—about which of us got to lie on the old wicker chaise lounge to read our books. Papa's house, built during the boom of the 1920s (in relative disrepair by the 1950s), had a long screened porch on one side. (We moved in with him, my grandfather, in the 1950s when my father died.) There was a very old wicker chaise lounge with a green flowered cover. Here's where we read. I walked to the library two blocks away, and like my mother and sister, probably, over a period five to six years, read most of the books in the small library. I remember the literal and metaphorical trips the books took me on. I loved the fantasy of magical tales and the believable action and resistance in biographies. The science topics interested me, but always in the contexts of the human dynamics—the struggles, successes, and barriers. These books helped me ask questions and see some complexities related to those I didn't understand in my environment of the Old South.

As a child, I never understood the unquestioned practice of separation of the "races." What was my race? My mother and I were as dark, darker than many Cubans I knew, while my father and sister were light with light blue eyes. "White, of course," my mother always replied and looked away.

What's left out? What did Papa, my grandfather, do on all those trips to Havana in the 1930s and 1940s? Why did my mother know nothing about my father's family? Where were they from? Who was my father's father? All I saw was a dark, high cheek-boned face in a photograph. Was it his face I inherited? Did he belong to a tribe? I tell students to always ask the questions about whose stories and options are left out of every textbook, every research study, every news report. Yet, personal story is complicated.

I have tried not to feel anger and shame that my family (the few I knew) communicated through secrets and things not said. At a small education conference in Madison, scholar and activist Carl Grant asked me whether I would tell my story for a book he was preparing (*Educating for Diversity*), which I later used in my teaching. He needed a Cuban American perspective of struggle and survival. "I can't," I said. "Why not?" He was surprised. An astute observer, he was probably thinking of our ten-minute conversation there in front of the fireplace after Lourdes Diaz Soto, a colleague and friend, had introduced us. Florida, Texas, Mexico, the surname, the names of my sons. The underlying family focus in my work. "No, I can't," I apologized. "I wasn't raised Cuban American. I wasn't raised anything." Other than one of two sisters raised by a single mother, dark skinned with green eyes and curly hair, who became bent by the dominance of others.

I told Carl Grant, "I'm a mongrel, who is clearly different from the white mainstream, but with only gotas (drops of Latina, maybe Creek Indian, maybe black), I don't know. I can really not claim any identity other than me." He looked at me. "You could pass for several," he said with a twinkle in his eyes. "There are more and more mixed ones like you coming up these days." This was almost two decades before our President Obama smilingly referred to himself as a "mutt."

I began traveling to new places early in my life. My father was in the U.S. Navy, so before I was five I knew that the waves of the Atlantic in Virginia were very different from those of Southern California on the Pacific. When my father was diagnosed with cancer, we moved to Guadalajara, Jalisco, Mexico, in hopes that the climate would help his health. I loved the huge, ancient hotel where we first lived in our new city. It was the first house I'd ever lived in with stairs. It had 143. My sister and I counted. And it was our "home" for a while. It didn't matter that there were only two small rooms that were really our family's. I had never seen tiles with paintings on them, centuries-old furniture, or pig brains served on a platter.

Sometime right before my sixth birthday my family moved to Chapala, a smaller town of about four thousand people, about sixty miles from Guadalajara. Here we lived in a small pink adobe house with a flat roof with a tiny flower garden on top. I could see Lake Chapala in one direction and the dirt and cobblestone streets and tiny adobe houses in all other directions. Marisa, my friend, had six brothers and sisters and an aunt and a grandma living with her and her mother and father. When I visited her family the first time, I didn't even notice until I got back home when my mother asked whether I understood what everyone said in the family. I knew a little bit of Cuban Spanish from early years in Tampa, Florida, but we had been in Mexico for only about three weeks.

I majored in literature in my undergraduate study at Florida State University and immediately after graduation began working with young children. I earned a master's degree in Early Childhood Education at the same university while I taught preschool in the morning and kindergarten and first graders in a parent cooperative school in Tallahassee, Florida.

Years later in the Southwest, after more work in different settings, as I observed the communication of monolingual English-speaking children, of African American children both in rural schools and in inner-city schools, of monolingual Spanish-speaking children in Mexico, and of Spanish-English bilingual children in Texas and New Mexico, I saw the "roots of literacy" as an integral part of what children do as they understand and take part in their world. It was exciting to see their literacy develop through a child's painting about "una piñata" (a birthday party with a huge number of family and friends and activities), through a collaborated effort of Lego building for the purpose of replicating the spacecraft *Discovery*, through the teaching and learning of a rap song, and through the practice of the songs for a Posada (a Christmas ceremony in Mexico and parts of the southwestern United States). Literacy was spreading roots across and through the cultures of children in my world. I knew that I was witnessing the roots of *literacies*.

During these times of observation and reflection about these developing literacies, I had the opportunity work with the parents of many young children as we collaborated about the task and pleasure of positively influencing the children's lives. Children come to early childhood programs straight from the influence and "cariño" of their parents' arms. Every parent I had met—

from a diversity of circumstances, from difficulty to comfort—cared deeply about his or her child that was being entrusted in my care.

As I came to know more and more parents, I read with skepticism the research that implied that parents who lacked formal education would negatively affect the education of their children (Stitch & McDonald, 1989). Because I had met numerous parents who with only three to five years of formal schooling had raised intelligent, successful children who are now attending the country's most prestigious universities (Quintero & Velarde, 1990). I had begun to see the social context in general, as the important factor for a child's learning success.

So, in the process of addressing these issues in my work, I collected ideas, assumptions, and hypotheses about multilingual children's roots of literacy and the effect that their parents and early teachers could have on this development. I had the opportunity to collaborate on the design of an intergenerational program, which became Project FIEL in El Paso, Texas, so I could use what I was sure about. I knew the strength of the child/parent relationship. I knew that the innate enthusiasm of every child to learn and flourish in a secure and meaningful social context would make a literacy class, in which parents studied alongside their children, dynamic and interesting. And I felt more and more certain that the family bond and the opportunity to engage in appropriately flexible and meaningful activities would make it possible to transcend difficulties such as different patterns of language dominance, different literacy abilities, and different learning needs.

I see my experience with bilingual family literacy as tangible evidence of what Maxine Greene (1992) was touching upon when she made the following comment: "It seems clear the more continuous and authentic personal encounters can be, the less likely will it be for categorizing and distancing to take place. People are less likely to be treated instrumentally to be made Other by those around," (p. 13).

As mentioned previously, my passion for working with refugee and immigrant learners began when I had the opportunity to work with a group of parents and teachers in a Bilingual Family Literacy Project in El Paso, Texas. Later, I initiated a similar project with another group of teachers and families to create a family literacy project in Minnesota with Hmong and Somali families. In summer of 2002, in Ankara, Turkey, I met refugee families on the run, seeking asylum, who taught me a lot about strengths of human spirit and determination for learning and positive family support in deplorable conditions. In London, in early 2004, I met families of Asylum Seekers from 68 countries who, with the collaborations of the Refugee Council, private foundations, and committed teachers, had created one of the most dynamic and exciting elementary schools in the one of the poorest neighborhoods in London. On an ongoing basis, in New York City while I was a faculty member in the Department of Teaching and Learning at New York University, my students and I worked with families from Chinatown to Brooklyn to Queens to the Bronx—Latino, Syrian, Palestinian, Pakistani, Orthodox Russian Jewish, and Central American families. Sometimes the work took the form of a family literacy project, sometimes it took the form of parent support groups, sometimes it took the form of parents designing curriculum through art and history to augment a school's standard curriculum. All encounters involve participants' use of critical literacy and personal historical and cultural knowledge.

Student Participants' Personal Stories

Many students from various backgrounds want to belong and to not appear different. Some of the teachers and student teachers I work with have past experiences similar to the experiences of the children who are now in school. There is complicated conflict surrounding the issue of family loyalty. In 2003, a teacher education student in a graduate program wrote:

> I came from India when I was four and started kindergarten when I was five. Neither one of my parents spoke English, so when I started school it was a difficult experience for me. I felt so different from the other children and wanted to quickly learn English so that I can be a part of their world. I would run home after school so that I could finally be in a world that was familiar to me, with language and customs I was an expert of. However, at the same time I was angry with my parents for not knowing and therefore not being able to teach me English. I felt very alone in my experience. When my mother would pick me up after school I would beg her to not speak to me in Hindi. I was embarrassed about who I was.
>
> What a shame for a child to be embarrassed about who they are because of the fear of rejection and because of the pressure to assimilate and build a new, acceptable identity for the new world they are a part of.

Moll, Gonzalez, and Amanti (2005) declare that "funds of knowledge" of families in our communities must be recognized and built upon. To begin to understand a culture, teachers and learners must study the folktales, legends, history, and current culture of that group of people. By the year 2030 over half of the students in schools in the United States will be students of multicultural and multilingual backgrounds. Acculturation and language acquisition are affected by the process of aligning new societal expectations and requirements with previous cultural norms, individual perceptions, and experiences preeminent in immigrants' lives. Yet, these urgent issues are often ignored (Ullman, 1997; Zou, 1998). Franken (2002) reports research documenting that when students are faced with a topic on which they have little content and domain-specific knowledge, interaction is significantly helpful for understanding text. By virtue of the fact that many immigrant students come from such a variety of backgrounds with such different "funds of knowledge" as Moll, Gonzalez, and Amanti (2005) report, it is almost inevitable that many occasions will arise in the literacy classroom when one or more students have a lack of background knowledge on a topic. Critical theory and critical literacy bring all these variations of story to the learning event.

Moll, Gonzalez, and Amanti (2005) give long-awaited documentation to the theoretical and practical issues of *Funds of Knowledge* as important contributions to our knowledge in the various fields of education. One reviewer (Carney, 2005) of the book pointed out that there are not enough accounts of this type of work outside of the contexts of the southwestern United States. The research presented here in this book modestly attempts to address the funds of knowledge of educators (families and community members) in a variety of contexts from a variety of cultures, continents, and situations of living. It is through the use of critical theory and critical literacy that the histories, languages, and multiple forms of knowledge from around the world come into our lexicon.

In a research study of literacy teachers (Rummel & Quintero, 1997) we learned about these teachers' family histories. They showed us how positive it is when educators are informed by families' knowledge. They brought the effects of their own families to their relationships with their students and to their teaching. Many teachers, like many well-known writers and visionaries (Allen, 1991; Walker, 1990), talked about the importance of the passing on stories by parents and grandparents. Family knowledge and literacy are interwoven fabric of cultural practices. The art of this family knowledge and related literacy practice promotes strength, encourages nurturance, and supports risk-taking. This is the ultimate, authentic way to personalize literacy.

Personalizing Literacy for Teacher Education Students

As explained, my issues of teaching and research revolve around paying attention to parents' and children's strengths. By doing this, I believe educators and leaders in all arenas can learn more about how culture, language, and varying concepts of family affect child development, community development, learning, and ultimately our ability to live with each other with respect and peace. I ask students in all of my classes to listen to and speak with each other, their families and community members, and authors from all over the world through their own reading and writing. In order to do this I use a problem-posing format.

In terms of teacher research, this use of critical theory and critical literacy is a natural fit for teachers researching their own practice, for teacher educators researching the practice of their students, and for researchers looking for information about more meaningful curricular models than have been prevalent during the era of No Child Left Behind. In terms of pedagogy, this methodology, with its strong theoretical and philosophical underpinnings, encourages teachers not to limit their teaching to units and lesson plans. It encourages curriculum development to use a point of departure the background funds of knowledge the children bring from their lived experience rather than from a written form of normalization. The method encourages integration of the community funds of knowledge, language, and culture with the standard school curricula.

As Pinar (2004) reminds us, "Information must be tempered with intellectual judgment, critical thinking, ethics, and self-reflexivity. The complicated conversation that is curriculum requires interdisciplinary intellectuality, erudition, and self-reflexivity" (p. 8).

I, with my teacher education students, address what such understandings might mean for creating environments for learning and for developing classroom practice. The teacher education students document their journey as they experience the method in their teacher education classes and as they use the method with young children. They practice using this critical literacy framework for focusing on story and multicultural children's literature and creating literacy opportunities that extend beyond the classroom to use the words of their families and communities for literacy education.

For example, in Ms. Rafiq's first grade, every child has come to this country from another country, recently. Ms. Rafiq's own family had come from the Middle East, and while she had spent post of her years in the northeastern United States, she has a commitment to honoring and building upon all learners' cultures and histories. Some never spoke English before kindergarten last year. Some spoke the English of Guyana and don't qualify for English language services, but the dialect is so different that it is as if the children are working with a second language. Some children are from Central America, some are from India, some are from Russia, and others are from Haiti. And they all love the poetry that Ms. Rafiq adores and introduces them to. She involves them in writing their own poetry through her literacy program. They make dioramas for a social studies project. The dioramas are set in a country where their families come from, and after a mini-lesson on voice as a part of the week's Writers Workshop, the children plan what the characters in the dioramas are talking about in their own voice.

They write the words, sometimes in English, sometimes in the home language of the families.

Findings

Findings reveal the myriad of ways that, through critical literacy, artful story connects learning, teaching, and integrated curriculum. The themes that have emerged are addressed in the chapters of the book: Artful Story to Connect with Others; Artful Story Illustrating Meaning through Language; Artful Story Supporting Critical Reading; Artful Story to Investigate Myth, Legend, and History; Artful Story and the Arts; and Artful Story as a Frame for Activist Work. The themes and meta-themes of the chapters overlap because of the nature of the interdisciplinary work. Therefore, the case study excerpts and examples could arguably have been grouped differently. However, when having *complicated conversations* about integrated curriculum the readers are encouraged to rearrange case study examples as they choose.

Finally, in a concluding chapter the findings are considered together, across cases, to illustrate the potential of critical literacy and story based on learners' lives and interests as dynamic curriculum at different age levels from pre-K to grade 3. The findings are addressed in each chapter through the categories of Participant's Histories, Multiple Forms of Knowledge, and Transformative Action.

References

Alarcón, F. X. (1997). *Laughing tomatoes and other spring poems/Jitomates risueños y otros poemas de primavera*. San Francisco: Children's Book Press.

Allen, P. G. (1991). *Grandmothers of the light: A medicine woman's source book*. Boston: Beacon Press.

Anaya, R. (2004). *Serafina's stories*. Albuquerque, NM: University of New Mexico Press.

Anaya, R. (2006). *Curse of the ChupaCabra [sic]*. Albuquerque, NM: University of New Mexico Press.

Bakhtin, M. (Voloshinov, V. N.) (1988). *Marxismo e filosofia da linguagem*. São Paulo: Hucitec.

Banks, J. & Banks, C. (1995). *Handbook of research on multicultural education*. New York: Macmillan.

Bartlett, L. (2005). Dialogue, knowledge, and teacher-student relations: Freirean pedagogy in theory and practice. *Comparative Education Review, 49*(3), 344–364.

Bateson, Mary C. (1994). *Peripheral visions: Learning along the way*. New York: Harper Collins.

Bateson, Mary C. (1997). *Learning from our lives: Women, research, and autobiography in education*. New York: Teachers College Press.

Benjamin, W. (1984). *Origem do drama barroco alemao*. Sao Paulo: Brasiliense.

Benjamin, W. (1987). *Obras escolhidas I, Magia e ténica, arête e poítica*. São Paulo: Brasiliense.

Bransford, J., Brown, A., & Cocking, R. (1999). *How people learn: Brain, mind, experience and school*. Washington, DC: National Academy Press.

Brooker, L. (2006). Interview. London, England. January 11, 2006.

Bruner, J. (1990). *Acts of meaning*. Cambridge, MA: Harvard University Press.

Cannella, G. S. (1997). *Deconstructing early childhood education: Social justice and revolution*. New York: Peter Lang.

Carney, N. (2005). Review: Applied Ling: Gonzalez, Moll & Amanti (2005). *The Linguist List*. Eastern Michigan University and Wayne State University. http://linguistlist.org/issues/16/16-3224.html.

Clandinin, D. J., & Connelly, F. M. (1996). Teachers' professional knowledge landscapes: Teacher stories—stories of teachers—school stories—stories of schools. *Educational Researcher, 25*(3), 24–30.

Ely, M. (2003). Personal communication. New York: New York University.

Franken, M. (2002). When and why speaking can make writing harder. In S. Randall & M. Barbier (Eds.), *New directions for research in L2 writing*. The Netherlands: Kluwer Academic Publishers.

Freire, P. (1973). *Education for critical consciousness*. New York: Seabury.

Freire, P. (1985). *Politics of education*. Granby, MA: Bergin & Garvey.

Freire, P. (1997). *Pedagogy of hope*. Granby, MA: Bergin & Garvey.

Freire, P., & Macedo, D. (1985). *Literacy: Reading the word and the world*. Granby, MA: Bergin & Garvey.

Geertz, C. (1988). *Works and lives: The anthropologist as author*. Cambridge: Polity Press.

Giroux, H. (1988). *Teachers as intellectuals: Towards a critical pedagogy of learning*. Granby, MA: Bergin & Garvey.

Goldstein, L. S. (1997). *Teaching with love: A feminist approach to early childhood education*. New York: Peter Lang.

Greene, M. (1992). The passions of pluralism: Multiculturalism and the expanding community. *Educational Researcher, 22* (1), 13-18.

James, A., Jenks, C., & Prout, A. (1998). *Theorizing childhood*. New York: Teachers College Press.

Kincheloe, J. (2000). Certifying the damage: Mainstream educational psychology and the oppression of children. In Lourdes D. Soto (Ed.), *The politics of early childhood education*, pp. 75–84. New York: Peter Lang.

Kincheloe, J., & Steinberg, S. (1997). *Changing multiculturalism*. Philadelphia: Open University Press.

Kramer, S. (2001). Can teachers be sheherazade? The role of memory, storytelling, reading and writing in teacher education. In A. Tamar, A. Keinan, & R. Zuzosky (Eds.), *The ongoing development of teacher education*. Tel Aviv: The Mofet Institute.

Lee, Carol D. (2008). The centrality of culture to the scientific study of learning and development: How an ecological framework in education research facilitates civic responsibility, *Educational Researcher, 37*(5), 267–279.

Leonardo, Z. (2004). Critical social theory and transformative knowledge: The functions of criticism in quality education. *Educational Researcher, 33*(6), 11–18.

Lunge-Larsen, L. (1999). *The troll with no heart in his body and other tales of trolls from Norway*. Boston: Houghton Mifflin.

Mallory, B., & New, R. (1994). *Diversity and developmentally appropriate practices: Challenges for early childhood education*. New York: Teachers College Press.

Moll, L. (1994). Funds of knowledge: A look at Luis Moll's research into hidden family resources. *CITYSCHOOLS, 1*(1), 19–21.

Moll, L. C., Gonzalez, N., & Amanti, C. (2005). *Funds of knowledge: Theorizing practices in households, communities, and classrooms.* Mahwah, NJ: Lawrence Erlbaum.

Paley, Vivian G. (1986). *Boys and girls: Superheroes in the doll corner.* Chicago: University of Chicago Press.

Paley, Vivian G. (1993). *You can't say you can't play.* Cambridge, MA: Harvard University Press.

Paley, Vivian G. (2000). *White teacher.* Cambridge, MA: Harvard University Press.

Pinar, W. (2004). *What is curriculum theory?* Mahwah, NJ: Erlbaum.

Quintero, Elizabeth P. (2004). *Problem-posing with multicultural children's literature: Developing critical, early childhood curricula.* New York: Peter Lang.

Quintero, Elizabeth P. (2009). Young children and story: The path to transformative action. In S. Steinberg (Ed.), *Diversity: A reader,* p. 3. New York: Peter Lang.

Quintero, E., & Velarde, M. C. (1990). Intergenerational literacy: A developmental, bilingual approach. *Young Children, 45*(4), 10–15.

Reed-Danahay, D. (Ed.) (1997). *Auto/ethnography: Rewriting the self and the social.* Gordonsville, VA: Berg Publishers.

Ringgold, F. (1995). *Aunt Harriet's underground railroad in the sky.* New York: Dragonfly Books.

Ringgold, F. (1996). *Tar beach.* New York: Dragonfly Books.

Rogers, Annie G. (1993). Voice, play, and the practice of ordinary courage in girls' and women's lives. *Harvard Educational Review, 63*(3), 265–295.

Romo, D. (2005). *Ringside seat to a revolution: An underground cultural history of El Paso and Juarez: 1893–1923.* El Paso, TX: Cinco Puntos Press.

Rumi (Translated by Coleman Barks with John Moyne, A. J. Arberry & Reynold Nicholson). (1995). *The essential Rumi.* Edison, NJ: Castle Books.

Rummel, M. K., & Quintero, E. P. (1997). *Teachers' reading/teachers' lives.* Albany, NY: SUNY Press.

Rymes, B. (1991). *Conversational borderlands: Language and identity in an alternative urban high school.* New York: Teachers College Press.

Sfard, A., & Prusak, A. (2005). Telling identities: In search of an analytic tool for investigating learning as a culturally shaped activity. *Educational Researcher, 34*(4), 14–22.

Spencer, M. B. (2006). Phenomenology and ecological systems theory: Development of diverse groups. In W. Damon & R. M. Lerner (Eds.), *Handbook of child psychology* (6th ed., Vol. 1), pp. 829–893. New York: John Wiley.

Stitch, T. G., & McDonald, B. A. (January 1989). *Making the nation smarter: The intergenerational transfer of cognitive ability.* [Executive Summary] San Diego, CA: Applied Behavioral and Cognitive Sciences, Inc.

Tolkien, J. R. R. (1977). From a letter by J. R. R. Tolkien to Milton Waldman, 1951. In C. Tolkien (Ed.), *The Silmarillion,* pp. x–xxiv. London: Harper Collins.

Ullman, C. (1997). Social Identity and the Adult ESL Classroom. *Eric Digest.* National Clearing house on Literacy Education, October 1997, EDO-LE-98-01.

Walker, A. (1990). *The temple of my familiar.* New York: Scribner.

Willis, A. (1995). Reading the world of school literacy: Contextualizing the experience of a young African American male. *Harvard Educational Review 65* (1), 30–49.

Wolcott, H. (1990). On seeking-and-rejecting-validity in qualitative research. In E. Eisner & A. Peshkin (Eds.), *Qualitative inquiry in education: The continuing debate,* pp. 121–152. New York: Teachers College Press.

Zou, Y. (1998). Rethinking empowerment: The acquisition of cultural, linguistic and academic knowledge. *The Teachers of English to Speakers of Other Languages Journal.* Vol. 7:4 (Summer), 4-9.

CHAPTER TWO
Artful Story to Connect with Others

You do not even know that you "have" a culture until you encounter other ways of thinking and behaving ... Today we are challenged ... to think more inclusively about other cultures and species, about the biosphere as a whole, to be unafraid as we make new meaning. (Bateson, 2004, p. 2)

Complicated Conversations—Artful Story to Connect with Others

As Lisa Delpit (1995) states, "We all carry worlds in our heads, and those worlds are decidedly different" (p. xiv). We educators set out to teach, but how can we reach the worlds of others when we don't even know they exist? Growing up as members of a family and community, children learn explicitly and implicitly the rules and expectations of their cultures. Individual children may be members of more than one cultural group and may be embedded in their cultures to different degrees. The cultures borrow and share rules, and cultures change over time.

Educators around the world have been facing stark challenges that seem only to become more complex as the months go by. On the one hand, all over the Middle East, the Balkans, Africa, and parts of South America and North America successive generations have handed down a legacy of loss, desperation, and betrayal to their offspring. This is also true in the "developed" world and technologically advanced societies where unregulated capitalism has created terrible inequalities in wealth and poverty. The political and economic conditions affect all aspects of education. On the other hand, economic globalization—with all its disadvantages and advantages—has uprooted families and brought people together under unforeseeable circumstances.

Many educators (Moll, Gonzalez & Amanti, 2005; Quintero & Macías, 1995; Quintero, 1994) believe that we can learn from families in several situations. We have conducted qualitative research in various communities where refugees and immigrants have settled and in other communities of migration around the world. The information gleaned from the interviews with the participants informs both educators and policy makers about the strengths and needs of immigrant and refugee families and students in terms of critical literacy and learning. This information can be used around the world in creating pedagogy for literacy, using local knowledge of particular sites, and drawing on a range of strengths and histories for families to advocate for their rights to literacy and learning in difficult times.

Today no region or continent lacks refugees—people caught between danger at home and loss of identity in a strange land. Millions have fled their homes in fear and sought safety in strange societies where they may be isolated, different, and often impoverished. The new refugees are different from refugees in the past in that the new refugees are culturally, racially, and ethnically vastly different from their hosts. They come from less-developed countries, at a greatly different stage of development than the host, and they are likely to lack kin, potential support groups, in their country of resettlement. These are reasons that schools and agencies assisting refugees in daily life and in resettlement need as much information as possible about them.

A conjunction of issues illustrated by migrating families and their strengths and needs combines critical theory and issues of place—where people live their lives. Gruenewald (2003) presents a critical pedagogy of place as a much needed framework for educational theory, research, policy, and practice. He advocates for place-based pedagogies so that the education of citizens may have direct influence on the well-being of the social and ecological places people actually live. I agree that critical pedagogies are needed to challenge many assumptions, practices, and outcomes taken for granted in conventional education in the United States and in other countries. In these changing times it is urgent that we reexamine several assumptions. Should education mainly support individualistic and nationalistic competition in the global economy? Is an educational competition of winners and losers in the best interest of public life in a pluralistic society?

Clarification of Terms

Immigrants are people who move from one country to another for the purpose of permanent residence. It has become accepted knowledge that a refugee is a person seeking asylum in a foreign country in order to escape persecution. Those who seek refugee status are sometimes known as asylum seekers, and the practice of accepting such refugees is that of offering political asylum. The most common asylum claims to industrialized countries are based upon political and religious grounds. Refugee status may be granted on the basis of the 1951 Convention Relating to the Status of Refugees.

Refugees are a subgroup of the broader category of displaced persons and are distinguished from economic migrants who have left their country of origin for economic reasons, and from internally displaced persons who have not crossed an international border. Environmental refugees (people displaced because of environmental disasters) are not included in the definition of "refugee" under international law. The practical determination of whether a person is a refugee or not is most often left to certain government agencies within the host country. This can lead to abuse in a country with a very restrictive official immigration policy. Under the 1951 Convention on Refugees and 1967 Protocol, a nation must grant asylum to refugees and cannot forcibly return refugees to their nations of origin. However, many nations routinely ignore this treaty (http://www.unhchr.ch/html/menu3/b/o_c_ref.

As stated in the previous chapter, for my work, I define critical literacy as using language, both oral and written, as a means of expression, communication, and transformation for ourselves and for those around us. Critical literacy is an especially effective approach to learning that addresses complexities of learners from migrating families who may have a variety of sources of background knowledge. The connection between background knowledge and power through critical literacy are complex. The power of critical literacy relates to comments by the late Edward Said about the responsibilities of writers and intellectuals and the potential of learners. Many participants in programs based upon critical literacy become writers we can learn from.

> I think it is generally true that in all cultures writers have a separate, perhaps even more honorific, place than do "intellectuals"... Yet at the dawn of the twenty-first century the writer has taken on more and more of the intellectual's adversarial attributes in such activities as speaking the truth to power, being a witness to persecution and suffering, and supplying a dissenting voice in conflicts with authority. (Said, 2000, p. 11)

My feelings about the importance of intellectual and inventive capabilities lead to my affiliation with critical theory and critical pedagogy. Critical pedagogists and other postmodern scholars speak often of the importance of educators taking on the risk and responsibility of being intellectual participants. By attending to both the sense of opposition and the sense of engaged participation, intellectuals can explore the possibilities for action. Said (2000) reminds us of the assumption that even though one can't do or know everything, it must always be possible to discern the elements of a struggle or problem dialectically, and that others have a similar stake in a common project. He reminded us that at least since Nietzsche the writing of history and the accumulations of memory have been regarded in many ways as one of the essential foundations of power.

A young child labeling a drawing of himself and a friend in his home language and in English, a refugee parent recently in a country demanding that information from her child's school be written in her home language, and a musician using his songwriting and performing to address issues of a past life as a child soldier in Africa are all forms of critical literacy that speak truth to power.

In her writings, Mary Catherine Bateson discusses the many ways that she was influenced by both the anthropological and scientific writings of her parents (Margaret Mead and Gregory Bateson). She believes there is always a strong connection between cultural context and environment. She writes:

> I continue to feel that the concept of "culture," which Mead did so much to in-
> sert into the thinking of ordinary Americans, is indispensable in working for under-
> standing across lines of difference. I continue to feel that Bateson's call for systemic
> thinking is key to developing non destructive environmental policies. (2004, p. 11)

Also, regarding understanding across lines of difference, Mary Catherine Bateson (2000) reminds us, "Curiosity and respect. We all fall short in these disciplines" (p. 12).

Curiosity and Respect

By respecting, studying, and learning from the stories of people who have migrated from one country or culture to another, we can learn to participate in cultures different from our own. By eliciting and by paying attention to newcomers to our communities, we, as academics and teachers, can discover information that is not currently available. We can disseminate information about our findings in academic journals and through sources broader than these journals so that communities and educational institutions around the world can begin to provide more knowledgeable support for refugees.

Regardless of the country or community we work in, this issue of connecting with people from a culture different from one's own is much more than reading multicultural literature or following court cases on affirmative action or learning new histories. It's more than the fact that since the 1990s more people have migrated all over the world than ever before. And at the same time, this curious, respectful participation is all of those things as well. Curiosity and respect are personal. Curiosity and respect are communal. Schools and curricula are a composite of personal learning and teaching that occurs among students and their teachers. So how do we do it? The answer is very complicated. The only "non-answer" is not to think about it and not to do anything.

The Personal

People want to belong. Some of the teachers and adult student teachers I work with have past experiences similar to the experiences of different migrating families that show the complicated conflict surrounding the issue of family loyalty. A teacher education student wrote about her memories in a journal entry.

> Racial identity has been a running theme in my life. For the first decade of my life I didn't think about being Hispanic. I just was me. When I moved from an urban area on the East coast to a suburban area all that changed. Being the only Hispanic in an entire K-6 school was devastating to me. All of a sudden I was "different." I quickly learned how cruelly "different" can be treated. My goal for that whole year was to do every thing I could to blend in. Before I knew it I had begun the process of hiding who I was. I changed my dinner on my nutrition logs. I stopped talking Spanish and wouldn't listen or dance to the music. I pretended that race was only the color of my skin.
>
> This process ranged at different levels of intensity and different periods of time. I remember that towards the end of high school there were several Hispanic girls in my class. They all hung out together, but I didn't. By this time my race, my cultural ties, were so suppressed that I didn't fit in socially with them. Yet, I didn't completely fit in with my "white" friends either. (Quintero, 2007, p. 117)

Another student from a different background wrote:

> My memories of Brazil are quite cloudy because my family and I immigrated to the United States when I was about six or seven years old. We left most of our family in Brazil in search of a better life filled with a wealth of opportunities, in search of "the American dream" some may say. The United States not only offered my family and I the American Dream, but also the United States offered me some confusion.
>
> As a young girl in an effort to assimilate to the culture that I now found myself part of, the American culture, I rejected the culture that I once called my own. This rejection came in the form of silence about my Brazilian culture. Some of this rejection can be attributed to the negative outlook the United States has on third world countries. As the writer, Gloria Anzaldúa (1999), writes in her book, *Borderlands: The New Mestiza/La Frontera*, "The U.S.-Mexican border es una herida abierta where the Third World goes against the fires and bleeds" (p. 3). I felt that as a native from a third world country my culture was not good enough for my new "American" friends to share. As the years passed the silence only grew and grew. This silence was quite discomforting because I was constantly reminded of a culture that had as much to offer as the one I now called my own. My experiences are much like Anzaldúa's.
>
> I wanted to reject my Brazilian culture, through rice and beans, samba, Capoeira, and Guarana, I was constantly reminded that rejection would not be a possibility. I had daily reminders of my Brazilian culture because it was evident in my life at home …, I was living in and am still living in a borderland, "a vague and undetermined place created by the emotional residue of an unnatural boundary. It is a constant state of transition (1999, p. 3)." My borderland is between Brazil and the United States rather than Anzaldúa's Texas and Mexico borderland.
>
> While I learned to speak English shortly after I arrived in the United States, the main language spoken at home was Portuguese, our meals during dinner almost consisted of rice and beans, salad, some form of meat, and Guarana. Every so often

we ate the more typical American meals from McDonalds and Burger King. These constant contradictions were quite unsettling, but I came to terms with it, or I thought I did, until I returned to Brazil with the university. (She went on to describe her hurt and confusion over her new classmates' misunderstandings of her native people and their ways of life.) (Quintero, 2009, p. 6)

Educators, teachers and researchers alike are relatively uninformed about the complex struggles of the families of students in our schools. Through several in-depth interviews, we learned a bit about the complex story of Mariam,[1] a woman I met in Minnesota. She, a Somalian, gave birth to twins in her home city in Somalia literally in the middle of civil war. When she woke up after almost dying from the difficult birth, she was told by her husband's family that both baby boys had died. She eventually gained asylum in the United States, and twelve years later, she settled in a small city in Minnesota with a preschool child and a toddler. She took advantage of Head Start for her children and various social services for her health issues that included Post-Traumatic Stress Disorder. Her life was complicated. Then Ali, age thirteen, was brought to her door step by a cousin who had been raising the boy in Texas. This was one of the twins that she didn't know had survived his traumatic birth back in Somalia. The relative left the boy with her. She had no information about his past years, his history, his life. She had no financial support from the child's father. And as one might imagine, the boy had many issues of his own. Life as a teenager in a new community with a family he'd never met was difficult. This family exemplifies issues of complex history from a war-torn country, a contentious relationship among extended family, childrearing issues, cultural conflicts and misconceptions in a new country, and a desperate need for empowerment and advocacy skills.

Pa, from Laos, by way of refugee camps in Thailand was in a family literacy class, also in Minnesota. Through interviews and her autobiographical writing we learned that for her whole life, in Laos and later in the camp in Thailand, she grew the food for her family. She also grew herbs for medicine and flax for making the cloth to make the clothes. Imagine her frustration with the climate, the soil, and ecosystem in her new home in frozen northern Minnesota.

These stories are not particular to the United States. Emmanuel was born during war in Sudan. At age seven or eight, he was taken from his family and forced to fight as a child soldier. A few years later he escaped to Kenya, where he was adopted by a British aid worker. In spite of being free of the army, Emmanuel still had a soldier's mentality and found it difficult to

---

[1] All names have been changed to protect privacy.

adjust to his new conventional and more loving life. "It's hard to experience love when you've never had any" (STAR, 2005, p. 1).

Emmanuel Jal started writing and performing songs to cheer up his fellow school mates. It was during his time as a student at the University of Westminster in Kenya that Jal's music became known and he was made an international music star. Yet, he is still haunted by his experiences as a child. At the same time, he is enormously positive about his life and his future. He believes, "The normal people [of Sudan] are for peace" (STAR, 2005, p. 1).

Migration affects millions of people every year from all corners of the globe and virtually every nation state, yet rational analysis and policy discussion on migration and its effects on families are severely lacking. Often policy and educational forums consider the topic of migration to be too politically sensitive or overwhelming to address. As a result, countries are unprepared to deal with recent developments in international migration and generally make decisions related to migration in an uninformed manner without the benefit of a participatory dialogue.

Meanwhile, the children are in our classrooms and teachers and educators must not assume the "the government" is taking care of the urgent needs of the families. Sadly, no international migration institution or mechanism manages the rights of people who move between countries. At the national level, policies tend to focus overwhelmingly on the legal exclusion of unauthorized migrants, making the need for a policy framework to guide this phenomenon ever more urgent. As population and poverty trends continue to further divide the world into stark divisions of poor, young, and overpopulated states on one hand, and wealthy, aging, and declining population states on the other, migratory pressures will only intensify, making the need for a policy framework to guide this phenomenon ever more urgent. These needs for policy considerations directly affect education (http://www.eginitiative.org/).

It is specifically the complex needs and strengths of migrating people and the continually more pluralistic makeup of communities that demand the use of critical theory and critical literacy in the design, implementation, and resulting research in diverse communities.

In its early stages, critical pedagogy grew out of the efforts of Paulo Freire and his literacy campaigns among peasants in rural Brazil who had virtually no access to education, or, in a few rare situations, access to a standardized form of teaching and texts that had no relationship to their educational needs and personal and community agendas. Many recent generations of North American teachers and cultural workers who have been influenced by Freire's work have used the theoretical framework and methods with urban minority populations in major metropolitan centers. Proponents of critical pedagogy often fail to acknowledge that culture is based in ecological systems. Furthermore, place-based education formats have developed an ecological and rural emphasis that is often addressed separately from the cultural conflicts in mainstream, dominant American culture. The focus on local, ecological experience of place-based approaches is sometimes hesitant to link ecological themes with critical themes such as urbanization and global capitalism and the homogenization of culture (Gruenewald, 2003).

Gruenewald (2003) tells us that place becomes critical because it focuses attention on analyzing how economic and political decisions impact particular places (Berry, 1992; Haas & Nachtigal, 1998; Orr, 1992; Theobald, 1997). Place, in other words, relates to local and regional politics that is attuned to the particularities of where people actually live and that is connected to global development trends that impact local places.

However, these different contexts and emphases of each tradition don't negate the contextual and theoretical relationships between the two. McLaren and Giroux (1990) addressed migrant education, issues of race, class, gender, and corporate hegemony as they affect rural community life and education (Lopez, Scribner & Mahitivanichcha, 2001). Similarly, some place-based educators are undoubtedly Freirean "cultural workers" (Freire, 1998). These teachers often embrace urban contexts and are involved in ecological projects such as naming environmental racism, organizing community gardens, and initiating other community development activities that make urban and rural, social and ecological connections (Hart, 1997; Smith, 2002; Smith & Williams, 1999). Articulating a critical pedagogy of place is a response against educational reform policies and practices that disregard local and regional histories and preferences and leave unexamined the relationship between education and the politics of economic development. Such alternatively built approaches to learning can be encouraged through the use of personal and community story and history and critical literacy, beginning with the early childhood classroom.

Curiosity and Respect in the Classroom

Many teacher education students I work with reflect in their teaching journals about ways their history and ongoing personal experiences with diversity have the potential to provide some meaningful bridges for students and families in the community of a school. One teacher education student wrote at the beginning of her student teaching experience in Chinatown in New York City:

On the first day of class, most of the parents and all the students in the entire elementary school gathered in the cafeteria on the first floor. As I waited for our class to arrive, a father approached me and began speaking in a Chinese dialect I regretfully could not understand. I explained that I could not understand and he apologized. Thinking back, I should've asked him in Mandarin if he spoke Mandarin because it is a fairly universal dialect. We could have made that important instant connection instead of creating distance.

On another day, I walked a student down alone because he was the last one to copy down his homework. As we approached our meeting ground on the playground, the student's father asked me if I spoke Mandarin. I smiled and replied, "Yes!" The father continued on to express his concern about his son and homework. Basically, he never saw his son do homework; his son just played video games all the time. Last year, he found his son's desk drawer stuffed with papers and thought he might be doing the same this year. To sum up our conversation, I informed the father that we did indeed assign homework every day and I would make sure to check to see he had completed it each and every day. We discussed other topics and concerns but his main worry was his son's homework. As they departed, the father asked me what my surname was (I'm not sure how to translate, but when you ask this question, it implies that you have a Chinese surname). I told him that I was mixed blood, but my mom's name is Lin. He then asked me if he should call me Lin Xiao Jie (Miss Lin) and I said, "of course." It felt really amazing to feel his trust in me and to have established this connection.

At the early morning meeting, I helped one of the parents translate my cooperating teacher's concerns, thoughts and answers to questions. By the end of the conference, … I was able to calm some of their fears and assure them their son or daughter was doing great and would excel. One mother was worried about her daughter needing speech therapy, so we visited the speech therapist together and I helped her translate that her daughter improved so much last year, therapy wasn't necessary this year. Needless to say she was very pleased. It made a big difference being able to speak their native tongue and I'm really glad I was placed in a bilingual school.

Another teacher education student, who is very knowledgeable about her particular community, acknowledged that we always have more to learn. She reported to the class:

I had a chance to speak with my mother's hairdresser this weekend. Her name is N. and she is from Senegal. N. lived in Senegal most of her life. She has been in the United States for only two years. I was actually fascinated with her story, because she accomplished so much in just two years. Learning a different language as an adult is difficult and N. speaks Senegalese and English. She works as a hairdresser and she is a student at the local community college. She says she is taking math and English courses. She said she's good in math but she's struggling with English. She said, "I get all As in math, but English is too hard." N. works in Flatbush; many people from Africa work and live in this area. N. said she used to be embarrassed by her accent when she's speaking English. Now she says she is more confident. I feel confidence is an important factor when acquiring different languages. Schools and teachers have to support and encourage English Language Learners just like English-speaking students. English Language Learners students should be a part of the classroom community and not isolated from it.

Some time ago, a friend and I (Rummel & Quintero, 1997) studied effective literacy teachers and found that teachers bring their past experiences and present values and priorities into the schools. Teachers' beliefs and their life experiences cannot be separated from what they do in the classroom. Outstanding educators show an interest in and acceptance of many students' families, cultures, and differences. We (Rummel & Quintero, 1997) found that teachers who support children and their cultural, linguistic context in school have some common approaches to pedagogy. They all exhibit a belief that it is their responsibility to find ways of engaging all their students in learning activity. They accept responsibility for making the classroom an interesting, engaging place. They work to provide students the opportunity to make connections on many levels. For example, one said:

> Using literature and music are other ways that can expose children to educational material. Instead of reading the Disney's *Cinderella*, why not pick up a copy of the Korean version? Not only does it create a chance to expose children to different types of literature, but it can also lead to other topics like different foods, celebrations, music, clothing, and so on. In order to create well-rounded, critical thinkers we need to expose children to more than just chalk on a blackboard.

One group of teacher education students read the storybook *Madlenka* by Peter Sis (2000). The story is about a little girl named Madlenka, whose tooth is loose. She visits her friends and neighbors around her block to let them know. The book introduces each of them and shows a little about their culture, language, and customs. The illustrations display different symbols, monuments, and geographic locations that are representative of the countries mentioned in the book. In the beginning of the book there is a map of Manhattan that shows exactly where Madlenka lives, and at the end of the book there is a map of the world, showing the locations of countries of the people that she interacts with without even leaving her city. Then, the assignment was to go out into the community near to their current teaching placement and bring back information that could stimulate a tangible learning experience for students of various ages.

One teacher education student wrote after the experience:

> While on my Madlenka journey, it was almost impossible to escape visual art. I collected a lot of menus from all the restaurants in this neighborhood. I was attracted to all the drawings and small sketches on the covers. It isn't the type of art that will make it into a museum, but it does represent a small piece of the community. Graffiti seems to be the most abundant form of art in this neighborhood, and although it can be a nuisance at times, some of it is lovely and shows that someone took a lot of time and energy to put it there.

Curiosity and Respect in the Community

A teacher education student from the same group working in another neighborhood in New York City wrote this about her experience as she went on a walk around the block: "How amazing is it that all the ideas and connections among us are right before our eyes and we don't see them unless we are asked a specific question exploration?"

Then she added:

> While I was walking, I stopped for a cup of coffee. I sat down at the counter and immediately took note of two young Asian children who were ripping up construction paper. I waited a few minutes and watched them with interest. Then, I asked them what they were doing. They told me that it was their great-grandmother's birthday and "because she's old" she likes these kinds of old things. I asked them what they meant and they explained that you couldn't always go in to a store and buy cards or even writing paper, and the people in Tokyo invented a way to make paper, and that every year that is what they make their great-grandmother as a gift. One of the children pointed above the counter and showed me another card that they had made. Right there before my very eyes was a culturally rich history/geography/art lesson with a practical product.

Another teacher education student who participated in the *Madlenka* storybook and follow-up activity visited her grandmother's neighborhood and learned from some experts. She wrote about her experience:

> I visited two hair-braiding shops in Brooklyn. I gathered some information and background knowledge. I thought about history, science, math and art, building community and relationships. Not only did I learn more about people, their customs, and history, I learned more about myself as well. I was born here in America, I am of African descent with roots from the West Indies. In school I never really learned much about multiculturalism. I never learned a great deal about African civilizations, art, history, etc. African/black history is in fact very important in American history ... Schools help shape one's identity and culture and vice versa. Self-concept has everything to do with how one views her/himself and how others view that person. How can one possibly go through life with marginal knowledge or misrepresentation of who they are and where they come from?

Curiosity and Respect in the International Context

Acknowledging the need to examine the relationship between education and politics of economics, the current sociopolitical context of the early 21st century, we may look to the work being done on an international level around the issue of global migration. The Global Commission on International Migration was launched by the then United Nations secretary-general Kofi Annan in December 2003. The Commission's aim was to analyze gaps in current policy approaches to international migration and provide a framework for a coherent, comprehensive, and global response. The Commission was committed to "reframe the current debate on migration in a way that grips the public and political imagination."

The Migration Policy Institute (MPI) was an independent, non-partisan, non-profit think tank in Washington, DC, dedicated to the study of the movement of people worldwide. MPI provided analysis, development, and evaluation of migration and refugee policies at the local, national, and international levels. It hoped to meet the rising demand for pragmatic and thoughtful responses to the challenges and opportunities that large-scale migration, whether voluntary or forced, presents to communities and institutions in an increasingly integrated world. The project conducted a set of coordinated activities carried out by a membership of research, policy, and non-governmental organizations who share a vision of strengthened migration policy by means of applied academic research. The Metropolis membership was composed of representatives from more than twenty countries and a number of international research and policy organizations representing a wide range of policy and academic interests. Members worked collaboratively on issues of immigration and integration, always with the goal of strengthening policy and thereby allowing societies to better manage the challenges and opportunities that immigration presents, especially to their cities (Migration Policy Institute, 2004; http://www.migrationpolicy.org/ retrieved November 21, 2005).

In the United Kingdom, the Refugee Council operates a number of programs for the vast and urgent needs of migrating families. This is the largest organization in the United Kingdom working with asylum seekers and refugees. The Refugee Council is governed by a Board of Trustees, which includes strong refugee representation. It is an organization consisting of various member organizations. Since 1983, the Council has increased its membership base from 50 to nearly 180, a significant number of which are refugee community organizations. The Council regularly consults with its membership base.

The Refugee Council is a strongly independent organization and registered as a charity. It is funded by local, central, and European government grants, grants from trust funds and corporations, and funds provided by individuals through one time donations, standing order arrangements, legacies, and their attendance at Refugee Council events.

The Refugee Council's work includes the following:

- giving advice and support to asylum seekers and refugees to help them rebuild their lives;
- working with refugee community organizations and helping them grow and serve their communities;
- caring for unaccompanied refugee children to help them feel safe and supported in the United Kingdom;

- offering training and employment courses to enable asylum seekers and refugees to use their skills and qualifications;
- campaigning and lobbying for refugees' voices to be heard in the United Kingdom and abroad; keeping them high on the political agenda and discussed in the media;
- producing authoritative information on refugee issues worldwide, including reports, statistics, and analysis.
- (http://www.refugeecouncil.org.uk/refugeecouncil/therefugeecouncil.htm,retrieved January 21, 2006)

While the work of the Refugee Council is by and large very effective, a critical perspective requires a closer look at difficult issues affecting the work of the organization. The Refugee Council has the complex job of being strong advocates for asylum seekers and criticizing the Home Office for not enough support and strong enough action, while at the same time working with this political, government bureaucracy (Maw, 2006).

To name a few of the many services provided for asylum seekers and refugees in the London area: there is a One Stop Service in which assistance is given based upon Geneva Convention 1951 (with the assistance of a staff of interpreters of a wide array of world languages) in the tasks of registration for needed services, application issues, and multiple family supports. There is a large Children's Sector that provides general services for families with young children and, through their work with the Medical Foundation for Victims of Torture, very specific services for children and unaccompanied minors.

The office in Brixton supports a large Day Center where a staff cook and a few volunteers provide hot meals for 250 people a day. The Day Center has hot showers, toys for children, and space and volunteers for various classes such as English as a Foreign Language. The staff organize get-togethers for youth every Tuesday evening where these young people can listen to music, eat, and talk with others their age in similar situations.

Learning from Migrating People

As we consider needs of migrating populations, rights, issues of neighborhood including cultural and ecological place, and critical literacy, a look at recent work in New Literacy Studies is useful. In terms of theory, Brandt and Clinton (2002) have warned of the limits of focusing only on the local contexts as many New Literacy Studies projects have done. They advocate recognizing the extent to which literacy does often come to local situations from outside and brings with it both skills and meanings that are larger than the emic perspective favored by New Literacy Studies. Brandt and Clinton's (2002) work provides a way of characterizing the local/global debate in which everyday literacy practices play a central role. Therefore, we educators working on local literacy issues can draw from new efforts to learn globally. The question raised in the early New Literacy Studies work concerning how we can characterize the shift from observing literacy events to conceptualizing literacy practices does provide both a methodological and empirical way of dealing with this relationship, thereby taking account of Brandt and Clinton's (2002) concern with the "limits of the local." Collins and Blot (2002) believe that while New Literacy Studies has generated a compelling series of ethnographies of literacy, there is a danger of simply accumulating more descriptions of local literacies without addressing general questions of both theory and practice.

I believe that by viewing literacy issues surrounding the complex lives and learning in immigrant and refugee families through a lens of critical theory and critical literacy and by taking guidance from a critical pedagogy of place and New Literacy Studies we will be able to get at a more authentic consideration of literacy theory, practice, and advocacy. For example, issues regarding bilingualism and biliteracy are always complex. Mr. Quintanilla told us,

> I was curious because I went across the border. My cousins in Mexico, across the border, were learning to read in Spanish. They had all these magazines lying around. I can still remember reading, *La Bruja*, and many others. Spanish seemed really easy to me. I learned to read and not to write. There is a difference because we were right on the border. We were sometimes criticized because they would say you can't speak English correctly and you can't speak Spanish correctly … Like still in the 8th grade, I'd turn the radio on and I'd be listening to a song and I still couldn't understand what they were saying; it was too fast. Because when we went home from school you know, we didn't speak English at home. Because the parents didn't speak any English and it would be disrespectful. The other thing was that we were all Mexican American and you spoke English and your brothers would say, "Hey, he thinks he is a big shot, because he knows English." It was kind of a shame thing to do. That doesn't help you when you are learning the language. I didn't have trouble with reading and comprehension because I had very good teachers. I think. I learned the library quickly…(1997, pp. 165–166)

These are issues that are at the center of some developments in New Literacy Studies. Maybin (2000) connects New Literacy Studies to other social-critical work, offering a way of linking Foucauldian notions of Discourse, Bakhtinian notions of intertextuality, and work in Critical Discourse Analysis with the recognition from New Literacy Studies of the articulation of different discourses which are dynamically interwoven in people's everyday literacy activities. Janks (2000), located in South Africa, also relates literacy studies to broader social theory as a means of synthesizing the various strands of critical literacy education. Freebody (2003), in Australia, writes of the relationship between New Literacy Studies and critical literacy as an approach to the acquisition and use of reading and writing in educational contexts that takes account of relationships of power and domination.

Also in the United Kingdom is a unique organization giving university students and young people the opportunity to learn from and be advocates for migrating families. This group, Student Action for Refugees or STAR, has a threefold mission to

- learn about and raise awareness of refugee issues in innovative ways;
- support refugees in a practical way in their local communities through volunteering; and
- campaign with and for the rights of refugees everywhere.

The STAR network is made up of university-based student groups, other young people involved in the STAR Youth Network, and Friends of STAR (individuals and organizations who support the work of STAR). The group believes that refugees and asylum seekers are a vulnerable group of people who often have a long and difficult struggle to secure their safety in another country. As people fleeing persecution, torture, and prejudice they need and deserve support. Furthermore, as a new generation it is vital that students and young people have a positive attitude toward refugees, asylum seekers, and displaced people (King, 2006). Natasha King, the Student Outreach Officer for STAR, said in response to a question about maintaining and sustaining work in contexts where the needs are so great and the issues so complicated:

> At the national level of issues, racism, lack of information, fear on the part of native Britons about their jobs being "taken" by asylum seekers is really depressing, but that at the local university-by-university level the small projects can be so effective that it is really encouraging ... (2006, p. 2)

Freire states in his last published work (1998),

> There are times when I fear that someone reading this…may think that there is now no place among us for the dreamer and the believer in utopia. Yet, what I have been saying up to now is now the stuff of inconsequential dreamers. It has to do with the very nature of men and women as makers and dreamers of history and not simply as casualties of an a priori vision of the world. (p. 55)

There is no question about the power of personal histories, art, and imagination that has a definite role in creating a sense of place, a community. A few years ago, a colleague at Middle Eastern Technical University in Ankara, Turkey, and I began interviewing refugee families in Turkey. The interviews were framed by the following questions: In what ways are caregivers able to educate their children within the context of refugee camps or other refugee contexts? Are programs available to support the children's learning? We were interested in documenting parents' strengths and challenges. We found that those fifteen interviews just barely touched on what are grave and dramatic worldwide problems for refugees and their children. We were struck by the severity of the needs and the lack of information both for the refugees themselves and the agencies and educational institutions that may be in a position to ultimately provide some assistance (Quintero, 2004).

We interviewed the director of the Turkish Office of United Nations Higher Commission on Refugees. We learned that the 1951 Geneva Convention dictates that refugees can be in Turkey temporarily as asylum seekers, and that they must apply to be recognized as refugees in order to receive services. On average, the refugees register within ten days of being in the country (Turkey, in this case). There are three steps to process: First there is an interview, and then the refugee must wait two to three months for a decision. The second phase is the waiting period for resettlement in the United States, Canada, Australia, and Scandinavian countries and other countries that accept refugees. The average time for resettlement is one and a half to two years. There is an appeal process when refugee status is denied. There is a limit to the number who can be asylum seekers. Estimates of refugees granted and denied asylum status indicate that only one in ten of refugees who apply for asylum status are granted the status (Icduygu, 2000). If asylum status is granted, the refugees have financial, medical, social, and psychological counseling. If asylum status is not granted, the refugees receive nothing. No money, no medical assistance, no schooling, no work permits. Nothing.

In August of 2002, our interview informants for the most part had been denied status. The first woman we interviewed, whose husband had been a police officer in Iran and who because of refusal to carry out an "unethical and inhuman" procedure, was, along with his family, driven out of Iran at gunpoint. The family applied for asylum status and was denied. I asked the interviewee whether they were told why they were denied: "No. Not even when I tried to find out, they wouldn't talk to me. They said my file was closed" (Quintero, 2004, p. 51).

Yet this woman did her best to educate her two children and the young children of other refugees who were in a similar situation. She said:

> I borrow books (in Farsi) that some other refugees have or have made for the children. I use the books so that my children don't forget their culture and language. And it is important to have contact with other refugees…(Quintero, 2004, p. 51)

Her children were not permitted to go to school. Because they feared for their safety, they could not return to their country.

Another woman we interviewed explained that her family has been in Turkey for four years. She has three children: twin boys and a daughter. They were rejected for asylum status by United Nations High Commission for Refugees, so she slept in front of their office door for forty days and nights to learn why they were rejected and to protest their decision. She was never told. She explained:

> We are political refugees. My two brothers were sentenced to death and killed. They were members of Halkın Mücahitleri which is an opposition organization. My other brother ran away from Iran without a passport. We are not members of that organization, but because of my brothers the government always bothered us. My kids could not go to school freely. Then we had to run away from the country to be safe…My sons forgot their mother tongue. I cannot teach them because my stress level is very high. I also have to work because my husband is sick and he cannot work. (Quintero, 2004, p. 52)

We interviewed another family. The mother did not speak English or Turkish, so her husband interpreted. They are from Iraq. They have four children of ages seven, nine, twelve, and fourteen. They had been in Turkey for eighteen months at the time of the interview. The UNHCR denied the family asylum status and closed their case. The husband could not find a job because people did not want somebody who does not have an identity authorized by the Turkish government. At the same time, they didn't have anybody who could help them find an illegal job. The church paid their rent and gave them eighteen dollars for food every two weeks. They could buy only bread with that money.

The father said he tries to teach the children English. He said, "There is no play, no pictures, no picnics…nothing for my children." The only activity they engage in is coming to church, but sometimes they cannot come because they don't have money to pay for the dolmu (bus). Sometimes they have to walk a long way. When we asked what were his hopes for his children in the future, he said, "To have a country." He went into detail about his reasons for being a refugee.

> I could not betray my conscience and become a spy working for the Iraqi regime. All my problems were due to the simple fact that I did not deceive and surrender three persons working for the UN Oil-for-Food programme as inspectors to the Iraqi intelligence on espionage over Iraq. My torturers told me that they would be accused of espionage working for the Americans against Saddam. Every Iraqi working for the projects under Oil-for-Food programme has been expected to report on international staff back to Baghdad. As I refused to collaborate in that, I was being accused of espionage as well and I was severely subjected to torture and ill-treatment by the Muhabarat. (Both he and his wife were assaulted and thugs broke the arm of his seven-year-old son. When agents showed him his death warrant signed by Hussein, he and his wife and children fled.) I had been working for the United Nations under contract for four and a half years, I had a very good life, house, a shop, a car. I had to leave all that and flee to Turkey seeking asylum. (Quintero, 2004, p. 52)

Unaccompanied Minors

An often unpublicized aspect of world migration that is particularly complicated and disturbing is that of unaccompanied minors. In the United Kingdom alone in April 2004 there were an estimated 6,500 unaccompanied minors under age eighteen in social services care and 2,500 separated young people over eighteen entitled to leaving care support (services to support their living after they begin to live indepently) (NRUC, 2004). The majority of young people who have been separated from their families are between sixteen and eighteen years of age. Although these young people in the United Kingdom are protected under the Children Act of 1989 and the Children (Leaving Care) Act of 2000, they face intolerable problems and barriers. For example, the housing made available to them is scarce and of poor quality, these children are prone to emotional or mental health problems, they lack English language skills, and they face racism and discrimination. They have difficulty in accessing services such as medical care, school, college, and they don't understand the workings of the social system they have entered. Often these youth have their age disputed and are treated as an adult, which in some instances results in them being held in immigration detention centers (Young Refugees, 2005).

Many people in the United States have experienced exile in one form or another. Edward Said (1990) explained, "Exile is strangely compelling to think about but terrible to experience. It is the unhealable rift forced between a human being and a native place, between the self and its true home ..." (p. 357). Keeping this poignant acknowledgment in the forefront, we can at the same time learn from the exiled peoples and those who have been uprooted. Bateson (2004) finds hope in families she has met:

> As I write about the lives of individuals, I hope to show how they both adapt to and create their environments so that they in turn are able to grow within them. Ultimately, I see this process as related to the question of how humankind is to make a home on this planet without soiling or incinerating its nest. (Bateson, 2004, p. 5)

Teacher Education Participants Delve into Curiosity and Respect

One of the many problem-posing activities that our student teachers participate in on their journey of learning about critical literacy in the early childhood classrooms is a version of the popular "Where I'm From" poetry activity that we have adapted from Christensen (2000). The activity gets at the critical literacy intention of recognizing personal history as a way to invite new learning from others' histories and connecting with others. The activity for the teacher education students set them thinking in terms of the possibilities they have. They submitted short stanzas of their own poetry as a part of the complicated conversation about connecting with others. The activity was structured using the problem-posing structure of critical pedagogy.

During the listening section the teacher education students were asked to write a few sentences about a childhood memory that involves a family (however you define family) celebration involving friends, food, and neighborhood. Then after a few minutes, during the dialogue section of the lesson, the participants discussed their memories with a partner.

Then, for the action activity the participants engaged in a "Where I'm From" activity using the following guidelines:

1. Make a list of items found around your home: stacks of newspapers, dirty socks, chewing gum wrappers, etc.
2. Make a list of items found in your yard or outside your apartment.
3. Make a list of items found in your neighborhood.
4. Make a list of relatives' names … especially ones that link you to the past.
5. Make a list of sayings you associate with your family.
6. Make a list of names of foods and dishes that recall family gatherings.
7. Make a list of places where you keep your childhood memories.
8. Discuss your lists.
9. Write … "I'm from"… poem.
10. Read Around.
11. Try it out with children in your classes.

A few excerpts from the student teachers' poems show the breadth of personal experience from which they could build upon for their "connecting with others" in their teaching.

I'm from a small island country.
I'm from Taiwan.

I'm from the delicious Taiwanese food.
Ma Po Tofu, Chow Mein, Spring Roll, Steamed Dumplings
Grandma is good at cooking.
We visited her very often.
I was wondering why Grandma couldn't read the newspaper.
I taught her ㄅㄆㄇㄈ when I was a first grader.
I taught her to write her name 袁黃逢妹.
I was also wondering why Grandma's name has four characters.
She explained that women in her generation have their husband's last name as their last name.

*****

Where I'm from is Jerusalem, sea talking girl,
Born to mid wives.
Where I'm from mother and father
Spoke to each another in a foreign tongue is
Where I'm from.

*****

I am from photo albums filled with memories
of relatives in a far off
distant place.
I am from Gyiagyia's stories and songs
from spanakopita, roast lamb, and cookies
made with love.

I am from a family seeped in culture and traditions
from a people blessed with faith, pride, and love.
I am from hard work and determination,
from struggle and success.
I am from a family of immigrants.

*****

I am from Halmoni, seven eemoes, three samchons, a never ending list of
tight knit cousins, loving parents, a musical family, a happy simple family of
three that I now longingly wish I could have again

I am from the affectionate "mani muk uhs" of eemo and halmoni, "mooh uhs
eedun yul sheem hee hae," "neehahrahwoo" of my halahbuhjee, and my parents comforting words of "I love you woo ree ddal"

I am from a traditionally rich and historically diverse Korean heritage,
from Koguryo to Shilla Dynasty, Confucian principles, a once oppressed
people who rose to become a globally recognized nation

*****

I am from the, "Ay bendito," "Ave maria"
and "Dios te bendiga hijita" phrases
from mom and dad
phrases I hear when they are happy and mad
I am from the "Si Dios quiere," and "Portate bien"
consejos that are daily reminders of my humble origins
of who I am, where I am from and what I believe.

Participants in this study continually discussed why and how our histories are important in our teaching and in our research. Moll, Gonzalez, and Amanti (2005) write, "The use of traditional pedagogical approaches to learning in public schools threatens the cultural frame and conflicts with cultural identity ..." (p. 82). Liz Brooker (2002) studied the pedagogical patterns of Bangladeshi families and compared them to those pedagogical patterns in native British families and those in the early years program in a quality school. She found that the Bangladeshi children did not have a "childish world." Bangladeshi children are used to intergenerational interactions in their families and when specific learning is required it is through rote methods. Before young children go to school for the first time at age four or five, their mothers tell them to "sit quietly and study hard" (Brooker, 2002). This directly conflicts with one of the most consistent expectations placed on primary children in Western cultures, which is to be actively engaged (verbally and kinesthetically) in their learning. Her research challenges early childhood educators to provide daily connections, human and pedagogical, for all learners.

However, the education of teachers in cultural matters does not stop there. Understanding children is only half the requirement for effective interaction with student groups. Teachers must understand the parents of the students, whose cultural and social histories are often very different from those of the teachers. Educators must take responsibility for participating in their newly composed classroom and school culture, which now involves people from many cultures. It has been the practice in the past to produce a document that details backgrounds on the pupils' countries of origin and that shows ways to adapt the curriculum. This information is vital but not put to adequate use. A document that sits stagnantly in a staff room is insufficient. The information must be shared, with historical facts and human story so that educators can connect with the knowledge and put it into immediate practice.

Schooling in these times is an experience in dissonance between two forces: on the one hand, a trend toward a global homogenization that brings people and countries closer than ever, and, on the other hand, the affirmation of what is specific and particular. This tension obviously has implications for decisions about teaching: Are we concerned with the education of the citizen for a globally patterned culture or for a particular cultural identity? Why are we not concerned with both? None of us lives or works in isolation, and we draw our inspiration from a world community.

What we call the familiar is built up in layers to a structure known so deeply that it is taken for granted and virtually impossible to observe without the help of contrast.

Encountering family issues in a strange setting is like returning on a second circuit of a Möbius strip and coming to the experience from the opposite side. Seen from a contrasting point of view or seen suddenly through the eyes of an outsider, one's own familiar patterns can become accessible to choice and criticism. With yet another return, what seemed radically different is revealed as part of a common space. (Bateson, 1994, p. 31)

As explained in Chapter One, excerpts from case studies are included to illustrate not only the themes as they emerged from research done in the early childhood classrooms with different ages of children, but also the aspects of critical theory—participant histories, multiple forms of knowledge, and transformative action. As Bruner (1990) reminds us, one way we learn is through our own and other people's stories to understand cultures and build relationships. These case study excerpts show some of the interactions in various classrooms when a critical literacy framework is used for designing and implementing curriculum.

Sometimes student teachers who are unfamiliar with Freire's work at first are confused by the term "problem-posing." They ask whether the method requires that there be a "problem." I then spend some time discussing the difference between calling something a problem and problematizing a situation or a set of ideas. The problem-posing comes from Freire's (1985) ideas about conscientization, which he defines as "the process by which human beings participate in a transforming act" (p. 106). He goes on to say that "conscientization thus involves a constant clarification of that which remains hidden within us while we move about in the world, though we are not necessarily regarding the world as the object of our critical reflection" (p. 107). The method encourages students to choose and examine voices in literature through poetry, fiction, academic research reports, and memory, focusing on authenticity of multiple experiences in multiple contexts.

To explain the concept, I ask student teachers to think of incidents in their past or present lives that might be considered critical literacy and then to observe an example of a child in their classrooms using critical literacy. After this assignment, one student wrote:

I remember this occurred for me while I was in ESL (English as a Second Language) class. My ESL teacher first read us the story of the three goats and they had to cross over the bridge. While doing so, they each encountered a troll. I forget the rest of the story, but I can see now how the listening piece comes into play. I also remember writing something about the story (I was too young to remember exactly what it was that I wrote). The best part came about when we each had to act out the play.

I remembered playing the strongest goat. I loved playing the strongest, tallest goat because I had that confidence. I was fearless and I could be anything I wanted to be. I acted the character out with such passion that my teacher was impressed.

The next week, I wanted to continue acting the character, but my teacher let someone else play the role to be fair. I played another role, but I loved playing the lead. So I was reminded of Grace (in Mary Hoffman's storybook, Amazing Grace) when listening and seeing the story. Reading about critical literacy brought this experience that was long dormant in my memory. I did not realize then that I was involved in listening, dialogue (even written dialogue), and action. Now I know, and I feel grateful to my ESL teacher for teaching me in this method.

Critical Literacy in Action—Connecting with Others
Case Study One
The following synopsis is from a case study of a teacher education student implementing a critical literacy for a group of first graders in Brooklyn, New York. The findings are summarized according to the sequence of activities of the pedagogical model: Listening, Dialogue, Action. This case study illustrates the importance of personal history and story in learning and in connecting with others.

The participants were kindergarten children from a variety of cultures living in the same neighborhood in Brooklyn, New York, and their student teacher. Some children were recent immigrants to the United States and a few children had moved to New York from a different state. A number of students were bilingual English/Spanish speakers. Sustained observations and interviews over three months' time revealed that the children were inquisitive, active, and particularly enjoyed literacy activities. Many enjoyed lessons centered on visual art and music. Some were interested in mathematical concepts and activities centered on collecting data.

Listening:
The student teacher began the lesson by asking the children whether they or members of their families were from other countries. She had displayed a world map. As the children named a country or place their family lived or had lived in the past, each one came to the map to mark his or her country or place with a post-it note with his or her name on it.

Then the teacher read the storybook *Madlenka* by Peter Sis (2000). The story, as explained earlier in the chapter, is about a little girl named Madlenka and her friends in her neighborhood of different cultures, languages, and customs. The illustrations display different symbols, monuments, and geographic locations that are representative of the countries mentioned in the book. In the beginning of the book there is a map of Manhattan that shows exactly where Madlenka lives, and at the end of the book there is a map of the world, showing the locations of countries of the people that she interacts with without even leaving her city.

Dialogue:

The student teacher led a discussion asking the children about the story. She asked questions such as, "What did Madlenka see on her neighborhood walk? What things was she learning from her friends?"

A discussion was then held about who the children meet in their communities. After starting with naming familiar shopkeepers and neighbors, the teacher reminded them that some of the characters in Madlenka's story were from specific places. For example, the baker was from France and the greengrocer was from South America. The teacher asked whether anyone knew a baker who is not from France. She also asked whether anyone has a friend from South America who has a different profession than that of greengrocer.

Several children knew of bakers from Mexico, from Israel, and from Mississippi. She continued with all the shopkeepers represented in the *Madlenka* storybook, all the while writing on a large chart tablet the categories of shopkeepers and the different countries they came from that were known to the children.

This is an example of critical theory and critical literacy. The teacher was using the children's experiential knowledge, the storybook that they love, and asking critical questions to give children opportunities to explore stereotyping and ways to avoid it.

The student teacher wrote a reflection about this in her journal:

> I think using *Madlenka* as part of a child's reading experience could also evoke personal connections for children and could be used as a springboard for writing. Also, given that we are living in such a multicultural society, especially here in New York City, this book depicts different cultures. When looking at the book in class, my attention and personal interest doubled when I saw the Indian newsagent. I felt represented. This personal connection acts as a springboard for further learning experiences in school, such as writing.
>
> It is often that you see an Indian newsagent, Asian shopkeeper, and Latin American grocer. My initial reaction when I saw this book, as an adult, was to think of the stereotypes, but then I convinced myself to go a step further and try to look at the book objectively and also from a child's point of view. I rationalized that even though this book might represent these stereotypes, it does represent a reality that is often seen here in New York City and I can't deny that.

The student teacher went on to implement action activities with the children during choice time.

Action:

1. One center consisted of materials (cardboard boxes, glue, paint, etc.) for the children to create shops and shopkeepers according to their preferences. A copy of *Madlenka* by Peter Sis was available along with rulers and math manipulatives for mapmaking as seen in the storybook.

2. Another center consisted of the storybook of *Whoever You Are* by Mem Fox. This storybook illustrates differences in physical characteristics, languages, dress, food, and shelter for children around the world and, at the same time, stresses the human characteristics that all children—all humans—have in common. Art materials and geography books, hand mirrors, and writing materials were used for the children to explore their own and their friends' origins. Some created self-portraits for a *Who We Are* Wall for the classroom.

3. Using a world map, the student teacher worked with small groups of children in a "Where I'm From" poetry activity. The student teacher began by asking a few girls what they thought a poem was. One said, "it's like a song, it rhymes." Another added, "yeah, it's like a story but it rhymes." The student teacher then told them that she was going to read them a poem that she had written about where she is from, about her home. As she read, the children listened attentively.

I am from the comfy black leather sofa, the magazines—Filmfare, Movie, Society, Indian movies that took me to another world, and ah most importantly Hindi music that always filled the air.

I am from congested streets, street vendors selling clothes, accessories and water chestnuts that gave a sweet aroma to the streets.

I am from fast food restaurants, shops at every nook of the street, bakeries selling sweet bread and creamy fruit cakes.

I am from Nani who had a special way of showing to each of us that we are her favorite grandchild.

I am from "always have a sense of humor—it's one of the most valuable things you can have in life."

I am from my mom's homemade dal, rice, paneer and roti.

I am from diaries hidden alongside the stack of books on my desk, letters and photographs hidden in salad bags in my chest of drawers.

The student teacher reported that

When I said I was from "bakeries selling sweet bread and creamy fruit cakes," the girls said "yum!" I then asked them what they heard. S. excitedly said, "you are from crowded streets and movies!" O. added "sweet bread." L. said "you are from your mom's rice." I then told them I was going to act out something that I like doing at home and I pantomimed reading a book. They said "you are reading." I told them that we were going to take turns and they would act out something that like doing at home which we then would make into our group poem. O. thought for a moment and hesitated before she started. She then pretended to read a book. S. and L. said, "you are reading a book" and O. said "yes." L. acted out stroking a cat. None of us could guess what she was doing and she finally said "I am from stroking a cat!" S. then said, "how can you be from stroking a cat?" L. said "well, that's what I do at home and that is where I am from." S. then acted out watching TV and O. guessed what she was doing. S. then said "I am from watching TV at home." I wrote down all their thoughts. We then read the poem together and then to the whole class.

The student teacher reported that she had been supported by the cooperating teacher, her mentor, in creating these lessons that are very much child centered. They both agreed that method gives the children the chance to express their own views and opinions and connect with others the knowledge they bring from their own families and cultures. The self-portrait was also related to valuing diversity because the children discuss how no one is really "white or black" and it gave the children power to create their identity. The self-portrait, with special cultural construction paper designed to be used to represent different skin colors, provided "transformative action" opportunities for these five-year-olds. Furthermore, the cooperating teacher mentor and student teacher documented that through this series of activities, the content subjects of social studies, literacy, math, and art were addressed. She wrote:

> What each child has to say is valued. There are many chances for class discussions, and other class activities were integrated into this series of "Connecting with Others" problem-posing activities.

References

Anzaldúa, G. (1999). *Borderlands: The new mestiza/La frontera*. San Francisco: Spinsters/Aunt Lute Press.

Bateson, Mary C. (1994). *Peripheral visions: Learning along the way*. New York: Harper Collins.

Bateson, Mary C. (2000). *Full circles, overlapping lives*. New York: Ballantine Books.

Bateson, Mary C. (2004). *Willing to learn: Passages of personal discovery*. New York: Steerforth.

Berry, W. (1992). *Sex, economy, freedom and community*. New York: Pantheon Books.

Brandt, D., & Clinton, K. (2002). Limits of the local: Expanding perspectives of literacy as social practice. ERIC EJ672867.

Brooker, L. (2002). *Starting school: Young children learning cultures*. London: Open University Press.

Bruner, J. (1990). *Acts of meaning*. Cambridge, MA: Harvard University Press.

Christensen, L. (2000). *Reading, writing, and rising up: Teaching about social justice and the power of the written word*. Milwaukee, WI: Rethinking Schools.

Delpit, L. (1995). *Other people's children: Culture and conflict in the classroom.* New York: New Press. http://www.eginitiative.org/

Freebody, P. (2003). Critical literacy. In R. Beach et al. (Eds.), *Multidisciplinary perspectives on literacy research,* pp. 433–454. Cresskill, NJ: Hampton Press.

Freebody, P. (2003). *Qualitative research in education.* Thousand Oaks, CA: Sage.

Freire, P. (1998). *Teachers as cultural workers.* Boulder, CO: Westview Press.

Freire, P. (1985). *The politics of education.* Granby, MA: Bergin & Garvey.

Gruenewald, D. (2003). The best of both worlds: A critical pedagogy of place. *Educational Researcher, 32*(4), 3–12.

Haas, T., & Nachtigal, P. (1998). *Place value.* Charleston, WV: ERIC Press.

Hart, R. (1997). *Children's participation: The theory and practice of involving young citizens in community development and environmental care.* London: Earthscan, Unicef.

Icduygu, A. (2000). The politics of international migratory regimes: Transit migration flows in Turkey. *International Social Science Journal,* vol. 165, 357-367.

Janks, H. (2000). Domination, access, diversity and design: A synthesis for critical literacy education. *Educational Review, 52*(2), 175–186.

King, N. (2006). Interview at STAR offices in London, England. January, 2006.

Lopez, G., Scribner, J., & Mahitivanichcha, K. (2001). Redefining parent involvement: Lessons from high-performing migrant-impacted schools. *American Education Research Journal, 38,* 253–288.

Maw, E. (2006). Interview at One-Stop-Service Refugee Council Office, Brixton, London, England. January 2006.

Maybin, J. (2000). The New Literacy Studies: context, intertextuality and discourse. In D. Barton, M. Hamilton & R. Ivanic (Eds.), *Situated literacies: Reading and writing in context,* pp. 197-209. London: Routledge.

McLaren, P., & Giroux, H. (1990). Critical pedagogy and rural education: A challenge from Poland. *Peabody Journal of Education, 67*(4), 154–165.

Migration Policy Institute (2004). (http://www.migrationpolicy.org/ retrieved November 21, 2005).

Moll, L. C., Gonzalez, N., & Amanti, C. (2005). *Funds of knowledge: Theorizing practices in households, communities, and classrooms.* Mahwah, NJ: Lawrence Erlbaum.

NRUC (National Register for Unaccompanied Children) (2004, Winter). *European Regional and Local Authorities on Asylum and Immigration.* Brussles, BE: Brussels Liason Office.

Orr, D. (1992). *Ecological literacy.* Albany, NY: SUNY Press.

Quintanilla, R. (1997). Raul Quintanilla. In M. Rummel & E. P. Quintero, *Teachers' Reading/Teachers' Lives,* pp. 161–170. Albany, NY: SUNY Press.

Quintero, E. (1994). Magic and risk: Lessons for the future. In G. Weinstein-Shr & E. Quintero (Eds.), *Immigrant learners and their families: Literacy to connect the generations.* Washington, DC: Center for Applied Linguistics/Data Systems.

Quintero, Elizabeth P. (2004). Problem-posing with multicultural children's literature: Developing critical, early childhood curricula. New York: Peter Lang.

Quintero, Elizabeth P. (2007). Critical pedagogy and qualitative inquiry: Lessons from working with refugee families. In A. Hatch (Ed.) *Early childhood qualitative research,* pp. 109-130. New York: Taylor & Francis.

Quintero, Elizabeth P. (2009). Children Using Story to Connect with Others. In Naidich, Fernando (Guest Editor), *Educação,* themed issue on Multiculturalism and Education, Rio de Janeiro, Brazil.

Quintero, E. & Macías, A. H. (1995). To participate, to speak out...: A story from San Elizario Texas. In R. Martin (Ed.), *On equal terms: Addressing issues of race, class and gender in higher education.* New York: SUNY Press.

Realizing rights. (2005). The ethical globalization initiative. http://www.eginitiative.org/ retrieved, October 10.

RefugeeCouncil.(2006).
    http://www.refugeecouncil.org.uk/refugeecouncil/therefugeecouncil.htm,
    retrieved, January 21.

Rummel, Mary K., & Quintero, Elizabeth P. (1997). *Teachers' reading/teachers' lives*, p. 165. Albany, NY: SUNY Press.

Said, E. (2000). The end of Oslo. *The Nation*, October 30, 2000, p. 12.

Sis, P. (2000). *Madlenka*. New York: Farrar, Straus and Giroux.

Smith, G. (2002). Place-based education: Learning to be where we are. *Phi Delta Kappan, 83*, 584–594.

Smith, G., & Williams, D. (1999). *Ecological education in action: On weaving education, culture, and the environment.* Albany, NY: SUNY Press.

STAR. (2005). Who stays? Who goes? Who decides? In *The National Newsletter of STAR.* pp. 1–2

Theobald, P. (1997). *Teaching the commons: Place, pride, and the renewal of community.* Boulder, CO: Westview Press.

United Nations Higher Commission on Refugees. (2006).
    http://www.unhchr.ch/html/menu3/b/o_c_ref.htm (retrieved 2-3-06)

Young Refugees. (2005). *Young refugees: A guide to the rights and entitlements of separated refugee children.* London: Save the Children.

CHAPTER THREE
Artful Story Illustrating Meaning through Language

Francisco tells me of his Spanish/
English poems translated into Irish poems.
His Dublin audience
would not speak English.
He could not speak Irish.
So he read in Spanish
and they all understood ...

—Mary Kay Rummel (2003, p. 2)

Complicated Conversations—Artful Story and Meaning through Language
Casey (1993) tells us, "Language is the way which human beings make meaning" (p. 3). She adds that worldviews are socially constructed in the process of making meaning with language. Where and when do our ideas about worldviews begin? Certainly, before age five. Language learning and perspective taking are in full swing by kindergarten.

A teacher education student talks about the children in her field placement.

> There are nineteen cheerful, bouncing kindergarteners in my classroom. The school itself is located in the colorful mural-splashed neighborhood of Spanish Harlem, and the students are reflective of the surrounding area. In Room 208 there are ten boys and nine girls. One student is first generation Chinese, two students are black, and seventeen students are of Hispanic/Latino background.
>
> In terms of home language, fourteen students speak a language other than English at home (Chinese or Spanish). In conversations among children Spanish is often used. In the beginning of the year there was, in fact, quite a lot of "code-switching" between school and home languages. There was also quite a bit of mixing of languages. For example, when I asked Tony to tell me about his picture, he responded. "It's a *mao*." (Chinese for *cat*). Mari, when reading, pointed at a picture and told me, "This is a mariposa" (inserting the Spanish word for butterfly into her sentence). I wonder if she even realized she was speaking Spanish versus English and whether or not she assumed I would understand.
>
> At this point, there is less mixing of languages happening in the classroom when the students speak with their teachers. It is almost as if they realize that there is a time and a place for one language and a time and a place for another. Four of the students have very limited English and receive pull-out English as a Second

Language tutoring weekly. Two of the students also meet with a speech therapist for help pronouncing certain sounds like *s*, *r*, and *l*.

Then, in the student teacher's reflective writing, she begins to think about critical questions about what is really going on in this classroom in terms of language and learning. She notes,

Academically, the class is very mixed in experience and ability. Some of the students have attended Pre-K and Head Start prior to kindergarten. They know numbers, shapes, and letters. Other students are just learning these concepts for the first time and hold their crayons and pencils with their whole hand versus using a pincer grasp. One student has difficulty focusing, and another has difficulty processing information. Both are scheduled to have evaluations performed at some point in the year. All of the students are learning how to sit nicely, raise their hands, and be members of a classroom community. It's a long day for many, I observe, and there is a lot of time and expectation that the students sit still and listen. This is difficult because they are still quite young and sitting cross-legged on a rug for forty-five minutes is not physically pleasant.

These teacher expectations are compounded by the fact that the students get no gym time or recess (after lunch the kids watch cartoons and movies—with more cross-legged seating—until the block time is over). These are major weaknesses on the teachers' and school's part. The children's strength is that they have so much energy and enthusiasm.

She dreams of what could be better for the children:

It would be wonderful instead to see the children exploring math hands-on, retelling stories with drama, and having periodic activities that incorporate the whole body for those kids who are still developing their gross motor abilities. Unfortunately, there is an overabundance of sitting quietly and listening to teachers talk.

Another class strength is how involved the parents are. Many attended the parent meeting and ALL wanted to chaperone the class field trip! Unfortunately, the teacher does not recognize the linguistic diversity of the families. At the parent meeting when parents did not ask questions the teacher said, "This is the quietest parent meeting I've ever held" failing to realize that perhaps language barriers were presented.

It's unfortunate that while the class community has many strengths to offer, these strengths are not highlighted and accommodated by the teacher and school. This failure, while it presents itself as a class weakness, is not their fault, but is that of the school's.

For many students and their teachers in the United States and around the world, there is confusion and often dissonance concerning multiple language use, learning, and the academic requirements for success. A bilingual graduate student, originally from Colombia and currently living in New York City, reflected on the issues of language, culture, expectations, and schooling. She has personal experiences of being an immigrant from South America. She came to New York as a young girl, and grew up in a loving, supportive, family and community. Unfortunately, the schools and other institutions she learned successfully to negotiate her way through as a student and young adult weren't always so supportive. The complexity, difficulty, and possibility influenced the lens through which she observed and interacted with children at the Star School in London, a school in East London that serves the largest number of children from families of refugees and asylum seekers in the city. She commented:

> Bilingual education is a sensitive topic in the United States, but I feel that children need to learn both languages. After speaking with a boy from Venezuela in the Star School, I was amazed at how quickly he learned English in the short time since he and his family arrived in England. Even though he was quiet, he communicated the English language very well. He is living proof that children can be successively bilingual without giving up their native language.

Participation in any learning event involves language. Sadly, in the United States it is still almost heresy to acknowledge that while English Language Learners are learning the new language of English, they should have opportunity to share their own lived experiences and prior knowledge. This involves using the learners' home language in certain instances. Issues of language and critical literacy in the context of home culture and culture of English Language Learners' new learning environments in both schools and communities are important to consider. Research (Baker, 2000; Cummins, 2000; Skutnabb-Kangas, 2000; Quintero, 2002) documents ways in which students learning English as a new language can become more effective writers, readers, and participants in English literacy as well as in their native language literacies.

Acculturation and Multilingual Learners

It has been shown that acculturation and language acquisition is impacted by the process of aligning new societal expectations and requirements with previous cultural norms, individual perceptions, and experiences that are preeminent in immigrants' lives. Yet, these urgent issues are often ignored (Ullman, 1997; Zou, 1998). Franken (2002) reports research documenting that when students are faced with a topic on which they have little content and domain-specific knowledge, interaction is significantly helpful for understanding text. As many immigrant students come from such a variety of backgrounds with such different "funds of knowledge," as Moll (1994) reports, it is almost inevitable that many occasions will arise in the literacy classroom when one or more students have a lack of background knowledge on a topic.

According to Bakhtin (1988), the production and reception of meaning is what truly establishes language. Language has a dialogical and intellectual scope that is historically determined and built. Comprehension implies not only the identification of the formal aspects and signs of language but also the sub-texts, the intentions that are not explicit. We humans do not just speak; we tell stories. Discourse always has a live meaning and direction. At the same time, meaning and communication imply community. One always addresses someone, and that someone does not assume a purely passive role; the interlocutor participates in the formation of the meaning of the utterance, just as the other elements of speech do. Bakhtin (1988) says that language is constitutively intersubjective and social. Language is essential to human existence. Thus, human intersubjectivity becomes actualized through particular and specific speech. It is not experience that organizes expression. On the contrary, expression precedes and organizes experience, giving it form and direction.

Cummins (2000) believes that students must develop critical language awareness that involves exploring the relationships between language and power. He says,

> In short, a focus on formal features of the target language should be integrated with critical inquiry into issues of language and power. Also to be effective, a focus on language must be linked to extensive input in the target language (e.g. through reading) and extensive opportunities for written and oral use of the language. (p. 32)

Bourdieu's (1991) perspective about language is that dialects within languages have evolved historically out of differential power and status relationships between groups of people in society. He believes the dialects are not a chance occurrence, but rather are grounded in the different ways of life of various groups and are embodiments of the social and cultural knowledge of those who speak each linguistic form. Identity and "station" in life, through the use of language, are actively engaged in the process of reproducing the social relationships embodied in the different language forms that have emerged over time. "The social uses of language owe their specifically social value to the fact that they tend to be organized in systems of differences...which reproduce, in the symbolic order of differential deviations, the system of social differences" (Bourdieu, 1991, p. 54).

Comber and Kamler (1997) state,

> If critical literacy is to mean anything to educators in the nineties, a greater self consciousness about language will need to be developed; a metalanguage for talking about how language constructs both a representation of experience and a positioning of readers and writers in relations of power. (p. 1)

The issues of power, what students learn to read and write, and their access to transformative use of their literacy skills are exaggerated in the classroom contexts of multilingual learners.

Languages and Possibilities

Bakhtin (1988) says that language is constitutively intersubjective and social. Thus, human intersubjectivity becomes actualized through particular and specific speech.

Kuiken and Vedder (2002) show that when a writing task involves collaboration there are a number of pedagogical advantages. This collaboration helps to assure the language skills are integrated rather than practiced in isolation. The theoretical construct used by Cummins (2000) to describe instruction for language learning and academic achievement has three components: (1) Focus on Message, (2) Focus on Language, and (3) Focus on Use. Cummins (2000) maintains that the Focus on Language component should put controversial issues such as the appropriate ways and time to teach second language grammar in a context of Language Awareness. Cummins advocates that under this category of Language Awareness, students must develop critical language awareness that involves exploring the relationships between language and power. Critical literacy includes critical approaches to languages. Once again, I define critical literacy as a process of constructing meaning and critically using language (oral and written) as a means of expression, interpretation, and/or transformation of our lives and the lives of those around us.

All over the world critical literacy is being studied in terms of theory, practice, policy, and research (Comber & Kamler 1997; Muspratt, Luke & Freebody, 1997; Freire & Macedo, 1987). The widespread attention does not mean scholars agree upon the definition or the extent to which the theory and the practice can or should be separated.

The use of critical literacy as a teaching method is a way to facilitate student choice and generative work that is integrally related to students' lives (Freire, 1985). The importance of personally meaningful contexts for writing activities for all learners has been argued by many (Giroux, 1988). In many settings where students have been previously unsuccessful in school, the need to create meaningful links between school and community has been proven effective (Reyes, 1992; Trueba, 1991). Evidence shows that the social context of the setting in which critical literacy and problem-posing are implemented enhances the opportunity to focus on the often dramatic transitions that the students experience as they move from one sociocultural context to another (Rummel & Quintero, 1997; Shor, 1987).

Comber and Kamler (1997) maintain that we must continue to examine the different versions of critical literacy that emerge and show the complex pictures of what pedagogies for critical literacy look like in different settings and educational contexts. These researchers believe that detailed narratives that show the negotiations of critical literacies in sites around the world are needed. In addition, they (Comber & Kamler, 1997) say that it is urgent that we continue to discuss the way in which power is exercised through textual practices during these times of demands for accountability in the production of students with particular sets of competencies and in the context of managerialist discourses that threaten to inhibit the freedom and power of individual and group student text in the literacy classroom. The issues of power, what students learn to read and write, and their access to transformative use of their literacy skills are exaggerated in the classroom contexts of multilingual learners.

The contextual reality of many English Literacy classrooms in the United States and all over the world is that there are many native languages present. This is a plus when a classroom teacher speaks the native language of the students. However, it is almost always impossible for each teacher to be knowledgeable of every language represented in the classroom. Reyes (1992) documents that rarely is it crucial for the classroom teacher to be proficient in all languages represented by students in the classroom. Yet, by using critical literacy, any classroom teacher can orchestrate a meaningful English Literacy lesson that includes writing in the students' native language—even when the teacher does not know the native language. This approach, critical literacy using native language writing as a scaffolding technique to promote English literacy, while exposing students to important content information, gives value to each student's personal experience. This approach allows for adaptations to be made regarding language and background knowledge such as cultural experience and experience in formal literacy instruction. It also allows for flexibility in terms of educational aspirations of the students.

Critical literacy can be a powerful tool for learning and instruction for English Language Learners. Problem-posing, a methodological aspect of critical pedagogy, combines reflective thinking, information gathering, collaborative decision making, and personal learning choices (Quintero, 2002). This method helps students express their voice in oral and written ways (Torres-Guzmán, 1993). Kuiken and Vedder (2002) show that when a writing task involves collaboration, there are a number of pedagogical advantages. This collaboration helps to assure the language skills are integrated rather than practiced in isolation (Kuiken & Vedder, 2002). This approach is not a prescriptive lesson-planning format, but is a way to facilitate student choice and generative work that is related to students' lives whatever the age or context of the students.

A congressionally mandated longitudinal study (Ramírez, Yuen, Ramey & Pasta, 1991) more than a decade ago found that in many, if not most, of bilingual and English as a Second Language classrooms in the United States students were forced to be passive learners with teacher dominance of virtually all classroom activities. The researchers reported the following.

> In over half of the interactions that teachers have with students, students do not produce any language ...When students do respond, typically they are providing simple information recall. Rather than being provided with the opportunity to generate original statements, students are asked to provide simple discrete close ended or patterned responses. Not only does this pattern of teacher/student interaction limit a student's opportunity to create and manipulate language freely, but it also limits the student's ability to engage in more complex learning...(pp. 421–422)

In the area of language development, we now know that children at age six have not yet begun to complete cognitive development in their first language (Collier, 1989). When children's first language development is discontinued before cognition is fully developed, they may experience negative cognitive effects in their second language development; conversely, children who have an opportunity to learn in their native language and learn a second language reach full cognitive development in two languages and enjoy cognitive advances over monolinguals (Collier,1989). Making the issue of learning in a student's first language more urgent, research now shows that it may take as long as seven to ten years for non-native speakers to reach the average level of performance by native speakers on standardized tests (Collier, 1989; Collier & Thomas, 1999).

In bilingual program evaluations, comparison groups of students being schooled exclusively in the second language typically never reach the levels of students schooled in their first language (Collier, 1989). A sense of urgency in teaching English to non-English-speaking children and concern about postponing children's exit from bilingual programs are unfounded according to linguists Hakuta and Snow (1986). There is no evidence that native language instruction holds students back. Lily Wong Fillmore (1991), a researcher in second language learning and early education, spearheaded a nationwide research project regarding the effects of inappropriate early education efforts to teach very young children a second language. The findings of this study show that not only do most of these children lose their first language in the process, but there are very tragic losses in family communication. Cultural values and traditional childrearing principles are not communicated. Give and take conversations that are the backbone of relationships cease to exist. Fillmore (1991) contends,

> Teachers and parents must work together to try to mitigate the harm that can be done to children when they discover that differences are not welcome in the social world represented by the school. Parents need to be warned of the consequences of not insisting that their children speak to them in the language of the home. (p. 345)

One teacher education student studying early childhood education wrote about an article introducing some of the above research data in relation to the students she is working with:

> ... here in New York, there are so many different languages all over the place. From what I have seen in the classroom that I work in now, is that all of the children are all very culturally different. I have not seen any lessons or sharing time to have children discuss their home language. However, I am aware that the kindergarten teacher has discussed a couple of different places where children are from, or where their parents come from, and their cultural differences. For example, one of the student's parents is from Ethiopia, and the teacher has discussed this on several occasions. I think that this is so great because then the child feels proud about his origins.

Yet, she made the critical comments,

> This is similar to but different from language use, ... both culture and language should be shared and taught whenever possible ... Within our use of language is our value system ... if English is the only language accepted in school, this implies other languages are not as valued.

Native Languages in Curriculum

There is not enough discussion and exploration in teacher education circles regarding ways in which native language use can be used to enhance English literacy instruction. The most convincing evidence of alternative theoretical propositions regarding bilingual writing comes from research of dual language or two-way bilingual immersion programs (Cummins, 2000). Evaluations of these programs have consistently revealed success over the course of elementary school for both language minority and language majority students. For example, outcomes from the Oyster Bilingual School in Washington, DC, illustrate this. The bilingual program involves instruction in both Spanish and English for about half of the lesson time. Students read and write in both languages each day so that development of literacy in both languages is simultaneous. The academic results of this program shows, for example, in grade 3 level Reading, Mathematics, Language, and Sciences scores were 1.6—1.8 median grade equivalents above norms (percentiles 74–81). The grade 6 level equivalents were 4.4—6.2 above norms (percentiles

85-96) (Freeman, 1998). Freeman (1998) provides detailed discourse analyses that illustrate how the interactions between educators and students in Oyster Bilingual School "refuse" the discourse of subordination that characterizes the treatment of minorities in most conventional schools.

DeSilva (1998) maintains that children can develop their knowledge of second language writing and speaking conventions by using what they understand about writing in their native language. Many researchers and classroom teachers have shown that language interaction in the form of student-centered discussions and demonstrations, language experience story writing and reading, and holistic literacy development allow for native language literacy to enhance English language literacy development (Hakuta, 1986; Hakuta & Garcia, 1989; Hudelson, 1994). In academic contexts, the notion that the first language interferes with the learning of the second language is known to not be supported by research evidence (Larsen-Freeman & Long, 1991). It is clear that the first language serves a function in early second language acquisition, but it is a supportive role rather than a negative one (Ovando & Collier, 1998). Ovando and Collier (1998) go on to state the importance of educating school staff and parents who are unfamiliar with this information about the importance of students using native language in learning.

As can be seen in many teacher education students' responses to their new ability to tune in to critical literacy in young children, many issues and important questions began to arise about home language, bilingualism, learning academic English, and related issues. For example, one student teacher said:

> Last week I was walking around the classroom during independent writing time, when F.'s piece caught my eye. The title, "M E X I C O" was in bold letters that colorfully stretched across the top of the page. I stopped and I asked her if I could read it. She happily agreed. I noticed that Spanish and English intermingled throughout the whole piece, quite an accomplishment for a second grader. Some of the words were written in Spanish, with the English words in parenthesis: "My tio Jose (Uncle Jose) picks us up at the aeropuerto Mexican (airport)." I was very impressed by her usage of Spanish words within an English sentence. She had the great insight to put the English words in parenthesis. It was obvious that she wanted to share her knowledge of Spanish words, while not alienating non-Spanish speakers. (Quintero, 2004, p. 27)

Another student teacher commented on the relationship between some of the background knowledge reading information about language acquisition.

> The other day J. was showing me one of his toys and he said, "This es mio." I knew he was trying to say "this is mine" or "Este es mio." I understand basic Spanish and

therefore I don't find it difficult to understand J. when he switches from one language to another. At times it seems to me that he is confusing the two languages. However, some days J. seems to speak only Spanish and other days only English. I have learned from the research J. was the part about code-switching (mixing languages). J. was code-switching and using appropriate "critical literacies" in his world. (Quintero, 2004, p. 27)

Languages and Local Knowledge

The perspective about literacies that exemplifies critical literacy in the context of home culture and culture of learners' learning environments can be transformational in both schools and communities. Local knowledge relates to reading and writing in all classrooms. These critical issues affect Hmong immigrant learners in U.S. schools, Chicanos in California schools, Turkish students in Eastern Europe and Central Asia, Welsh and Irish students in England, Black South Africans in newly created, post-apartheid schools, and many other learners. These issues influence how literacy is used, learned, and taught in many languages and in many forms of media.

Hmong parents commented in an evaluation of a Hmong/English bilingual program in a local school:

> All persons in the home speak Hmong. Their writing and reading of Hmong is fair but progressing. I am only happy for them because it can only help them to read and write Hmong.

The parents also acknowledged wanting their children to study and learn English. They commented:

> They both are very enthusiastic about their work and I am sure their English skills are great. But they speak only Hmong in the home. They can speak fine to Americans. Learning English is good for job to help their future.

Another wrote about the complexities of being bilingual and bicultural and the interactions among different generations. Critical reading, critical questioning, and knowledge from multiple perspectives are intertwined in this student's story about three generations of family members.

> L. and I are twenty-two years apart. We're the special girls on my mom's side of the family because we are the only granddaughters out of six grandchildren! L.'s mother (my aunt Eva) and I are only seventeen years apart. When Aunt E. moved here to the U.S. with the rest of the family she was only ten, so of all her siblings, her English is the best. When L. was born, she tried to teach L. some Mandarin, but that idea was quickly abandoned because L.'s father only speaks English. L. seemed to have a preference for English anyway. When she does try to speak Mandarin, she is unable to distinguish tones; our grandpa joked that L. speaks [Chinese] like a pure American!

L. learned how to speak at an early age, and she is a witty child. This is a conversation I had with her once when she was almost four years old: (taken from my own personal journal)

L. (points to an advertisement written in Chinese): What does that say?

Me: I don't know.

L. (shocked look on her face): What?! Can't you read??

Me (hiding my amused look): Yes, I can read ENGLISH. But those are Chinese characters. I can't read Chinese.

L. (even more shocked look): But aren't you CHINESE?!

Me: Yes, I'm Chinese, just like you. We're from the same family. But no, I don't know how to read Chinese. How come you don't know how to read, if you're so smart? (I gave her a wink.)

L. (very serious): Because I'm not even four yet! I'm not supposed to know how to read right now!

Now, it was my turn to be shocked. What do you say to that? ☺

I recall my mom and her sisters comparing our development, and they all agreed that L. is by far the wittiest and has the sharpest tongue, much like her mother. Each of us began talking early, but of all the cousins, only L. is not bilingual. There's still hope for her yet. I think she needs to overcome her self-consciousness first.

Very recently my mom noted that I speak Mandarin and use Zhe Jaing phrases like my grandma (her mother) used to. She seemed pleased that I remembered these sayings even though my grandma passed away ten years ago. I just always thought I was speaking Mandarin, not realizing I was really speaking my grandma's dialect!

Another teacher wrote about language and local knowledge within the family:

My fiancé's grandmother does not speak English. English is the prevalent language in the upper classes of Indian society. I feel that this is in some way the after effects of colonization. My fiancé told me that as a child he would be embarrassed to bring his friends home and did not want his grandmother to speak or interact with his friends. His grandmother loved making treats for all his friends but he tried to keep her away from his friends. He also did not like going out with his grandmother and certainly didn't like her coming to his school. I think his grandmother understood his predicament and kept her distance from his friends and school environment. However, as he grew up his mother saw his behavior and talked to him about his behavior towards his grandmother who we affectionately call "baaji." She told him that by shutting out his grandmother he was shutting out an important part of his roots and heritage. She made him realize that his grandmother was a part of the family and that he should be proud of her. His mother talked to him about all the hardships his grandmother had faced while bringing up his father and that he should celebrate and not shun her.

As my fiancé grew up he began to take pride in his culture and heritage. "Baaji" is now his favorite person to spend time with at home and he absolutely dotes on her. All his friends too love spending time with "baaji" and listening to her stories about the pre-partitioned and colonized India. In fact my fiancé has also taught "baaji" a little English and she is able to talk in the language albeit in broken sentences. I feel that schools and teachers can help by making children cognizant of their culture and by teaching them the regional languages in India so that they do not feel that these languages are inferior. Schools and teachers can celebrate the Indian culture and heritage so that the children do not feel pressured to ape the West. In much the same way as my fiancé's mother talked to him teachers can have conversations with their students so that no child feels embarrassed of people in their family that they should actually be proud off.

Another teacher education student participant interviewed a friend, and they both agreed that understanding multiple languages gave us a great advantage; this allows people to gain multiple perspectives. Certain ideologies are easier to express in one language over another or cannot be crossed over into another language at all. For example, it is easier to express past tenses in Spanish, whereas tenses and verb conjugation do not exist in Chinese. On the other hand, there are many four-character idioms in Chinese that although concise are very rich in meaning. She commented:

> Interestingly, during his interview, my friend happened to mention that he gestures a lot more when he speaks one language over another, "I speak Spanish with my hands!" He noted that when he spoke English or Mandarin, he gestured very little or not at all, but when he switched over to Spanish, he gestured animatedly. This notion led me to wonder if the use of gestures and signs might be related to language acquisition.

> My friend started to take Spanish in middle school and continued through high school and college. During his senior year, he decided to add Mandarin Chinese and ended up studying it for years. Today, he is fluent in English, Spanish, and Mandarin; he is more conversational and literate in Spanish than he is in Mandarin, but continues to practice both languages whenever he has the opportunity. Understanding different languages has helped him relate to his friends better. It gives him a different perspective when he thinks in a different language because certain ideologies are easier to express in one language over another or cannot be crossed over into another language at all. He also finds that the way things are named in Chinese "make more sense" than that of Romance languages. According to him, Chinese has "cool: phrases—four-character idioms/proverbs that are concise, but very rich in meaning." Another difference he noticed in himself is that the frequency of his gestures increases when he speaks Spanish than when he's speaking either English or Chinese. "I speak Spanish with my hands!" he exclaimed.

Finally, an early childhood teacher participant planned a bookmaking project with her preschoolers and their families. She explained:

> I wanted this to be a storybook-making project that included children and their families so I asked children and parents to contribute a song, a poem, or a nursery rhyme that was special to their family in some way. I asked them to try to think of something the parents had grown up with, a favorite tradition or something they would like to share with their child.

She added:

I wanted to do a project that promotes literacy and encourages multilingual language use among our families and children. I wanted to include parents, grandparents, aunts, uncles, and siblings so that I would receive contributions from many different languages and cultures. I wanted this to be a project that included children and family stories so I also asked that everyone who contributed do some kind of picture or art work with their child to put in the book.

I received many different forms of literacy. I received songs that families sing but had never written down. I received poems that they had recited from childhood memories. I received poems and nursery rhymes that they picked out of books, and I received pictures the family members and children drew interpreting their contributions.

Just a few of the examples of family contributions to the book are as follows:

Sam's mother brought in a counting song from her native country of Romania. Sam spends a lot of time with his grandparents and they sing this song to him quite frequently. His mother informed me that Sam loves the song and I should ask him to sing it for me. I had no idea that Sam even spoke Romanian! During circle time we shared the song with the other children raising their hands want to sing songs, most, of course, were in English, but we had one boy sing a song in Spanish and a girl who sang in Farsi.

One little four-year-old boy who was with us in circle time went home and told his mom that he needed her to bring a song to me for the book and it needed to be in Danish. So she translated a song for me and brought it in the next day with a picture that her son drew. She really didn't understand why she was bringing in the song but her son was so adamant that she did as he requested. I was, of course, ecstatic. She later conveyed that the process of picking a song with Andy and trying to translate it into English was a lot of fun. Many of the words don't translate directly into English and they laughed and laughed over the translation.

Luis and Julio's family is from Mexico. Luis attended our school when he was younger, and Julio is in our Pre-K room. Both boys speak Spanish and English, and their parents are diligently working on their own English skills. The boys' mother explained to the boys what I wanted for my book, and both boys wanted to pick out songs for the book. They picked out songs from a book they had that contained both the Spanish and English translations of the songs. Luis and Julio drew pictures for me while their mother made dinner; their mother informed me that this has become a nightly ritual for them ever since. She makes dinner and both boys sit and draw pictures and discuss which ones we might use in the books. She also reports that when they read a story or poem that they particularly like, they want to bring it in and share it with me. When I showed the boys the book with their pictures included in it, I thought Julio was going to jump out of his skin, his face lit up and he squealed, "Looook Ms. J, it's meeee, it's my picture!" (Quintero, 2009, p. 18)

Critical Literacy in Action—
Artful Story Illustrating Meaning through Language

Case Study Two

A student teacher wrote about her work using critical literacy as a framework and how she was able to integrate other research-based perspectives that have influenced her as she has studied and worked in early childhood programs. She wrote in an introduction to her problem-posing plans:

> I can use the critical literacy framework of problem-posing and have opportunity to include in my research-based frame the principles and practices of the Reggio Emilia schools and some of the National Association for the Education of Young Children Position Statements. I have chosen the NAEYC standards because I feel that they are inclusive and are founded on early theorists whose work I find useful such as Piaget and Erikson. I chose Reggio Emilia principles and practices as another foundation for my research-frame based curriculum activities because I believe in the inclusion of ideas from emergent curriculum, theory of multiple intelligences, teachers as researchers, and documentation of artwork. Critical literacy gives me opportunity to include other research-based ideas.

She went on to describe her focus of activities:

> I focused my curriculum areas on Literacy Activities and Art. My main goals are to promote the oral language of English Language Learners and Native English speakers and to explore the aesthetic components of art and art appreciation. I hoped to help several of the children find confidence in their own storytelling abilities, to promote the self worth of all of the students through creativity and to foster competency in Literacy and Art.

She described the classroom context of the early childhood program where she works and implemented her problem-posing activities:

> It was the start of week three in the classroom and I was beginning to see cohesiveness among the children. They were already choosing their playmates regularly. There was a lot less solitary play and they were beginning to remember the names of their classmates. This year the tone of the class is very calm even though we have twelve boys and six girls. They are a very busy group and they want to explore everything. They flutter from station to station without hesitation.
>
> Eight of the children are Spanish speaking only and another eight are English Language Learners with a fair amount of English, one boy speaks Mandarin Chinese and is learning English and four children are English only speakers.

She goes on to explain how her observations of the children have influenced her choice of topics, activities, and materials for her problem-posing lessons:

> To address some of the literacy and math skills I observe in the children and how I know they know these skills is a bit difficult for me. I know they are demonstrating a skill but it is not always clear-cut. For example, one of the boys today created a

catapult out of two blocks (it looked like a teeter-totter) and he was bent on showing everyone his invention. I know he is manipulating geometric shapes, using symbolic representation, demonstrating memory and knowledge, cause and effect, measurement, timing and balance, being creative and showing competence, but I can't think of the scientific term for the demonstration of how he made an item fly through the air...maybe, aero-dynamics? Is it gravity? I wonder how to support the science when I know little about such properties.

I know Reggio would have me elicit questions from the child and further explore.

To address the literacy domain, many of the children are beginning to participate in our morning songs and chants. We repeat them for consistency and to give the children the opportunity to learn the songs and chants. In the library the children are demonstrating an interest in literacy and concepts of print by holding a book the appropriate way and by wanting me to read over and over again. Right now we are encouraging color recognition in Chinese, Spanish, and English. Many of the children who speak Spanish only are beginning to say the names of their colors correctly.

Social skills are the biggest area of development right now. Many are trying to solve situations such as sharing and waiting their turn. They are still regulating their minds and bodies. I see that the biggest strength of the group is their language. They are all big talkers. They can't wait to tell me their stories. This morning one little girl told me about a bug that hopped and hopped and with all her might she demonstrated her best hopping skills. I can tell that I will have no problem implementing the acting out of stories this year. I am truly making a note of all of their special interests.

Day One

Pre-listening Activity:
They went on a nature walk in search of sticks (for later activity) and collected objects, such as leaves, pine cones, stems, flowers, and other items.

Listening:
The student teacher introduced her own talking stick and told the story of how she got it and what it represents for her. This object is a tool to allow children to have a visual for when it is their turn to talk. She showed the children photos of different types of sticks from other cultures (Guatemala, India, Kenya) and described some of the interesting features of each. Although the main objective was to promote oral language and culture, it is within the confines of gentle, social structure that promotes active listening skills. It is always important to use your own story of an experience with a stick just to get things started and stress that the person with the stick is the one who gets to talk while the others listen.

Dialogue:
She passed her talking stick to each of the children and asked each of them to take turns telling a story or sharing some thoughts. She tape recorded and videotaped their stories for their listening pleasure. She encouraged students to tell stories in their first language and recorded for later translation that could be dictation for a book. "The Talking Stick." They further discussed the importance of the social rule of actively listening to others.

Action:
The student teacher then asked the children bring their own sticks to the art table to decorate using paint, yarn, material, and several other collage items. The children would share their creation on day three.

Action Extensions:
At the math center, the table had pre-drawn shapes (square, rectangle, diamond, and triangle) along with popsicle sticks for the children to create shapes and 3-D structures.

Science objects from the nature walk were placed on a tray with magnifying glasses.

At the literacy center, several fiction/non-fiction books related to natural and man-made things made from wood were placed. (Books on trees, building construction using wood, for example.)

In addition, the student teacher sent home a letter to parents asking them to find and create a stick that represents some aspect of their culture or bring in an artifact that is made from wood. They planned to share these artifacts on the fourth day during small group as an introduction to Celebrating the Family month.

Day Two

Listening:
The student teacher showed the children the items collected from the nature walk and lay them out in preparation for dialogue. She laid out ten sticks. They counted the sticks in English, Chinese, and Spanish. Then she introduced the chant "One, Two, Buckle My Shoe." Then they repeated the chant giving each child a turn to lay out the sticks and count them on, "Seven, Eight, lay them straight." They used all three languages for counting (child's choice of language).

Dialogue:
They discussed the different properties of the items found. In addition to these items, the student teacher had also brought celery sticks, popsicle sticks, carrot sticks, chopsticks, toilet paper, a wood block, and a strip of ply-

wood. She asked children to use their senses (touch, smell, vision, and hearing) to interact with the objects and encouraged the use of adjectives in English/Spanish/Chinese to increase vocabulary.

Action:

They separated the objects into either "natural" or "created by humans" categories. (This was a little difficult at first, but she explained it in part by asking the children whether they think the item grew on its own or whether it was made by someone. Then we talked about whether the item was made of wood and how did they know?)

At the art center, wooden objects were placed on a table with a flat piece of cardboard or plywood. Bottles of glue that had paint added for color and twist ties, yarn, and rubber bands for creating a 3-D group sculpture were available.

At the literacy center, a large area displayed an array of fictional and non-fictional books to explore, with topics such as woodworking and how trees grow.

Day Three

Pre-listening Activity:

The student teacher called the children to the carpet and they sat down together and repeated the chant, "One, Two, Buckle My Shoe."

Listening:

She read the book *Not a Stick* by Antoinette Portis (2007).

Dialogue:

They discussed the object the stick was turned into in the story by using the pictures in the book. She had brought the children's talking sticks to group time also, so after they talked about the story, she asked the children to tell or act out what their stick would be used for. The student teacher wrote down what each one said, for example, a baton or a lion tamer. She photographed each child and their stick to use with drawing activity (Art: Day Three) for the creation of a book.

Action:

At the art table, construction paper, crayons, and markers were available. She asked each child, "If you could be anything you wanted to be, what would you want to be?" Then she wrote their answer on their paper and asked them to illustrate their answer. Using the photos from Day Three Dialogue, the children pasted them onto their drawing and the student teacher wrote what they said their creation was on the photo. Then she laminated the drawings and made a book to use in the library.

Action Extensions:

During free time several different kinds of wooden blocks (ABC, Jenga blocks, and large wooden blocks) were grouped together on a table for the children to build with.

At the science center a project of making paper (using toilet paper, glue, food color, water, blender, and screen for pouring paper concoction onto for drying) was available with the help of a parent volunteer.

After the problem-posing lessons were complete, the student teacher wrote an anecdote about some of the children's responses to her lessons. Regarding T.,

> T. is at the art table creating her story stick with paint, beads, yarn, and feathers. When she finishes I am ready to take dictation and I ask her this question, "Can you tell me about your stick? And, how will you use it?" Her response is as follows: "I want a Pricerella house, and I want a Pricerella doll and I want a Pricerella dress." I reply, "How will you use your stick?" she responds with, "I gonna see Santa Claus." I can only surmise that she was using the stick to make a list for Santa.

Then she wrote:

> On the final day of my problem posing I brought the children's talking sticks to group time for them to share with their friends. Children were holding and playing with their sticks, and I asked each of them to tell the others about their stick. Or I gave them option of sharing a story again. The children were talking and sharing ideas, mostly unrelated to my request until I got to the last child M. M. had this to say, "Someone chase me, they take my stick. And turn into monster. In my closet." I asked him, "Did you have a dream about someone chasing you, taking your stick, turning into a monster?" He says, "Si, in my closet." I said, "There was a monster in your closet?" M. replied, "Si, but monsters no real." Just so you know, I followed up with the book, *There's a Nightmare in my Closet* (Mayer, 1992). I really felt some gratification at the fact that at least this child could demonstrate understanding about the whole idea behind a story stick. Overall, I felt over the course of the time spent with the problem-posing activities, my main goal was achieved by promoting oral language, vocabulary and self-expression.

Case Study Three

The following synopsis is from a case study of a teacher education student who implemented a critical literacy agenda for a group of kindergarten children in New York City. She was interested in the broad issues of culture and identity as they relate to language and learning. She commented that this issue of meaning through language is important to her. Her case reveals aspects of critical theory in the aspects of personal story/history, multiple sources of knowledge, and transformative action—with kindergarten students.

> A topic that has been of particular interest to me in early education has been that of responsiveness to family cultures, values, and languages. Having immigrated to the United States at a young age with my family, I have a personal connection with this topic. In my opinion, the incorporation of different cultures, values, and languages about each other's likenesses and differences via their culture, values, and languages should be a part of all teachers' curricula. Persons who come from different backgrounds can provide one another with new ideas or perspectives otherwise not explored. This lesson was planned for kindergarten or first grade early in the school year when children are learning about each other.

Listening:

She read *The Colors of Us* by Karen Katz (2007). The story is about a child whose mother is an artist who insists that there are many different shades of brown. Mother and daughter take a walk through their neighborhood thinking about friends and relatives and all of their skin colors. Their skin colors are compared to honey, peanut butter, pizza crust, ginger, peaches, chocolate, and more, conjuring up delicious and beautiful comparisons for every tint. Katz's pencil-and-gouache pictures convey the range of human pigmentation.

Dialogue:

She asked the children, "What did you see or notice about the story?" Then she asked them to talk more about the comparisons the author made about skin color and different foods. She then brought the discussion to the topic of language by asking whether the students could say or know about the language a person speaks by looking at skin color.

Action:

Then she read the book *Why Am I Different?* by Norma Simon (1993) and illustrated by Dora Leder. This book is about some of the things that make us all different and uniquely ourselves. The story invokes opportunities for discussions about the many differences that make people so unique from the way we look, to language, to food, to preferred activities.

Dialogue:

She then asked the children to explore ideas in the book by asking open-ended questions. She asked, what preferred activities did you see in the book? So the people who like that activity speak only one language: Are there people who always have the same skin color?

Action:

For action inside the classroom during choice time, she provided materials and activities at learning centers.

1. One center was equipped with dress up clothes from different cultures for children. There were also encyclopedias, *National Geographic* magazines, and a variety of books from UNICEF with pictures of people from different countries and cultures. There was also displayed a world map with the country names written on it.
2. At the art center, large sheets of butcher paper and markers (with an adult helper stationed there) made it possible for children to create life-sized outlines and portraits of themselves.
3. At a second art table, with partners and in small groups using a variety of art materials, children explored food comparisons for their own skin color. They drew or painted pictures of the food and wrote a few phrases or sentences about this comparison. There was an extension categorization activity that consisted of different fruits and vegetables and the various nutrition facts.
4. At the book center, there were different multicultural books on tape in English and in other languages that groups of children listened to.

For action outside the classroom, she asked children to bring in a family artifact, something that represents their culture or a certain tradition that they have with their family. The student teacher explained that she was interested also in things from their homes that had print in languages other than English. The children brought in these artifacts during the next few days and made an "artifact/language/family" exhibit in the classroom.

The student teacher wrote in a reflective journal about this group of learners.

> In this kindergarten class, out of the twenty-four students in the classroom, at least five were English Language Learners. Each student was at a different developmental stage of learning the new language, English, and I had the opportunities to see and work with these students as they learned to read.
>
> One boy's home language was Korean, and when he read he never said the 's' on plural words. If there were a bunch of apples, he would only say apple. I learned that because in the Korean language plurals are different words so he was confused with the s ending. S.1 and S.2 both spoke Spanish at home. S.2 was doing fine with reading and the problems she did have were not because she was an English Language Learner student. I did not know that S.2's first language was English until she helped me communicate with R. who was just learning English. R.'s family has just come to the United States this year and the kindergarten class was his first encounter with the language. It was interesting to see small steps of language acquisition by watching him.

I really wished the teacher did more for R. She speaks Spanish (she is Hispanic), and she was able to communicate with him when he did not understand what was going on, but that is where her support ended. R.'s family spoke minimal English and they could not read anything she handed out, so he was never able to do the family homework projects or the reading logs. The family asked for the handouts to be translated into Spanish, but the teacher thought that was not her job … I think what upset me the most was that the teacher speaks Spanish and she could at least have called the family and told them what the assignments were and they could write them down. The worst part was the reading journal; he was not getting practice reading books and talking about them because his parents could not fill out the sheet. I wish we had books in our classroom that where in Spanish because he could have taken those books home and his parents could have had conversations in Spanish about what happened and take their notes in Spanish. R. would have still be learning to read and practicing reading techniques, but it would have been in his home language and a language his parents understood.

Case Study Four

Another example of critical literacy and critical literacies was compiled with the help of a class of English Language Learners and their teacher. The school is in a neighborhood that is home to many recent immigrants. In this particular third grade class, the majority of students were native speakers of Spanish, a few from the United States, and more from Mexico and Central America. There were a few Hmong speakers, one speaker of Burmese, and one speaker of Somali in the class. The variety of ages, variety in proficiency of English language use, and variety of formal schooling experiences of the children demanded that the teacher plan learning activities that were supportive of the students' level of background knowledge (of course, including their home languages) as well as current learning needs. She used problem-posing with personal oral storytelling, native language writing, and English writing.

The varied backgrounds and languages of the students showed both the importance of personal history and multiple sources of knowledge. The focus on skills development through the lesson revealed students' participating in transformative action for their academic English development.

The teacher started the class with an introduction using the wordless picture book *Anno's Journey* by Mitsuamaso Anno (1997). The discussion centered around the artist/author choosing the illustrations to tell a story, but then leaving text off so that the readers could make their own stories from the pictures. The teacher then connected a few of the illustrations to historical facts that the author wanted to portray. After this, she led the students to a discussion centered around the variety of ways we can all tell our personal stories by using different languages. Then she began a problem-posing activity that connected personal story with native language and target language writing.

Listening:

The teacher showed the class a photo of herself when she was seven years old and then pulled out a map of South Dakota. She showed them the small South Dakota town where her own immigrant family lived when she was a child. Then she told a story of how when she was seven, her father lost his job on the railroad and there was no other work in their town. So the family decided to move to Arizona. Her dad went first and saved money, and then sent for the family some months later. Her mother, with her four young children, flew on an economy flight leaving at midnight and arriving in Arizona at dawn. "I still remember how impressed I was by the sight of the toy city below…and how happy my dad was to see us," the teacher explained.

The teacher then showed the drawing she had made in four parts that visually told her story that was drawn on one large sheet of butcher paper.

Dialogue:

Here the teacher asked the students, "What are the sentences to explain each of the pictures?" (They worked on keeping the story in past tense and had to learn a couple of new words like airport and toy.)

Action:

The teacher then gave students a lesson guide that included the following instructions:

Your story assignment:

1. Divide your drawing paper into four parts and make four drawings telling a story about a migration (or moving) event in your childhood.
2. Write a story about these pictures of the event in your home language. Write the story in the past tense.
3. Tell your story, using English, to three other students and one teacher.
4. Rewrite your story in English in the present tense. Now write the story using the past tense in English.
5. Turn in your work to your teacher.

This guide along with the required task of reading their stories to others satisfied an important component of providing opportunities for the development of academic English. Cummins (2000) outlines a framework for English Language Learners that highlights distinction between conversational and academic communication. He notes that persuading another person of one's point of view and writing an essay demands cognitively demanding skills necessary for academic language use. The teacher commented, "It was very interactive and encouraged the students to think and speak in meaningful complex sentences. I'll definitely do something like this again!" A student who had emigrated from Mexico to Minnesota told her story first with pictures, then she wrote the story in her native language of Spanish, and then she wrote the story in English. A student from El Salvador told his story of going from El Salvador to Mexico to the United States. His first work sample was in drawing form, the second was a story written in his native language of Spanish, and the third, a story as he wrote it in English. Similarly, Hmong students drew, wrote first in Hmong and then in English, their families' stories of immigrating to the United States from Southeast Asia.

Case Study Five

This excerpt is from a student teacher working in a first-grade classroom. She was interested in tying personal family story and language into the new learning contexts that are multilingual for many children. She had strong personal convictions about giving children opportunities to explore languages with others from different backgrounds. This case illustrates the strong links between personal history and multiple sources of knowledge in terms of language and culture.

Listening:

The teacher began by explaining to the children that in her family four languages are spoken at different times. Then she read *I Love Saturdays y domingos* by Alma Flor Ada (2002), which is a story about how a child has one set of grandparents who speak Spanish and one set of grandparents who speak English. The child describes her visits to both families and what they do and what they say, in both Spanish and English.

Dialogue:

Then after the story she asked, "What did you learn about the girl's family? What were some differences about the different grandparents? What did you learn about the family members that was the same? How did they feel about the girl?" The children noticed the different languages, the different ways of enjoying time together, and the different foods of each family.

Then the class had a group discussion about all the different languages used in their families and communities. The teacher extended the discussion in terms of sociolinguistics by asking, "How do you know which language to speak with which person?"

Action:

A variety of "action opportunities" were available at the classroom centers:

1. At one center, children could choose pictures to make a "family collage" to represent their family and write together a short story, in their home language or English or both, about the family depicted in the collage.
2. At another, there were recipe books from around the world, and materials for children to "write" recipes of dishes their family likes to eat. There were also math manipulatives related to measurement for exploration at the same center.
3. There were compact disks and tapes with music from around the world at the music center.
4. There was a variety of heavy card paper for children to write letters or invitations (in different languages) to family members.

For action outside the classroom,

1. She and the children went on a neighborhood walk and looked for different examples of print written in different languages. They stopped along the way and talked and showed each other bits of the script they saw. All children had clipboards so that they could draw or write some details about where the script was found, such as if it was a store, what was sold there, or if it was a place of worship, how did they know?
2. She sent a letter home to families with the children, asking permission for the children to bring one artifact (a cooking utensil, a photo, etc.) from the family to share the story of this artifact and the family memory with the class.
3. Then the class wrote a brief thank-you letter to all the families in the form of a newsletter with illustrations and examples from the families.

After this brief experience and several others from her fieldwork she wrote:

> In my experience in the classroom I have witnessed that children respond beautifully to learning about their classmates' cultures, values and languages. Singing in different languages or reading books about different cultures is thrilling for children. Children who are exposed to different cultures, values, and languages learn to respect one another and to appreciate their own cultures as well. I feel that children who are involved in a culturally supportive environment where they are encouraged to share their ideas become more confident about their own identity. When children develop their own sense of self they are more apt to respect others' differences.

References

Ada, Alma F. (2002). *I love Saturdays y domingos*. New York: Simon & Schuster.

Anno, M. (1997). *Anno's journey*. New York: Putnam.

Baker, M. (2000). Towards a methodology for investigating the style of a literary translator. *Target, 12*(2), 241–266.

Bakhtin, M. (1988). From the prehistory of novelistic discourse. In David Lodge (Ed.), *Modern criticism and theory*. New York: Longman.

Bourdieu, P. (1991). *Language and symbolic power*. Cambridge: Cambridge University Press.

Casey, K. (1993). *I answer with my life: Life histories of women teachers working for social change*. New York: Routledge.

Collier, V. P. (1989). How long? A synthesis of research on academic achievement in second language. *TESOL Quarterly, 23*, 509–531.

Collier, V. P., & Thomas, W. P. (1999, December/January). Making U.S. schools effective for English language learners, Part 3. *TESOL Matters, 9*(6), 1, 10.

Comber, B., & Kamler, B. (1997). Critical literacies: Politicising the language classroom. Paper submitted for interpretations. Language and Literacy Research Centre, University of South Australia, Underdale.

Cummins, J. (2000). *Language, power, and pedagogy: Bilingual children in the crossfire*. Clevedon, England: Multilingual Matters.

DeSilva, A. D. (1998). Emergent Spanish writing of a second grader in a whole language classroom. In B. Perez (Ed.), *Sociocultural contexts of language and literacy*, pp. 223–248. Mahwah, NJ: Erlbaum.

Fillmore, L. W. (1991). Second language learning in children: A model of language learning in social context. In E. Bialystok (Ed.), *Language processing by bilingual children*. Cambridge: Cambridge University Press.

Franken, M. (2002). When and why talking can make writing harder. In S. Ransdell & M. L. Barbier (Eds.), *Psycholinguistic approaches to understanding second language writing*, pp. 34–46. The Netherlands: Kluwer Press.

Freeman, R. D. (1998). *Bilingual education and social change*. Clevedon, England: Multilingual Matters.

Freire, P. (1985). *The politics of education*. Granby, MA: Bergin & Garvey.

Freire, P., & Macedo, D. (1987). *Literacy: Reading the word and the world*. Granby, MA: Bergin & Garvey.

Giroux, H. (1988). *Teachers as intellectuals: Toward a critical of learning*. South Hadley, MA: Bergin & Garvey.

Hakuta, K. (1986). *Mirror of language: The debate on bilingualism*. New York: Basic Books.

Hakuta, K., & Garcia, E. (1989). Bilingualism and education. *American Psychologist, 44*(2), 374–379.

Hakuta, K. & Snow, C. (1986). Summary of research in bilingual education, *California School Boards Journal 44*, 70, pp. 2-4.

Hudelson, S. (1994). Literacy development of second language children. In F. Genesee (Ed.), *Educating second language children: The whole child, the whole curriculum, the whole community*, pp. 129–158. Cambridge: Cambridge University Press.

Katz, K. (2007). *The colors of us*. New York: Henry Holt.

Kuiken, F., & Vedder, I. (2002). Collaborative writing in L2: The effect of group interaction on text quality. In S. Ransdell & M. Barbier (Eds.), *New directions for research in L2 writing*. The Netherlands: Kluwer Academic Publishers.

Larsen-Freeman, D. & Long, M. H. (1991). *An introduction to second language acquisition research*. New York: Longman.

Mayer, M. (1992). *There's a nightmare in my closet*. New York: Puffin.

Moll, L. (1994). Funds of knowledge: A look at Luis Moll's research into hidden family resources. *CITYSCHOOLS, 1*(1), 19–21.

Muspratt, S., Luke, A., & Freebody, P. (1997). *Constructing critical literacies: Teaching and learning textual practice.* Creskill, NJ: Hampton Press.

Ovando, C. J., & Collier, V. P. (1998). *Bilingual and ESL classrooms: Teaching in multicultural contexts.* New York: McGraw-Hill.

Portis, Antoinette. (2007). *Not a stick.* New York: Harper Collins.

Quintero, Elizabeth P. (2002). A problem-posing approach to using native language writing in English literacy instruction. In S. Ransdell (Ed.), *Psycholinguistic approaches to understanding second language writing.* The Netherlands: Kluwer Press.

Quintero, Elizabeth P. (2004). *Problem-posing with multicultural children's literature: Developing critical early childhood curricula.* New York: Peter Lang.

Quintero, Elizabeth P. (2009). Young children and story: The path to transformative action. In S. Steinberg (Ed.), *Diversity: A reader.* New York: Peter Lang.

Quintero, Elizabeth P., & Macías, A. H. (1995). To participate, to speak out …: A story from San Elizario Texas. In R. Martin (Ed.), *On equal terms: Addressing issues of race, class and gender in higher education.* Albany, NY: SUNY Press.

Quintero, Elizabeth P., & Rummel, Mary K. (2003). *Becoming a teacher in the new society: Bringing communities and classrooms together.* New York: Peter Lang.

Ramírez, Yuen, Ramey, & Pasta. (1991). *Final report: Longitudinal study of structured English immersion. strategy, early-exit and late-exit transitional bilingual education programs for language-minority children* (Vols. I and II). San Mateo, CA: Aguirre International.

Reyes, M. (1992). Questioning venerable assumptions: Literacy instruction for linguistically different students. *Harvard Education Review, 2*(4), 427–444.

Rummel, M. K. (2003). Histories. In Elizabeth P. Quintero & Mary K. Rummel, *Becoming a teacher in the new society: Bringing communities and classrooms together.* New York: Peter Lang.

Rummel, Mary K., & Quintero, Elizabeth P. (1997). *Teachers' reading/teachers' lives.* Albany, NY: SUNY Press.

Shor, I. (1987). *Freire for the classroom.* New York: Boynton/Cook.

Simon, N. (1993). *Why am I different?* New York: Albert Whitman and Company.

Skutnabb-Kangas, T. (2000). *Linguistic genocide in education — or worldwide diversity and human rights?* Mahwah, NJ, and London: Lawrence Erlbaum.

Torres-Guzmán, M. E. (1993). Critical pedagogy and Bilingual/Bicultural Education Special Interest Group update. *NABE News, 17*(3), 14–15, 36.

Trueba, H. (1991). From failure to success: The role of culture and cultural conflict in the academic achievement of Chicano students. In R. R. Valencia (Ed.), *Chicano school failure and success: Research and policy agendas for the 1990s,* pp. 151–163. London: Falmer Press.

Ullman, C. (1997). Social Identity and the Adult ESL Classroom. *Eric Digest.* National Clearinghouse on Literacy Education, October 1997, EDO-LE-98-01.

Zou, Y. (1998). Rethinking empowerment: The acquisition of cultural, linguistic and academic knowledge. *The Teachers of English to Speakers of Other Languages Journal.* Vol. 7:4 (Summer), 4-9.

CHAPTER FOUR
Artful Story Supporting Critical Reading

You can padlock a building, you can't padlock an idea. Highlander is an idea. You can't kill it and you can't close it in. This workshop is part of the idea. It will grow wherever people take it. (Horton, 1959, p. 28)

Complicated Conversations—Artful Story Supporting Critical Reading
Myles Horton (1959) was speaking about Highlander Folk School in Tennessee, where he supported critical ideas and social justice for decades. He met there with Paulo Freire, and the two activists found they had many ideas in common. Ideas are the foundation of critical reading. Young children, when given the chance, grapple with ideas to make sense of and make a difference in their worlds. In Chapter 1, we met the boy riding the crowded subway with his father. He had an idea to create his version of the train with enough seats for everyone to sit. In Chapter 3 we met another boy who had made a talking stick and then used the mechanism to talk about his fears in a nightmare about a monster in his closet. He was using new ideas to grapple with his world.

The history of the Highlander Folk School reflects the course of organized labor and civil rights movements in the South, as well as the struggles of Southern activists between the 1930s and early 1960s. Highlander's programs were based on the belief that education could be used to support people's using the knowledge they had gained from experience and work to implement actions toward a more democratic and humane society. This approach made the adult education center a source of inspiration and the most controversial school in modern Tennessee history.

The process of analyzing and responding to the problems was as important as the proposed solutions. Their generative learning activities have many of the components of critical literacy learning activities in this book. The school used visiting speakers, movies, audio recordings, drama, and music to identify common issues, offer multiple perspectives, and introduce promising strategies for action.

Workshop participants evaluated their findings, assessed their new understanding of their concerns, and made plans to initiate or sustain activities when they returned to their communities. The Highlander faculty considered the workshops as only part of a learning process that began before students arrived at the school and continued after they left. Once labor education, literacy training, leadership development, or voter education classes had been firmly developed, Highlander transferred responsibility for the programs to organizations with larger resources, thereby remaining both a resource and a catalyst for future action.

In the book *We Make the Road by Walking* (1991), Horton and Freire discuss social change and empowerment and their individual literacy campaigns. The dialogue between two of the most prominent thinkers on social change in the 20th century was momentous. Throughout their highly personal conversations, it became clear that ideas of these men had developed through two very different trajectories. Myles Horton was a major figure in the civil rights movement in the United States and the founder of the Highlander Folk School, and later the Highlander Research and Education Center. Paulo Freire, author of many books on critical theory and critical pedagogy, established the Popular Culture Movement in Recife, Brazil's poorest region, and later was named head of the New National Literacy Campaign until a military coup forced his exile from Brazil.

These two educators were giants in the critical literacy arena. They worked primarily with adult learners. However, many educators struggle with how we can help younger learners become critical readers and activist citizens. One important goal in literacy education is helping students critically "read" what they are learning in and out of school. How does the information relate to prior personal and family knowledge? How does the information differ from that knowledge?

In a previous study of the beliefs and practices of effective literacy teachers (Rummel & Quintero, 1997), we found that family history and literacy are an interwoven fabric of cultural practices. This family knowledge and related literacy practices promote strength, encourage nurturance, and support risk taking. The teachers in our study, like many well-known writers and visionaries (Allen, 1991; Walker, 1983), talked about the importance of the passing on of stories by parents and grandparents. They felt that this was an important legacy passed down through the generations. One teacher smiled as she reported that her West Indian grandmother passed on teachings through folktales. Another teacher talked about his grandfather and grandmother. He noted that passing on stories in his American Indian family during his youth was done orally. They gathered around a campfire, and the eldest would talk and tell stories.

Another family strength we found in this study (Rummel & Quintero, 1997) was parents' reading practice. While families did not always read bedtime stories, people read what they were interested in. This reading combined with the relationships among family members seems to be what matters. This often differs from much traditional literacy development advice, which stresses the importance of the "bedtime story." These teachers were as affected as the children were, in many cases not by storybooks being read to them but by the positive relationship of the parents and children and the exposure to parents reading what they wanted and needed to read for themselves.

A student teacher examining her own literacy history wrote in a journal entry:

> At home, my mother sometimes would read a story or tell a story of her own before I went to bed. I enjoyed the stories told by my mom, but I was particularly interested in her own stories, because through stories, I have the chance to meet the little girl who later became my mom across time. I felt I was closer to her, because she was once a little girl like me.

Another student teacher from a different country and culture wrote:

> I remember that my family had a lot of books, but not children's books. My grandfather and I had very good relationship and in fact, we are still very close. When I was young, we used to live together as a big family. It was always the night time, when I was going to bed, he told me the folktales. He didn't have a book. It was a real folktale that he knew from a long time ago. Those stories were amazing. I described all the characters; and I imagined all the happenings that came out of my grandfather's mouth. While I was thinking about the story, I fell into sleep and dreamed about it.
>
> On the other hand, my grandmother used to tell me her real-life stories. For her, it was real, but for me, it was a tale. She lived in a completely different society from mine. She talked about how her house, school, family, marriage, the Korean war … etc. It was all about her. However, it was also a culture and history lesson for me. When I was young, I used to sleep with her. When my grandfather was not able to tell me a folktale, my grandmother and I lay down together and had a nice conversation.
>
> Every night, I begged for a story from them. Often times, they said, "I already told you about that story, didn't I?" I replied, "Yes, but that's okay, I can listen one more time …" I still remember every single story and moment that we shared.

It is not often that the philosopher and scholar Foucault is brought up in a discussion of young children learning to be critical readers. Yet, Foucault (2001) said,

> … I call a theorist someone who constructs a general system, either deductive or analytical, and applies it to different fields in a uniform way. I'm an experimenter in the sense that I write in order to change myself and in order not to think the same thing as before. (pp. 239–240)

In my experience, children are experts at experimenting with story "in order not to think the same thing as before." Take the four-year-old who was afraid of his nightmare about a monster from Case Study Two in the previous chapter. He used his talking stick and the story the teacher brought in for him, *There's a Nightmare in My Closet* (Mayer, 1992), to not think the same thing as before.

Where's the "Critical" in the Method?

Louise Rosenblatt (1996) categorizes readers' involvement in text along a continuum. One end of this continuum is aesthetic reading, when a reader becomes involved in the story and identifies with the characters. At the other end of the continuum is reading to gain information. Of course, children operate all along the continuum and use books for enjoyment, critical analysis, and learning. Critical pedagogists and teachers using critical literacy are committed to giving learners multiple sources of knowledge for critical analysis and opportunities for transformative action.

The problem-posing method of critical literacy encourages students to experience and make conscious the transformations that often occur through the reading of and reflection on literature. This natural outcome is not causal, but our thinking, our understanding of events, and consequently our behavior are influenced by the process. It is always important to keep an open mind regarding what we are all learning, and we must always ask what is really going on here? This is true in terms of policy and politics, and it is true in terms of the multicultural children's literature we use in our classrooms. For example, when a teacher education student found the storybook *Knots on a Counting Rope* by. John Archambault and Bill Martin Jr. with Ted Rand as illustrator (1997), we were all happy to see the beautiful book and have the opportunity to further our knowledge of American Indian people.

The story is about an American Indian boy and his grandfather. The boy is blind and his grandfather tells him the story of when he was born and how his family discovered that he was blind. The grandfather's story helps the boy to deal with his blindness. The grandfather uses a counting rope and adds a knot to it for each time he tells the story—when the rope is filled with knots the boy will know the story by heart. The grandfather tells the boy that he does this because he will not always be here to tell the boy himself. In addition, the story seemed to be a way into information sessions with children about issues of ability and disability, potential and barriers.

Then the student teacher and her collaborator found an article by a Navajo scholar and learned about inaccuracies in the book. They explained that Ted Rand's illustrations suggest primarily that the story is set in the Navajo nation, but his pictures show a mix of material culture from other nations as well. For example, traditional Navajo men in the story have a variety of hairstyles of the Atsina, Blackfeet, Mandan, and Piegan nations. Also, Pueblo people are shown at a horse race wearing traditional ceremonial clothing that would be inappropriate for such an occasion. Whereas these inconsistent details may seem insignificant, they are very important in terms of critical literacy and of history.

So, should the book be totally censored and never used? I think not. I think it is a good way to engage young children in critical literacy and a starting point for them to learn to be critical researchers (Quintero, 2004).

A student teacher planned such a problem-posing lesson with a multicultural storybook. The book she chose for her lesson was *Magda's Tortillas (Las Tortillas de Magda)*. In this first-grade class, some of the children were from Latin backgrounds and all children were learning Spanish in the school. Therefore, the teacher had chosen to use the book *Magda's Tortillas (Las Tortillas de Magda)*, by Becky Chavarria-Chairez, which is about a family's traditions of beginning to teach children to make tortillas on their seventh birthday. The teacher began the lesson by introducing the concept of "rites of passage." This included some examples from different cultures such as a Bar Mitzvah or Bat Mitzvah in the Jewish culture, driving, dating, or babysitting in the United States, or even going into kindergarten.

In our university class, we read and discussed some reviews of the storybook, some of which were positive, others of which were critical of the quality of the translation. In our process of problematizing, we discussed dialect differences in different geographical locations and different vernacular ways of speaking in different communities. We reviewed a copy of *Are You My Mother?* by Dr. Seuss, which had been translated into Spanish. The publishing information revealed that the translation had been done in Spain. This accounted for the fact that some of the vocabulary words in the story were different from words used for the same items in Mexico and Cuba. Nevertheless, the student decided to keep her original plan to use the book and raised some of our questions with her cooperating teacher and the Spanish teacher at her school (Quintero, 2004).

Controversial Books and Topics

During the past decade, as throughout history, there have been controversies about appropriateness of certain books and certain topics for children. A notable series of our times is the Harry Potter series by J. K. Rowling. While some parents and various special interest groups would like to censor the books, most communities and schools have embraced the books because of their compelling stories that interest even committed non-readers. A member of the International Reading Association has documented that children who had not read a book in years started to read the Harry Potter books and were asking for more. She says, "For the first time for them, a book was as exciting as a video game" (Hallet, 2004, p. 2). Relating the issue of book choice, censorship, and children's reading to critical literacy, it must be noted that children should be the key participants in their own learning and the choice of material must be their own. Furthermore, according to the Federation of Children's Book Groups, 84% of teachers surveyed said, "Harry Potter thathas helped improve child literacy and 67% claimed the series had turned   nonreaders   into   readers"   (http://news.scotsman.com/uk.cfm: id+765922005). Perhaps more important, according to the same study, 59% of students believe that the Harry Potter books have improved their reading skills and that these books are what has led them to read more.

One example of a teacher education student's tenacity of dealing with a controversial topic was her commitment to addressing the complex relationship between family pride and immigration. She planned and implemented a problem-posing lesson using multicultural children's literature with a critical literacy framework. The student was student teaching in a second-grade classroom. She used the storybook *La Isla* by Arthur Dorros (1995).

She explained:

> At the school where I am student teaching, the second-grade class' theme of study for the year is the history of New York. The students just finished a section on immigration. The focus of my problem-posing lesson further explored this topic and stressed family pride and some of the critical questions surrounding the media and political controversies about immigration.
>
> I began by saying "I know a few of you have immigrated here, to the U.S., from another country. By a show of hands, let's see who you are. Does anybody have parents who have immigrated to this country? Raise your hands. I have to raise my hand too because my parents came from Europe. How about grandparents? Does anyone have grandparents or great-grandparents that have immigrated here? Or does anyone know neighbors or friends who are immigrants (remember your friends in class count)? What about immigrants we don't know personally? Who are some immigrants that are in the news or on T.V. or in the movies?" (I will allow a few children to respond after each question.)

She then talked about the storybook *La Isla*.

> The grandmother of the girl in the story I am going to read is an immigrant, and she tells her grandchild about her homeland. The storybook is *La Isla* by Arthur Dorros. Some of you may be familiar with another of his books, *Abuela* (She showed them this book). This is a sequel to that book, which means it's like part two of the book.

Then she read the storybook and held a discussion revolving around these questions:

- In this story, how did the little girl come to appreciate the homeland of her grandmother? What are the kinds of things that we found about La Isla?
- If we wanted to find out about the homeland of immigrants we know or even about the homeland of people we don't know but would like to know about, what kind of things would you like to find out? (List responses on chart paper.)

She then asked the children to pair up and interview each other about homeland or the homeland of someone they know. She said that if they didn't want to share, they didn't have to; they could listen in on another's interview. She reminded them to look to the chart that they had made up here for ideas for your questions. She asked that they try and ask about at least two things. (She gave the example of if she were interviewing L., she might ask him about the kinds of places there are to visit in the Dominican Republic and what kinds of foods there are.)

Then she explained that after the interviews they would come back as a group and share some things that were learned. Then they had time to draw some pictures. For the pictures she asked that they draw (or write) something about their homeland or the homeland of someone they know. She said that if they couldn't think of anything to draw, they could draw something about their homeland or something in New York. She reminded them that immigrants have two homelands, the homeland of the country they moved from and the homeland of where they live now.

In her student journal, the student teacher wrote about the success of the lesson and her commitment to similar topics and approaches:

Isla was a hit. Although the lesson did not go exactly according to plan, the outcome was better than expected. Students were very engaged. My personal belief as to why this lesson was successful is related to its interactive design and the deep meaning of the topic for my children. Because students took an active role in the experience from the beginning, for each student, personal meaning was what gave the lesson its depth. They told stories about the good things about the homeland their families had left and they talked openly about the difficulties that they'd heard their elders discussing.

The students were able to extend on their theme study (related to immigration to New York), learn about a number of different countries and develop an appreciation of the differences among them. They talked about what was being said about immigration in their families and asked critical questions about things they had heard on television news about immigration.

When I have a chance to implement this sort of lesson in my own classroom, I will probably follow the same approach, as well as implement the original lesson I had intended (where the students would interview a person outside the classroom and conduct a mini-research of that person's homeland). (Quintero, 2004, pp. 145–147)

Critical Literacy Around the World

I have collaborated with teachers in a variety of contexts whose classrooms are active, vibrant sites for critical literacy development and learning. The insights learned from collaboration with the teachers include a deeper understanding of

1. the relationship of critical literacy to the political, social, historical strengths and tensions, and funds of local knowledge in "borderland" groups of cultures;
2. the extent to which those strengths and tensions affect literacy and language use, learning, and teaching in school;
3. the extent to which those strengths and tensions affect literacy and language use, learning, and teaching in the community;
4. the ways in which policy and practice could improve by acknowledging and using this information. (Quintero & Rummel, 2004)

These are the reasons that critical literacy is an integral part of the problem-posing process in our classes. It has been shown, over and over again, that writing and reading are transforming (Barone, 2000; Greene, 1992; Quintero & Rummel, 2004; Rummel & Quintero, 1997; Sherman, 2002). As students—children and adults—read and write, they change. A student's writing can tell us much about her/his personal, family and community contexts. It is the students' using these shared assumptions in their work that has led to corroboration of recent findings from practicing teacher interviews regarding related theoretical and pedagogical issues (Rummel & Quintero, 1997; Ladson-Billings, 2001).

Some educational programs around the world show prime examples of critical literacy even if they do not identify themselves as programs of critical literacy or critical pedagogy. Yet, the commitment and application of these programs to respecting and building on participants' cultural and historical backgrounds, to using and critically reading multiple sources of knowledge, and to providing students access to transformative action give critical pedagogists much to learn from.

Ilê Aiyê, Salvador, Bahia, Brazil

All of us have a long way to go to understand the complexities of race, class, gender, and nationality—and how we can learn from each other and live together in peace. Critical reading for children is one hopeful trajectory. A model that can inform us comes from an activist group in Salvador, Bahia, Brazil. As a community association, Ilê Aiyê has established itself as one of the most distinguished agents in recovering the self-esteem and the self-consciousness of the black community in the state of Bahia. The association is working at addressing the complex issues surrounding race, identity, history, and learning. The name of the group, Ilê Aiyê, comes from the Yoruba phrase for "House of Life." The group began as a music group, but Ilê Aiyê has gone beyond the production of Afro-Brazilian dance and music. It has started two schools that serve children who, as they explain, "are too poor to afford uniforms necessary to attend public schools." Education in these schools consists of both academic subjects and the arts, with a focus on African heritage (BrasArte, "History of Ile Aiye," September 9, 2006).

Each year the school develops a different theme that is later expanded into the carnival theme of the year. For each theme, school leaders create a textbook, which teaches students about the history of the subject and provides historical activities, poetry, essays, and songs that will be incorporated into dance and music lessons. The 2005 theme was Mocambique Vulturi, while in years past, it has been devoted to a variety of subjects including single countries such as Senegal (1998) and Nigeria (1999), the organization of the black resistance (1995), and the African nation called Bahia.

When the children experience this integrated curriculum they learn to be citizens to stand up for civil rights and to understand in layered perspective (Sandro, 2006). A new class specifically focused on the rights and responsibilities of citizenship has been recently created for students from eight years old to sixteen years old.

The Star School in Newham, East London, England
Critical reading, in English as well as in other languages, is urgently important for immigrant and refugee students. What are the aspects involved in educating children of refugee and immigrant families? In communities with a high population of refugee families, students who speak the language of the school as a second, third, or fourth language, and a high rate of poverty, what can schools do? How can a curriculum be designed and delivered that supports and respects the history, language, and culture of newcomers while providing students with knowledge and skills to give them an equal chance for success in their new homes? How can schools provide support for the entire family of its students? One school in East London is charting new inroads for our knowledge that addresses these issues.

Star Primary School is a community school for pupils aged three to eleven years. It is located in Canning Town in the East End of London, an area of economical deprivation, and surrounded by pre-war properties used mainly for social and temporary accommodation. The school provides education to pupils from a wide range of cultures, faiths, and languages. There are 650 students in the primary school and 75 in the nursery. Half of the pupils are speakers of languages other than English, and for those who are children in asylum-seeking families, their potential for resettlement causes additional complications and stress. Teachers have to become legal advisors, helping families negotiate the minefields of immigration and housing law and social security benefits.

The British National Curriculum had been put in place before Marion Rosen (2006) took over as principal at Star School. She said that the curriculum was very boring and not very well delivered. She is a great believer in using the arts, drama, music, and visual arts; therefore they used the arts from the beginning to make the curriculum engaging. She and the teachers set out to create a culturally inclusive curriculum. They included traditional information and other information—information that is culturally and historically important, and which is not always in mainstream curriculum. For example, in Year Two, seven-year-olds study Florence Nightingale and Mary Seacole in history, and have storytelling sessions with the Anansi stories. During Year Five, classes participate in different types of curriculum framework, for example, one based on dance and science, another based on the combination of history and theater. They use lots of music. For example, in Year Three students study the violin and recorders, and in Year Five students learn African drumming. The curriculum at Star School is process driven rather than content driven. The six key skills the curriculum addresses are questioning, making connections, describing their learning, evaluating their learning, personal connections, and problem solving. Rosen (2006) believes that these key elements will help to create adults who are creative, adaptable, flexible, and independent.

At Star School English Language Learners are pulled out of their regular classroom to attend special lessons in a different classroom or given assistance in the class. The school supports the students staying in the class, even if they come with only five words of English. This "doesn't mean they haven't got a language; it doesn't mean that conceptually they are not on the same level with some of our children in their numeracy. We take children who are new to the country who don't speak any English and we deliberately keep them in the classroom" (Rosen, 2006).

When a child arrives, the English teacher provides the child with a dictionary in his own language, and the staff also ensure that the teacher knows the level of English of the student. They provide the child with some basic words such as friend, teacher, bathroom, eat, home, school, and parent, and they provide the teacher with some basic words and information about some web sites. They are very deliberate about not grouping non-English speaking children by ability because there would be a tendency to group children because of lack of English. They mix the new language learners with other students until they can make an assessment.

Marion Rosen (2006) strongly believes that "Every 11 year old deserves to be at the national average in attainment. These children are entitled to achieve." She decided that it was not only the school's responsibility to provide critical reading and learning experiences for the children. She realized that she needed to "talk up" the school to the outside community so that the general public would begin to understand the positive work and potential of the students. So, every week she had an article in the local newspaper to show a positive learning event happening at Star School.

After the visit to Star School, a graduate student reflected:

> An assumption from my field that heavily guides my work is that human motivations and behaviors are largely determined by cognition. Something Ms. Rosen said about the impact of "talking up" the community that she works in really rattles me and hit close to home. Most of the time, we Mississippians spend so much of our time sharing all the negative aspects our community in an effort to find help for it and to possibly change things. I think if we spend more time "talking up" the more positive aspects and possibilities, it will encourage those within that community to help themselves rather than sitting around waiting on someone else to rescue them. This doesn't indicate that I feel their struggles should be forgotten, but rather use them to support their efforts and accent where they are now versus where they came from. (Quintero, 2007, p. 121)

Another graduate student was impressed with the Star School students' knowledge and understanding of people from around the world:

> Children have a compassion and empathy for the "other," and there is a danger of base propaganda and uninformed citizens. We need to expand foreign understanding of the human side of American, but moreover we need to bring understanding of other cultures here to the U.S. … As global citizens we carry social responsibility. (Quintero, 2007, p. 122)

And another was impressed with the mature, in-depth conversations that children were involved in as a part of their curriculum.

> Learning the language and history is not all you need to know to understand a culture. You need interaction, conversation, a true understanding of the individuals themselves in order to really learn. How does this individual use the language? How does the history of that area or group apply to that person's individual life and personal choices. … reading in texts cannot teach you about the individuals you have to try to integrate into a new culture. Only through sincere and empathetic cross-cultural conversations, can these adjustments take place.

New Literacy Studies

Other literacy research around the world supports the importance of critical reading. Brian Street (1988) makes a distinction between literacy events and literacy practices. Many scholars report their dismay that the accepted view in many fields, from schooling to development programs, works from the assumption that literacy in itself will have effects on other social and cognitive practices. In other words, by introducing literacy to poor, "illiterate" people, villages, and urban youth, the cognitive skills will be advanced thus improving their economic prospects, making them better citizens, regardless of the social and economic conditions that accounted for their "illiteracy" in the first place.

Research in New Literacy Studies challenges this view and suggests that in practice literacy varies from one context to another and from one culture to another and so, therefore, do the effects of the different literacies in different conditions. The alternative model that these and other critically based approaches support offers a more culturally sensitive view of literacy practices as they vary from one context to another. This model starts from the assumption that literacy is a social practice, not simply a technical and neutral skill and that it is always embedded in socially constructed epistemological principles.

Critical theorists, as well as New Literacy Studies proponents, believe that literacy is about personal and communal knowledge. We believe that the ways in which people address reading and writing are themselves rooted in conceptions of knowledge, identity, and being. Literacy is always contested, both its meanings and its practices; hence particular versions of it are always "ideological," and they are always rooted in a particular worldview and in a desire for that view of literacy to dominate and to marginalize others (Gee, 1999; Besnier & Street, 1994). The ways in which teachers or facilitators and their students interact is already a social practice that affects the nature of the literacy being learned and the ideas about literacy held by the participants, especially the new learners and their position in relationships of power. It is not valid to suggest that "literacy" can be "given" neutrally and then its "social" effects only experienced afterward.

Multiple Sources of Knowledge for Critical Reading

Bringing different sources of knowledge into the learning arena is paramount to better understanding of our cross-global realities and multiple realities of ethnic and historical complexities. On the one hand, educational researchers are methodologically bound to study homogeneous groups in an available setting to gain understanding about learning, pedagogy, and knowledge. Yet, on the other, how much of what is learned from such limited studies will really add to our knowledge on a worldwide basis? This reminds me of some uncritical and uninformed student teacher candidates I have met over the years. They are so convinced that they will go back to their home community (in northern Minnesota or Long Island or wherever) and teach there forever. Why do they need to consider multicultural and multiethnic realities in other parts of the world? This is so sadly shortsighted.

For example, a graduate student from India is often amazed that her classmates understand so little about her background. She explained in one journal reflection:

> I lived in a joint (extended) family until the age of fifteen. Even today we are an extremely close-knit family. I am the only child and still live with my parents and grandfather in the same house. My father is an entrepreneur who has built his own career from the beginning. In relation to most American families we are a very conservative close-knit family. My father realizes the value of education and hence he sent me to the United States to study despite opposition from other family members. We celebrate Indian festivals such as Diwali and Holi and believe in the god "Vishnu"... In Indian culture, family is paramount and it is key to develop relationships with all other family members. The basic culture in America is more about independence, while in India it is all about being together as a family and solving all problems together. Children in India may actually live in the same house with their parents for their entire life, while in America the concept of living with one's parents is essentially not accepted.
>
> Talk to me about the gender roles in India? In India, a woman's role is more of a matriarch who runs and executes all essential functions of a household ranging from raising children to running the household finances. There is a general expectancy for the men to be the breadwinners and the primary providers.
>
> However, as literacy levels increase in India and more people have exposure to the Western way of thinking there is a positive shift in the expectancy of a woman's role in the corporate world and there is a move towards a more balanced structure between running the house and building a career. A few decades ago a woman was not expected to pursue higher studies. However, today with increased awareness many women are pursuing their careers.

Teacher Education Students and Critical Reading

Reading the world through critical literacy and problem-posing helps us find ways to look at alternative ways of knowing and at people's real experiences and real achievements. The findings from this study dramatize the fact that teachers can create the context for learners to use autobiographical narrative to reflect upon their strengths and needs and to use critical literacy to address the barriers they face every day.

Student teachers realize that

> When I'm in the classroom I'll be challenged to find out where my kids come from. Do they have families with gender role expectations? Are the expectations healthy? How will conflicting expectations from different families reveal themselves in my classroom? How will I be sensitive to and help the class embrace the rich lives of their classmates?

Another challenge for me will be to decide what I will do when family traditions/role expectations conflict with what I believe is right. Will I want to simply follow a parent's guidelines when inside I feel a more complex dilemma? Who's to say that I know better than someone's parents? This makes me nervous.

Teacher education students in the study reflected on their own experiences of critical literacy in their own families and communities. A student teacher whose parents came to the United States from Colombia when she was a baby wrote about her early literacy experience:

My own memories of literacy were enjoyable. I remember heading to the library almost every week with my older sister and my mother. I would check out as many books as I could. Before I could read, my sister read to me. I asked her what books she read to me because I could not remember the exact books she read. She said she read fairy-tales such as Cinderella and Sleeping Beauty. When she told me that, another memory flashed in my head. I sat in my first-grade classroom, and I was waiting for my turn for some activity going on in the room. While waiting, I remember pulling out my Cinderella book that I had my father buy for me while shopping at the supermarket. Yes, the supermarket actually sold books! I read each page and examined the pictures in detail. I remember my sister really wanted me to learn to read before I entered kindergarten because I never went to preschool. She read me the Curious George books as well; however, I do not remember the Curious George books, so I will take her word for it. My parents were happy that I was just as interested in books as I was in watching television. My father encouraged me to read more books because he felt (and still feels) that television does not educate people.

My family definitely supported my literacy. My sister was most active by reading to me and exposing me to books. My mother supported me by taking me to the library when I wanted to go. My father supported me through his verbal encouragement. Sometimes he wanted to read with me. I remember teaching him the proper pronunciations of certain words when he had trouble reading some words to me. I especially remember reading The Frog and Toad series by Arnold Lobel. I loved reading those books. Whenever there was a Frog and Toad book that I did not yet read, I made sure to get it from the library. Early on, I learned that if we could not afford a whole library of books, the library was available for our use. To this day, I still pick up some books to read for fun, even though I have no time to read them. My family helped me love to read.

Another student teacher remembered her childhood in Southern California and wrote a reflection about her childhood literacy experiences.

I have always been surrounded by literacy in my life. I can remember as far back as when I was three years old or younger. I remember my dad listening to the Dodger games in Spanish over the radio. My dad would have me turn on the radio and he would tell me turn the dial until he was able to hear the game without static.

Another memory I have of my father was when I was four years old. My dad would sit me on his lap with a note pad on mine. He would write my full name in cursive and have me trace it. I also remember my dad teaching me English at home. He would say "Spoon," "Apple" and "Teacher." He would have me repeat it after him. My dad had very beautiful penmanship. My mother, on the other hand, did not know how to read or write. They had an agreement that my dad would teach us how to read and write while she taught us how to be honest and responsible people.

A memory I have of my mother with literacy is singing and dancing while doing chores. I remember her dancing around with broom and whistling. She taught me how to whistle and hum to music. My mother did not read or write but she would always sit down with us to do our homework. My mother would also buy the newspaper and read it, little did I know that all she did was look at pictures and cut the coupons. Now I understand a lot of things that happened when I was younger and appreciate my mother more.

Another student teacher voiced painful memories regarding early literacy, while at the same time, acknowledged her first memories of taking critical action. She wrote:

My experience with literacy before the age of nine was not a good one. Reading and writing did not come easy to me. I remember sitting in class praying that my teacher didn't call on me to read out loud. I felt the children looking at me impatiently and wondering why I couldn't read the words on the page. In the first grade I was tested for dyslexia and it was confirmed that I had that learning disability. I began taking reading classes everyday for an hour in the afternoon. The reading classes helped, but I still felt like I wasn't as smart as the other children in my class. In high school I tested out of the resource reading program and have been doing well in school ever since. However, my early literacy experiences still have an effect on me until this day.

Another student had different memories of literacy in her early life.

I do not recall anyone sitting and reading to me or encouraging literacy via reading. I do remember many times over the experience of music in my life. My older sister, Annette, was more or less the one who raised me. She must have had a passion for music because she shared that passion with me. I remember one occasion when we were living in a two-story house. We were upstairs and playing a record of Diana Ross and the Supremes. This one song, "Stop! In the Name of Love," would come on and I would throw my hand up as if to really mean it and then even when the word stop wasn't being said I would say it and swing that hand out in front of me. I would continue this over and over because my sister would be in stitches. I always enjoyed acting silly because it made her laugh...we made each other laugh. She and I both created our own choreography to the music, which always had a silly twist to it. Our personalities are much the same to this day and we both still act silly when we are together. But just between you and me...we still make each other laugh by creating our own choreography to songs. No, it wasn't reading a book but I listened to the words, I learned the words and I said the words. I became creative with my own words and oral language. I suppose the most important thing to remember is that I didn't even know I was learning...literacy at that. I was simply having fun.

Another student teacher wrote of her memories of literacy in her family.

When I was a small child, as with most things, we had very few books. The books we did have were passed down by my mother or grandmother and we *treasured them.* We took very good care of them and would not have dreamed of abusing them in any way. Until I was nine I was the only girl in the family and my mother gave me books that she had read as a child. I felt very special that these stories and books were something that my mother and I shared separately from my brothers. I still have these books and have shared them with my daughter and nieces. However, they don't seem to share my feelings about how special they are. I would surmise that I treasured these books so much because we had so little and most children nowadays have an overabundance of everything at their disposal.

I also have fond memories of dictionaries and atlases. Again these were special and we were to treat them with the utmost respect. We were always taught to be appreciative that we had these resources available to us. The library was also a special place to my brothers and myself as children. We were taken to the library at least weekly and we were encouraged to value and respect the opportunities and privileges the library offered us.

Thinking about all this has reminded me why I love books and reading so much.

Finally, a student teacher documented an observation early in her time in a Head Start program in which a four-year-old exhibited critical literacy for her very important purposes of the heart:

While I am student teaching at a Head Start program, every week I learn something new from a child every time I am there. While watching the children play out on the playground today, a girl named Tatiana came up to me and asked, "Teacher T., why are you coloring over words with that pink marker?" What she saw me doing was highlighting phrases on my observation notes.

I replied, "Well Ana, this pink marker is called a highlighter and I am coloring over these words with this marker because these words are IMPORTANT to me." While Ana sat with me as I continued to highlight words on my observation notes, I gave her a piece of paper so she could draw me a picture. After she was all done, she said "Look Teacher T., I highlighted something on my paper too." Astonished by the phrase "TriHODRB," I continued to ask her what that highlighted phrase said. She responded, "It says … I love you Teacher T., Teacher E., Teacher H., Teacher V., E., and Y … with ALL MY HEART." Because what she had written was important in her eyes, naturally she wanted to highlight it.

Critical Literacy in Action—Artful Story Supporting Critical Reading

Case Study Six

One teacher planned the following lesson for her kindergarten/first-grade classroom. She was particularly interested in using folktales and storytelling as a way to support children's critical reading. She showed her class that folktales and stories can enrich personal history, can be one of the multiple sources of knowledge, and can support critical reading and transformative action.

Listening:

The teacher reminded the children of the previous class discussion about the definitions of the word "critical" and how it applies to making classroom rules, to playing games of pretend, and to understanding books, jokes, and directions. She reminded them that for their purposes, "critical" meant asking "what's really going on here?" Then she discussed the different definitions of folktales with the students and then explained that, for their purposes, a folktale is a short story that comes from the oral tradition of families passing down stories from older people to children and others over the years. Folktales have to do with everyday life and sometimes feature peasants getting the better of their superiors. In many cases, the characters are animals with human characteristics. She then asked the children to listen to class members talk about folktales they knew, and they discussed whether there were any "critical" aspects to the stories. Then she read the folktale *Why Mosquitoes Buzz in People's Ears: A West African Tale* as told by Verna Aardem (1992). It's a story in which a lying mosquito sets off a chain reaction ending, finally, in the sun no longer rising. When the animals of the forest track down the reasons behind the sun's disappearance, they reach the conclusion that mosquito is the one to blame. Ever since, mosquitoes will sometimes ask people whether or not "everyone" is still angry at them. The answer is a big slap. It is a kind of cautionary tale about gossip and its tragic consequences.

Dialogue:

The teacher asked, "How does this story fit the definition of a folktale? What are some interesting things about the earth that might have folktales written about them. (For example, why is the sky blue? why do birds sing?) She then used open-ended questions to ask about the parts of the story that would encourage the children to think critically.

Action:

She reported,

> I sent the students off to "work time" also known as "center time." Students chose an activity to work with. They one had requirement of coming to the writing center at some point during the work time.

The choices for work time were:

1. Clay center—making one of the animals, locations, etc. from the story, a folktale the student knows, or one they are inventing. There were science books available showing pictures and giving facts of various animals. The children were encouraged to place their clay animals in an "imaginary ecosystem" and make lists of critical questions about ways the animals might live together.

2. Art center—drawing one of the animals, locations etc. from the story, a folktale the student knows, or one they are inventing. More science books, with the addition of fanciful fiction and art books were available here.

3. Blocks—building one of the scenes from the story, a folktale the student knows or one from a tale that they are inventing. Books with photographs and descriptions of shelters around the world were at this center.

4. Dramatic play—performing the story, a folktale a student knows or one they are inventing. Props in the form of dress up clothes, masks and other concrete objects were available here.

5. Writing center—writing/dictating their own folktale to explain something (the students can reference the book, as well as the suggestions from earlier in the dialogue). As a group, the children came up with critical questions, "Who buys the food?" or "Who cleans the house?" and "Who decides if that is the truth about the other animals?" for the folktales.

After the lesson, the student teacher reflected upon the structure of choice she'd used for the purpose of critical reading.

> I agree with Freire when he says that students' participation in the curriculum is important in achieving democracy and development. My cooperating teacher exemplifies this in her classroom. Although certain periods of the day are defined in terms such as Word Study or Writing Workshop, the children have choice time when they can choose which work to do. She feels that allowing them to participate in choosing the activities they do helps them to be more interested in the material, learn decision making, and helps them to be more productive. I see the children excited about and learning from what they do throughout the day and I believe it is because they are taking part in choosing and creating these activities. They are also confident to bring in critical facts about their stories even if their information is different from other students.

Case Study Seven

One teacher education student was studying the issues of both critical literacy and multicultural understanding through fairy-tales from different cultures. She decided to try a lesson with first graders using the Brothers Grimm *Little Red Riding Hood* (2004) and a storybook of *Lon Po Po* (Young, 1989), a Chinese interpretation of the Red Riding Hood story.

Listening:

She began by telling a story about herself: She said, "When I was younger, my brother used to tell me you could dig a hole to China. I later found out he was lying." She asked the children whether anyone had ever told them something that isn't true and listened to their answers. She then asked whether there was ever a time that they had to protect themselves from a dangerous situation. She listened to them describe the situations.

She then asked them to listen to *Little Red Riding Hood* and then *Lon Po Po*. She explained the origin of each tale and marked the countries on the world map.

Dialogue:

Using a Venn diagram, she asked the children to compare and contrast the book *Lon Po Po* to the cartoon on a video with the tale of *Little Red Riding Hood*. As the children discussed the comparisons, she wrote the characteristics on the diagram. When the elements of the story were the same, they were noted in the overlapping part of the diagram.

After this, she asked the children to describe aspects of both stories that they especially liked.

Action:

The children had two activities to choose from.

1. In groups of three or four children, they were asked to have a discussion of what each daughter would tell her mother when she returned from her visit. Short skits were used to share the ideas with the class.
2. Or, the other choice was creating their own interpretation of *Little Red Riding Hood*. Used costumes and props were provided for creating the new version and performing it for the class.

For action outside the classroom, the children were asked to interview family or community friends about a story that they remembered from their childhoods that may or may not have been true. They would be asked how they found out whether or not the information was true. The children reported their results the following week in class.

Children's author Lisa Lunge-Larsen (1999) tells us that literature in children's lives helps them become critical and comfortable in their worlds:

> Over and over again, in wonderful, fanciful stories these themes (of being human) are repeated in a predictable formula that exactly mirrors the child's view of the world. Children, like the heroes and heroines in these stories, perceive their lives to be constantly threatened. Will I lose a tooth? Will I be invited to play? Will I learn to read? By living a life immersed in great stories and themes, children will see that they have the resources needed to solve life's struggles. (p. 11)

Case Study Eight

A student teacher in Southern California, who is passionate about preserving the beauty of the environment, combined this passion, her feminist philosophy (which she reported was influential in her being a female surfer), with her beliefs about how children learn to be critical readers through a critical literacy framework. She wrote:

As an early childhood educator, I highly value NAEYC and what this professional organization stands for. In NAEYC's position statement, it states, "the first years of life are critical for later outcomes" (NAEYC, 2002). Through my experiences in early childhood classrooms (infant/toddler–1ˢᵗ grade), I've learned that "young children have a [natural] desire to learn" (NAEYC, 2002). What I've also learned is that children need time and space, attention, affection, guidance, and conversation. They need sheltered places where they can be safe as they learn what they need to know to survive. They need opportunity to function on the edge of their developing capacities, take on new social roles, attempt novel or challenging tasks, and solve complex problems.

Unlike learning from a textbook, children learn from hands-on experiences that are of interest to them. As educators, it is important for us to observe children and to determine from these observations what kinds of experiences the children are interested in. After seeing what the children are interested in, it is our job to provide the materials to foster learning. Through child-initiated activities, children learn to interact freely, ask questions, discover, formulate answers, and reflect on their findings. Only in this type of environment can we create "school readiness and build a foundation for later academic and social competence" in children.

With these beliefs, it is clear why the student teacher took such care in describing the children she was creating problem-posing lessons for:

From the second I walk into the classroom in the morning, the room buzzes with "noise" as the children sit down to eat breakfast. Although some might view this noise as a bit chaotic, that is the least of my worries. Personally, breakfast time is my favorite part of the whole day because this is where I get an opportunity to sit down with a group of children (group changes daily) and have meaningful conversations with them.

Currently, there are twenty-three students enrolled in the class. With twenty-three children come twenty-three different and defining personalities. When the children choose a center to play in, more than half of them end up in the dramatic play area (a.k.a. the "casita"—the little house). Sometimes I just observe the amazing imaginative play about planning for a Quinsañera or a Fiesta, other times I play with them and watch how they show their background knowledge through play.

For example, one day outdoors, I had the opportunity to interact with two four-year-old girls who were playing in the sandbox. As I was walking around, they invited me over for some posole (a Mexican stew or soup). "Teacher T., Teacher T.," they both hollered. "Do you want some posole?" As I walked over to the sandbox area, I instantly saw a bright red sand bucket with sand, sawdust bark (bark they had collected from the slide area), and water poured inside of it. After asking me again, I instantly replied "I would love some posole." "YUM … YUM … I said with a big grin … does it come with cilantro and lime?" After shoveling more sand in the bucket, they replied … yup … we just added some." After all the ingredients were added, they then served me up some of their delicious (didn't look so delicious) soup with an actual soup spoon. Because I had grown up with Mexican food, I had to request one more food item that I love eating with my posole … corn tortillas. As I was shoveling down the posole, I asked "do you girls know how to make fresh homemade corn tortillas?" With a smile, one of the girls replied, "Si, my grandma makes me tortillas at home." With that, she took a sand sifter from one of the bins, pushed it into the sand in a circular motion. She made me scoop up the sand from the sifter and put it on a plate and said, "There you go, now eat!" After eating my posole, which was accommodated by a tortilla, they each started to talk about the other cultural dishes their families make them at home. After they talked about some of the dishes, I told them of some of the dishes I grew up with. In all, I would have to relate this experience to critical literacy that began with the children's play about creating a meal. These two girls were using oral language as a means to express and use story as a way of learning.

As the semester progressed, the student teacher became interested in adding the standards from the Population Connection work on environmental education (Wasserman, *Sharing a Small World*, 2001) that have been correlated to the State California State Board of Education Content Standards.

Listening and Dialogue:

The teacher began by talking to the large group of four-year-olds gathered together on the carpet:

You might have heard people refer to our planet as Mother Nature. Can anybody tell me why you think people refer to our planet as Mother Nature? Many people call nature "mother" because the natural world gives people everything we need to live, just as your parents give many necessary things to you.

She then asked, "What things does mother nature give us?"

The question was a little difficult, so there was a slight hesitation on the children's part. So, the student teacher turned to the window and pointed outside. One child said, "Sun!" Yes, what else? "Rocks," a boy said. There were a few more answers and then she summarized,

From nature, we get air to breathe, water to drink, soil to grow crops for food, fabric for our clothes, and materials to build the houses we live in. The natural world is also home to all the plants and animals that share our environment and enrich our lives. Just as nature takes care of us, we must take care of our planet so it can go on giving us everything we need to live healthy and happy lives.

She went on,

Let's start with ourselves: What are some of the things you do each day to take care of yourself? Wash hands and take a bath, dress warm in cold weather, eat food, some said. What are some of the things you do each day to take care of your classroom? Pick up toys, clean up, some answered.

Then the student teacher asked,

What are some of the things we can do each day to take care our Earth? Some answers were—pick up trash, plant flowers, vegetables, recycle.

Listening:
She read *100 Things You Should Know About Planet Earth* by Peter Riley (2004)

Dialogue:
She then showed children a globe and explained to them that if the globe was rolled out, it would look like a flat map (show them both a globe and a flat map). This way, they can see how much land consumes Earth versus how much water consumes Earth.

She asked,

"This GREEN part right here, what is that?"
"What about this BLUE part, what is that?"
"Do you think there is more land or more water on our Earth?'
"Well let's take a look at this apple."
"If I were to cut this apple into four pieces, three out of four pieces represent how much water there is on Earth. The remaining one piece represents how much land there is on Earth."
"What are some of the foods we eat that are grown on land?"
(Answers include apples, oranges, pumpkins, and carrots)
"What are some of the foods we eat that come from our ocean?"
(Answers included fish, camarones, and shrimp)
Now that we have discussed what foods come from both the land and the ocean, we are going to make some bread that is made out of pumpkin, a vegetable grown on land.

Action:
The student teacher led a cooking activity, Making Pumpkin Spice Bread. The recipe below was transferred to a large chart with pictures and fewer written words so that the children could follow it as they cooked.

Ingredients:
1 2/3 cups all purpose flour
1 teaspoon baking soda
3/4 teaspoon ground cinnamon
1/4 teaspoon ground ginger
1/4 teaspoon ground cloves
PAM spray

1/4 plus 1/8 teaspoon kosher salt
1 1/3 cups sugar
1/3 cup canola oil
1cup unsweetened pumpkin
1 large egg

1. Preheat oven to 350 degrees. Grease and flour an 8 ½ x 4 ½ inch loaf pan. Sift together first 5 ingredients

2. Combine sugar, oil, and pumpkin in a large bowl; beat at medium speed with an electric mixer until smooth. Add egg, beating until well blended. Gradually add dry ingredients, beating at low speed until blended. Transfer batter to prepared pan.

3. Bake at 350 degrees for 1 hour 5 minutes or until loaf is golden brown. Let cool in pan on a wire rack for 15 minutes, remove from pan.

4. Enjoy and Eat (MAKE SURE ALL CHILDREN CAN EAT PUMPKIN BEFORE SERVING—no allergies).

Listening:
The student teacher showed the children the book *Eyewitness TREE* (2000) by David Burnie and read bits of explanatory text from under the illustrations.

Dialogue:
She then said,

> Let's recall: The natural world is home to all the plants and animals that share our environment with us and enrich our lives. Trees and plants provide us with clean oxygen so we can breathe. Let's think about "What are some of the things found in nature?"

She then passed around objects she had previously found and let the children explore (let the children know that they are going to be finding objects similar to hers on their nature walk).

Action:
1. She lined the children up.
2. She explained plastic bag rules. She stressed the importance of what NOT to do with the bag—DO NOT put plastic bag over head.
3. She explained that children are NOT to pick anything off of plants, bushes, and trees (no picking flowers).
4. NATURE WALK: They explored the outdoors (20–30 minutes). She gave children ample time to find objects such as sticks, leaves, bark from trees, pine cones, etc. She talked to them about what they are finding. She encouraged them to find as many items as possible (can be the same item of different sizes).
5. When inside, she put out butcher paper at each table (two long pieces taped together covering the whole table).
6. ART: Children used their creative abilities and glue the found natural objects onto butcher paper (no right way, no wrong way).
7. After children were done, they came back together as a group and discussed the activity as a whole. They recapped what the children did: each

helped in lending a hand to Mother Nature by picking up natural waste outside, and made art out of it.

Listening:
The student teacher read *Planting a Rainbow* by Lois Ehlert (1992).

Dialogue:
She asked the children to each think of one positive action they could take to protect the environment, and why it is important. She brainstormed with children and generated a list of ideas. (Answers included: pick up trash at the beach, recycle plastic, turn off lights when no one is using them, do not leave a refrigerator open.)

Then, she announced, "As a class, we are all going to create a garden of love by planting flowers outside of the classroom."

Action:
Materials:
1. 2 Bags LGM PLANTING MIX
2. 6 pack flowers (colorful)
3. Shovels
4. Watering cans

Steps for Activity:
1. Choose an area to plant.
2. Bring out 6 packs of flowers and demonstrate to children how these flowers are to be planted.
3. Let children each plant a flower.
4. Water plants thoroughly after planting.

After the planting was done, she emphasized that in big and small ways, we can each do something to lend a hand to Mother Nature. Even the smallest things can make a world of difference in helping to keep our planet clean and healthy.

The student teacher reported:

My "Gifts from Mother Nature" activity was a not only a big hit with the children, but with the teachers and the program director as well. When the class was done gluing all of their items found outside on three pieces of butcher paper, the class's artwork was hung floor to ceiling in the science center for display.

References
Aardem, V. (1992). *Why mosquitoes buzz in people's ears: A West African tale.* New York: Puffin.
Allen, P. G. (1991). Grandmothers of the light: A medicine woman's source. Boston, MA: Beacon Press.
Archambault, J., & Martin, B. (1997). *Knots on a counting rope.* New York: Henry Holt.

Barone, T. (2000). Introduction. In W. Pinar (Ed.), *Aesthetics, politics, and educational inquiry: Essays and examples* (Counterpoints Vol. 117.) New York: Peter Lang.

Besnier, N. & Street, B. (1994). Aspects of literacy. In T. Ingold (Ed.), *Companion Encyclopedia of Anthropology*, pp. 527–562. New York: Routledge.

BrasArte (2006). http://www.brasarte.com/modules/news/

Burnie, D. (2000). *Eyewitness TREE*. DK CHILDREN,1st edition. New York: Penguin.

Dorros, A. (1995). *La Isla*. New York: Penguin.

Ehlert, L. (1992). *Planting a Rainbow*. New York: Voyager Books.

Foucault, M. (2001). *Madness and civilization*. New York: Routledge.

Gee, J. (1999). *An introduction to discourse analysis*. New York: Routledge.

Greene, M. (1992). The passions of pluralism: Multiculturalism and the expanding community. *Educational Researcher, 22* (1), 13-18.

Hallet, V. (2004). The power of Potter. *US News and World Report*: July 25, 2005. http://www.usnews.com/usnews/culture/articles/050725/25read.htm.

Horton, M. (1959). http://www.uawregion8.net/Activist-HOF/M-Horton.htm

Horton, M., & Freire, P. (1991). *We make the road by walking: Conversations on education and social change*. Philadelphia, PA: Temple University Press

Ladson-Billings, G. (2001). *Crossing over to Canaan: The journey of new teachers in diverse classrooms*. New York: Jossey-Bass.

Lunge-Larsen, L. (1999). *The troll with no heart in his body and other tales of trolls from Norway*. Boston: Houghton Mifflin.

Mayer, M. (1992). *There's a nightmare in my closet*. New York: Penguin.

Quintero, Elizabeth P. (2004). *Problem-posing with multicultural children's literature: Developing critical, early childhood curricula*. New York: Peter Lang.

Quintero, Elizabeth P. (2006). Interview with Marion Rosen, Star School, Newham, England.

Quintero, Elizabeth P. (2007). Qualitative research with refugee families. In A. Hatch (Ed.), *Early childhood qualitative research*, pp. 109–130. New York: Routledge/Taylor and Francis.

Quintero, E. P., & Rummel, M. K. (2004). *Becoming a teacher in the new society: Bringing communities and classrooms together*. New York: Peter Lang.

Riley, P. (2004). *100 Things you should know about planet earth*. New York: Barnes and Noble.

Rosen, M. (2006). Lecture. Star School, Newham, England.

Rosenblatt, L. M. (1996). *Literature as exploration*, 5th ed. New York: Modern language Association of America.

Rummel, M., & Quintero, E. (1997). *Teachers' reading/teachers' lives*. Albany, NY: SUNY Press.

Sandro, A. (2006). Lecture. Salvador, Bahia, Brazil.

Sherman, D. (2002). *Passion and pedagogy: Relation, creation, and transformation in teaching*. New York: Peter Lang.

Street, B. (1988). Literacy practices and literacy myths. In R. Saljo (Ed.), *The written word: Studies in literate thought and action*, pp. 59–72. New York: Springer-Verlag Press.

Walker, A. (1983). *In search of our mothers' gardens*. New York: Harcourt Brace.

Wasserman, P. (Ed.) (2001). *Sharing a small world*. Washington, DC: Zero Population Growth.

Young, E. (1989). *Lon Po Po*. New York: Philomel.

CHAPTER FIVE

Artful Story to Investigate Myth, Legend, and History

Histories

A letter, a bill, a diary,
a scribbled note I call history.

The birthday card from my mother
addressed to the best of daughters,

given to me just before she died, words
I waited too long to hear, to see.

When I read my mother's writing
I hear her, see her hand shaking.

I am my own collector, docent
telling my survival, my subject,

the past looms while the future
shrinks on parchment scraps.

Give me texts I can take
as evidence of the world's love,

books I can see and hear
at the same time:

the Rabulla Gospel, the Lindisfarne,
A copy of the Qur'an, a Buddhist folding book.

Reading the way a child
reads a picture book,

reading a kind of eating
urging me to utterance,

urging me to read the body,
the holy text, the world.

(Rummel, 2006, pp. 33–34)

Complicated Conversations—Artful Story Investigating Myth, Legend, and History

Communication theory (von Foerster, 1993) claims that we can only learn what we already know at some level. Cognitive science tells us that knowledge is relative and depends on context. Especially when it comes to history, context is everything—there is always an interaction between the researcher and his or her object (von Foerster, 1993). Shissler (2006) says that the communicative interaction includes us as the observers, our audiences, and the past, present, and future that we explore. This interaction continuously changes the past through our interpretations. It influences the present, in which we position ourselves, and sets the state for an unknown future.

The events of the past decade have not only opened borders across the world, but also pointed out that we in the human service professions have urgent responsibilities toward newcomers in our communities. We have a responsibility to learn about the newcomers' history and their cultures. Stories are the nearest we can get to experience as we tell of our experiences. Some say that the act of our telling our stories seems linked with the act of making meaning, an inevitable part of life in a postmodern world. This process becomes problematic only when its influence on thinking and learning goes unnoticed or is ignored. Education, with all ages of learners, has the urgent task of supporting the development of a new consciousness that embraces the world.

Educators can learn from families in a variety of situations. I have conducted qualitative research in a variety of communities where refugees and immigrants have settled and other communities of migration around the world. The information gleaned from the interviews with the participants informs both educators and policy makers about the strengths and needs of refugee families and students in terms of critical literacy and learning. This information can be used around the world in creating pedagogy for literacy, using local knowledge of particular sites, and drawing on a range of strengths and histories for families to advocate for their rights to literacy and learning in difficult times.

Scheherazade in *A Thousand and One Tales of the Arabian Nights* faces the king's threat to kill her. Her sister comes to her rescue by asking her to tell more stories, thus preventing Scheherazade from being killed. Scheherazade arouses the king's curiosity and makes him eager to listen to the story. To make a broad stroke of metaphor, the king could symbolize the ineffective conditions in schools, curricula, and classroom interactions. And to carry the metaphor further, the sister in the *A Thousand and One Tales of the Arabian Nights* could symbolize the children who give educators a chance to stay alive. Scheherazade's triumph lies in her skill as a storyteller, in her knack to tell and create a story. To be Scheherazade means to overcome the threat of failure and consequent death. How? By becoming a storyteller.

A group of teacher education students studying literacy read *Serafina's Stories*, a novel by Rudolfo Anaya (2004). The novel has historical and cultural relevance for teachers in the southwestern United States and, in fact, the whole world today. The woman, Serafina, was the daughter of a pueblo tribal leader, a hereditary storyteller— a role passed down in her tribe from female leaders—and a courageous leader of her people. She and fourteen males from her tribe were captured by the Spanish colonists in what is now Santa Fe. The governor of the Spanish territory was curious and attracted to the young woman's presence, power, and storytelling ability.

One teacher education student taking part in a university class's critical literacy activities using *Serafina's Stories* to explore myth, legend, and history commented: "Serafina stands for all women who wish to stand up for their own ideals. She has an internal courage and is not afraid to voice her internal wisdom," The student went on,

> The native peoples are always being accused of being pagans. However tribal people are not violent in nature. More people have been killed under the umbrella of Christianity ... Can you see how wrong it is to come in and destroy civilizations, saying they are a threat to new movements and colonies. Are the colonists the ones who are the destroyers? This was always so puzzling to me as a child ... this kind of oppressive thinking.

Personal Histories as a Way to Approach History, Legend, and Myth

Students want to belong and to not appear different. Some of the teachers and student teachers I work with have experiences similar to the experiences of the children. There is complicated conflict surrounding the issue of family loyalty. In a graduate class, a group of teacher education students had the task of reflecting and writing about how they describe or define their racial or ethnic identity. Some starter questions were: What is important and not important to you about this aspect of yourself? If it is important, why? If unimportant, why? Is your ethnic identity tied to a particular place? In what ways? What are some of the details of that place that are a part of your life now or of a memory you hold dear?

A class of graduate teacher education students when asked about how they felt about a homework assignment on reflective writing, many of them said they were excited about the activities as these activities provided ways to connect personal experiences to issues they were studying. Yet, one woman said, "I don't like it!" (Quintero, 2007, p. 116).

She explained,

My mother tends to live in the present and you have to get her in a really good state of mind to even hear about things that went on in her past. Most of it is negative stuff anyway that was used to point out how she had suffered or how "if she had been taught better she would have gone further in life." Such short snippets only served to place upon me a burden which I should, but do not want to, bear. (Quintero, 2007, pp. 116–117)

After we listened to this student and critically analyzed her stance, we listened to each other's thoughts about the connection of her comments to particular issues of life for refugee and immigrant families. We discussed the complex task of remaining respectful and creative in our work because every activity in our work will not be embraced by everyone and for very good reasons. We must respect silence and choice. This is another important aspect of critical theory.

Then the teacher education students *who chose to share* stories discussed their personal stories. A few examples were as follows:

My racial identity has always been the word black. However, what that means is hard to say. My family is more religious than cultural, so no one ever really talked about our ethnic history. To be honest, most people my age where I come from don't even know about Zora Neal Hurston and Billie Holiday. They only have heard mention of those more noted leaders of our culture, like Rosa Parks and Martin Luther King, but still couldn't share much knowledge about their beliefs and struggles. It became more important for me to learn more about my culture once I came to New York, a place of cultural diversity. Being from a place where there is only white and black leaves little need for explorations of any culture. (Quintero, 2007, pp. 117–118)

Another teacher education student from the same group comes from different life circumstances and perhaps asks the most provocative questions at the end of her reflection.

I do not recall having any particular conceptions of it (racial identity) and the reason why I say this is because I did not feel disappointment like some immigrants who come to the U.S. and feel as if it was not living up to their preconceived expectations. I did have a picture in mind, but it is hard to put into words. I think that it does not solidify itself until after real-life experience ... I am still trying to reconcile what the difference is between personal philosophy, personality and culture. I find myself making statements about all, after seeing the actions of a few ... Unable to see, think or believe what is outside of the racial check boxes. Why do we have to check the box? Why are the boxes there in the first place? Who does it benefit? ... I feel that the process of migrating, in itself, changes the migrant,... The Jamaican culture is neither racial nor ethnic, but it is what I identify with most strongly. Yes, most of the population is black and so I guess many of us do not use the blackness as a unifying factor in the way we view potential friends. It is hard to understand the concept that those identifiers are now used to judge us when we do not necessarily do the same to ourselves. (Quintero, 2007, p. 118)

Another teacher education student from a different group of participants reflected,

> As a student, a future teacher, and most importantly a human being, I believe in preserving our own heritage (no matter what generation you are) as well as learning about other individuals' cultures and traditions. I am a firm believer in allowing children the opportunity to explore their own heritage so they can feel proud of where their ancestors and roots came from. I absolutely loved the learning ways students study the Maori language, cultural traditions, song and dance, and way of life in New Zealand through an educational approach in their school.

Another student teacher explained a family tradition that encouraged children's critical literacy, exploring history and imagination:

> In my family we have a "Magic Book." The magic book got its name because everyone in my family tells a different story every time it's told. In my family we have different types of levels of education and life experiences. My nephew has had this magic book since he was a few weeks old. My sister made it a habit to read to him this "Magic Book" every night. As my nephew got older he would carry his book and ask different family members to read him this wordless book. We explained to him that he could use his imagination and make up a story every time. The reasons we started this tradition was because children tend to memorize a story and when someone else reads the story and doesn't read it as they know it the child corrects the adult. My nephew is six years old now and he has a year-old sister. He continues the tradition with his younger cousins and his sister. The rest of the family also continues the tradition but now not as much because my six-year-old nephew likes to read them the "Magic Book." It's amazing to me that he never repeats the story; it's always different. What I find more interesting is that he individualizes the story according to whomever he reads the story to.

We discussed at length how her nephew was both creating and documenting family history.

History in the Making

In Britain there is a unique organization giving university students and young people the opportunity to learn from and be advocates for migrating families. This group, Student Action for Refugees, or STAR, uses story and encourages the use of personal histories of migrating peoples to exercise their potential for learning. They also help educate Britons about the new neighbors arriving in their country. The STAR network is made up of university-based student groups, other young people involved in the STAR, and Youth Network and Friends of STAR (individuals and organizations who support the work of STAR). The group believes that refugees and asylum seekers are a vulnerable group of people who often have a long and difficult struggle to secure their safety in another country. As people fleeing persecution, torture, and prejudice, they need and deserve support. Furthermore, as a new generation, it is vital that students and young people have a positive attitude toward refugees, asylum seekers, and displaced people (King, 2006).

Natasha King, the Student Outreach Officer for STAR, said in response to a question about maintaining and sustaining work in contexts where the needs are so great and the issues so complicated that

> At the national level of issues, racism, lack of information, fear on the part of native Britons about their jobs being "taken" by asylum seekers is really depressing, but that at the local university-by-university level the small projects can be so effective that it is really encouraging ... (2006)

The small projects often consist of documentary student-made films about migrating peoples' histories and legends presented through various art forms.

Other ways of exploring history have existed for generations. There is recorded history in easily accessible books and documents. And there is much history that is still passed along only through oral storytelling and music. Choctaw Storyteller and author Tim Tingle tells that even in this day of electronic communication, Native Americans live in a world that often accepts the spoken word as the authority. He says, "Even today, many Choctaws are likely to trust a story told to them by another Choctaw more than anything they read on the printed page" (Tingle, 2006, p. 38). His children's book *Crossing Bok Chitto: A Choctaw Tale of Friendship and Freedom* is what he calls an Indian book, written by Indian voices and painted by an Indian artist. The story was passed down the Indian way, told and retold by elders. The book *Crossing Bok Chitto*, Tingle (2006) says,

> in this new format—of language and painting, this book way of telling—is for both the Indian and non-Indian. We Indians need to continue recounting our past, and from this book, non-Indians might realize the sweet and secret fire that drives the Indian heart. (p. 39)

In addition, in the case of new refugees and immigrant students, this issue of which histories are studied, valued, and added to the curriculum is very important. The Hmong refugees who came to the United States in the 1990s had had little or no formal education or access to English instruction. Some were pre-literate. The Hmong culture is historically an oral culture; this was the first generation of Hmong who were using printed materials as a way to learn.

A bilingual family literacy program that was implemented in Minnesota using two languages—Hmong and English—at Poj Niam Thiab Meyuam (The Mother/Child School). Participants were encouraged to use their native language and to learn and practice their new language while participating in Intergenerational Literacy, and Adult English Literacy Activities. The women processed information and planned activities in small group discussions and then collaborated on parts of the lessons where they could use English. In their adult literacy class, the women designed and put together a bilingual book that is a collection of their family history stories, historical tales of Hmong culture from the past 5,000 years, and folktales. They decided midway through the project to record some of the stories, in both Hmong and English, on audiotapes to go along with the books. They came to this decision because of their worry about their children and grandchildren losing the ability to speak and understand the oral language of their ancestors. The decisions made surrounding this endeavor began the process of integrating all four components of best practices (Quintero, 2004).

The women had had little or no formal education previous to this project and were between the ages of sixteen years and late fifties. Some were preliterate. The challenge of the English literacy class was even more interesting than the usual situation of students with varying experiences and levels of ability in the subject matter. This was because the Hmong culture is historically an oral culture; this was the first generation of Hmong who were using printed materials as a way to learn.

The instructor in the Adult Basic Education English as a Second Language class asked the women what personal needs and issues concerned them and what information they would like the class to present (Larson, 2003). After a discussion, they decided to try to record their experiences in their home country of Laos and later in Thailand and now the United States. They thought that to write these experiences in English was a way to preserve and document them for future generations while improving their understanding of English. The participants and their facilitator agreed that the related objectives of the class were to establish camaraderie within the group; provide access to group problem solving skills; increase participants' comfort level with American people, culture, and institutions; preserve, honor, and respect the Hmong culture; preserve the Hmong oral and written language for future generations; understand the current generation of children; and deal effectively with cultural, generational issues.

The decision to record their personal experiences was a way to achieve these multiple objectives; therefore, the women decided to spend the year creating their personal histories. The stories began with their earliest memories. Some remembered homes in Laos; others remembered the refugee camps. They chose topics to write about together, and then each woman ended her entry with her hopes for her children and grandchildren. The text was written in both English and Hmong for all the women. By the time they finished collecting and organizing materials, the original objectives changed to become a composite story—this was at the women's request because they wanted what each woman contributed as part of their own collections.

Key to the success of this project was the participation of a group member who could translate and provide a sort of cultural bridge between the Hmong and American cultures. Y., who agreed to serve in this role, was extraordinarily gifted in her ability to effectively fill this difficult position. Any problem or question that the participants had, they were always comfortable bringing up because they were comfortable talking to Y. in Hmong, and she then either translated or helped communicate the issues in English. With the collaboration of Y. and the permission of the participants in the class, the class completed this project with a compilation that provides a contemporary social history of the experience of Hmong women who immigrated to America as refugees from the war in Vietnam toward the end of the 20th century. It is a composite story that begins in Laos, travels through the war years, journeys through the refugee camps of Thailand, and ends in America. They also included a chapter of traditional folktales. They were able to locate resources to have the folktales written and recorded in Hmong and to get copies of the collection printed for all the participating families and their relatives, in addition to making copies available to local human service providers who serve Hmong clients (Larson, 2003).

During the process of the storytelling and the writing and editing of the stories, the teacher could see the women changing their feelings about their culture/themselves as they interacted more with American culture. In the beginning of this project, not a single woman was telling her children about her childhood; now several of them regularly reported telling their children about the stories they had told in class, and they were always proud when they talked about them. Some of their older children began asking when the next stories would be ready for them to read.

At the beginning stages of the process, the instructor was worried about whether the women would be comfortable sharing stories. She learned, and documented in her journal, that her worries were unfounded:

> … as the Hmong women have been sharing stories and experiences orally in groups for as long as they have been able to meet together. They settled into a routine that included a snack on storytelling day and complete openness. Stories were audiotaped for reference and the women were free to tell their stories in their native language. (Larson, 2003, p. 158)

Myth and Legend as Historical Perspective
J. R. R. Tolkien wrote in his letter to his publisher at Collins, Milton Waldman, in 1951 (Tolkien, 1977):

> After all, I believe that legends and myths are largely made of "truth," and indeed present aspects of it that can only be received in this mode; and long ago certain truths and modes of this kind were discovered and must always reappear. (p. xvi)

These ideas can come alive through literature and problem-posing.

When thinking about legend, myth, and history in some of our university classes we investigated folktales and fairytales. For our purposes, a folktale is defined as a short story that comes from the oral tradition. Folktales often have to do with everyday life and frequently feature sly common people getting the better of their superiors. In many cases, the characters are animals with human characteristics. In their original versions, most folktales are not children's stories (or at all appropriate for children) because they are bawdy and often violent. However, the tales we choose to use with children have themes of little ones having power, venturing out into the world, and good triumphing over evil.

How are fairytales different from folktales? Fairytales are a subgenre of folktales and almost always involve some element of magic and good triumphing over evil. A graduate student reflected about using fairytales with her second-grade class.

> Our fairy-tale unit was a class favorite. To prepare for the unit I gathered as many different versions of the Cinderella story possible. These stories came from a variety of different countries and cultures. I introduced the unit by asking the students what they already knew about fairy-tales. We made a list on the board. Their ideas were very limited to what they'd seen in Disney movies and books. I then gave the students a compare and contrast chart. For the next several days the students read the Cinderella stories in pairs. After each book they had to fill in the following categories on their chart: title, country/culture, main character, evil characters, magic person or objects, and the reward. When the charts were complete, we made a class list of the elements found in all of the fairy-tales the students read. The students then wrote their own Cinderella tales based on the list of elements:
>
> 1.   The story starts with, "Once upon a time" or a similar phrase.
> 2.   Magic events, characters, and objects are part of the story.
> 3.   At least one character is wicked or evil.
> 4.   At least one character is good.
> 5.   There is usually someone of royalty involved.
> 6.   The main character always gets a reward in the end (goodness is rewarded).
> 7.   The story ends with, "They lived happily ever after."
>
> (Green, 2003, p.88)

This model was used by several study participants as a part of their problem-posing curricular activities.

Regional and historical fiction provides opportunities for young people to live vicariously in times and places they cannot experience any other way.

Well-crafted stories can provide lived-in experiences that encourage the development of attitudes that lead to caring for and appreciation of others unlike themselves in the actual world. Some critical questions must be considered in the study of stories, legends, and myths. Some of the questions and issues relate to the authenticity about a sense of place in story, whether or not the historical fiction is highly romanticized, and the accuracy of minor background details in historical fiction.

History through Children's Literature

After a reading the publication of *Brundibar* by Tony Kushner and Maurice Sendak (2003) a student teacher reflected:

> When the woman introducing Sendak mentioned the connection of the story to the Nazi period in European history, I came home and did some research on the internet about this book and found out that not only does it have artistic appeal for the children but it is a book of historical accuracy. One of the reviews that I read online about the book made me reflect on the issues of authors being concerned about historical accuracy. The review stated, "It's a great kids story about bullies and how they can be dealt with. On a more adult level, it is about how World War II and the Holocaust affected the children of Europe, Christian as well as Jewish" (http://children.bookbest.com/node/index_3.html). While this reviewer feels that this book gives a sense of what it was like for children who were affected during the Holocaust at an adult level, I think children too have the capacity to take that message. I think as early childhood educators, it is important for children to enjoy books that bring in some relevance into their life, but also give them a chance to be exposed to other realities besides their own. I truly believe we live in a multicultural society, and if our aim is to strive towards this common goal, we must bring historical accuracy in which our reflections and perceptions hold some solid ground.

Another student teacher discussed her students' connections to history and legend:

> Recently I started to see how children are anxious to share anecdotes of their personal lives with me; they talk about "Mi Abuela in Puerto Rico" and their dogs, cats, brothers, sisters and toys. One day I put up a piece of butcher paper in an area with a bucket of crayons. I asked the children to come up as they finished breakfast to draw something on our "message mural" that they would like to share with the class. The response was amazing. One girl said she drew a ball and when she talked about it she told the class, "I play with a ball with my brother." Another drew a Yu-Gi-Oh card with his name on it and talked about how "my little brother always be trying to eat my Yu-Gi-Oh cards." Each child drew a symbol of something important in their life, and this drawing in turn elicited language from every child. Moreover, I feel that it encouraged the children to take a risk as they spoke in front of all their classmates.

After a class session on the topic of "Rethinking Columbus" (Bigelow & Peterson, 2003), another student wrote:

Since I was young, I always have known that the winners wrote history especially when wars are involved. I thought it was good that the article addressed that there are two types of history: reading and creating. I think it is good for students to hear multiple points of view on the same topics, so that they can learn how to create their own history. It is important even as adults not to believe everything we read or hear as true, for we have to come to our own conclusions.

Bateson (2004) warns about research and work that breaks new ground:

> So many ghosts to be entertained without belief. The ghost at the typewriter or the ghostly interlocutor fade, but they have played a crucial role in the formulation of thought and the transition to the page. They remain in that place in memory from which all of the honored dead speak to enrich our thought, so that even when we speak, we echo many voices. (2004, p. 16)

The voices I hear and sometimes echo are many—voices in this actual study and voices that I have studied from the past. I am reminded of the ghost of Leonardo da Vinci. In the British National Library, parts of Leonardo da Vinci's notebooks have been preserved. In one section are architectural designs for a new city that the King of France had asked him to create. Among the drawings are comments in his handwriting that say, "Let us have fountains in every plaza," and "Let the country folk inhabit the new houses in part when the court is absent." He was dreaming and documenting his hopes for a more egalitarian use of his creations. As we know, this new city was never built. Yet, to find evidence of a great thinker using imagination and creativity to suggest positive transformation is inspiring and relevant to the work of our building a more civil society.

I have recently been informed by another artist who searched for knowledge and found it through some ghosts. David Dorado Romo (2005) says of his ghost, "I've been looking for Pancho Villa for the last four years. I didn't intend to" (p. 3). He began a quest of creating a psychogeography of the El Paso, Texas/Juarez, Mexico, border cities. He explained that he was inspired by the Situationnistes, an obscure but now-defunct group of French urbanists, artists, and anarchists who, in the 1950s, would travel the streets of Paris noting its various types of ambience. He thought it was a bit "out there" but it resonated somehow. So he tried it—not in Paris, but in El Paso, Texas, and Cuidad Juarez, Chihuahua, Mexico, where he had grown up years ago. In his resulting book *Ringside Seat to a Revolution*, he explains:

> *Ringside Seat to a Revolution* deals not so much with history as it does with microhistory ... Microhistory at its best is more about small gestures and unexpected details than grand explanations ... Ultimately, microhistory is a method of study that focuses on the mysterious and the poetic than on the schematic. (2005, p. 14)

As he searched for Pancho's ghost to teach him about the Mexican Revolution, along the way, he learned about the important contributions of journalists, curanderas (healers), radicals, saints, inventors, jazz musicians, human rights activists in the persona of domestic workers and day laborers, and many others who had important lessons for us all.

Another ghostly interlocutor in the United States who had much to say about the issues of human rights, literacy, and our paying attention to others' histories and strengths both in and out of school was Septima Clark. A child of former slaves, Septima went to high school in South Carolina. She had to attend private school because public high schools would not admit black students—and then began her teaching career. In 1916, the city of Charleston would not hire black teachers in its public schools. So she was hired as a teacher at a school on Johns Island, off the coast. The island was accessible only by boat at that time.

Although a stranger, she was able to communicate with the islanders in Gullah, so she quickly fit in. It was here that she first became involved in adult education. In 1918, Septima Clark left Johns Island to teach sixth grade at the Avery School in Charleston. She joined a campaign of community activism to demand that the school board change its policy, and in 1920, black teachers began to teach in the Charleston schools that taught black children.

She later became instrumental in the NAACP efforts to agitate for equalization of teacher salaries. She later said:

> My participation in this fight ... was what might be described by some ... as my first "radical" job. I would call it my first effort in a social action challenging the status quo ... I felt that in reality I was working for the accomplishment of something that ultimately would be good for everyone ... (Clark, 1962, p. 82)

In 1947, Ms. Clark returned to Charleston to teach. However, after the Supreme Court issued the *Brown v. Board of Education* desegregation decision in 1954, South Carolina school officials required teachers to list their organizational memberships. Septima Clark listed her membership in the NAACP, and as a result, she lost her teaching job. Ms. Clark then accepted a job offer from social activist Myles Horton and became Director of Workshops at the Highlander Folk School in Tennessee (discussed in Chapter 4), where she would play a role in helping to educate adults for citizenship.

Over the years, Septima Clark developed a method of teaching based on relating subjects like math and English to the kinds of problems people faced in everyday life. She would teach adults to read by beginning with street signs and newspapers (Brown, 1990). In many ways the challenges she faced involving racism, fear of unknown newcomers to our cities, multiple languages, and lack of students' formal education parallel the challenges refugee and immigrant groups and their teachers and advocates face today. In many ways, the principles she based her work on reflect those of critical theory and critical literacy. And in many ways, her method of teaching reflects many similarities with critical literacy methods.

Critical Literacy in Action—Artful Story to Investigate Myth, Legend, and History

Case Study Nine

A student teacher who is a native of Southern California comes from a family of immigrants. Her father is from Colombia and her mother is from the Philippines. The family is multilingual in terms of speaking Spanish and speaking the language of music. Through the mother, classical music, in particular the violin and the guitar, has always been a part of the family's history, and in recent history when the student teacher's oldest brother began teaching high school music in a poor neighborhood in Southern California. Approximately 90% of the students were poor, many from families who had very recently emigrated from Mexico and Central America, and more than 90% were Spanish speakers just beginning to learn English in spite of a rich background of life experiences. In an effort to find a way to build relationships with his students, build their self-confidence, show respect for their history, and teach music at the same time, he got the idea to form a Mariachi Band. He recruited his mother, his two younger brothers, and his very young sister who is now the student teacher to form a band. They implemented a Mariachi Band at the high school. This was eight years ago. The band formed by his family is still active and performs across Southern California; the high school music teacher is now teaching high school in Washington State and working with high school musicians in that state for the creation of this historical musical form. One of his younger brothers now teaches at the very same high school where this idea was first put to form those years ago, and his youngest sibling, his sister, is the student teacher who conducted a problem-posing lesson for over several weeks in a Head Start classroom in the same neighborhood where the Mariachi Band began.

Reflecting on how by using critical literacy as a framework she could also incorporate other research relating to development and learning as she planned and implemented her problem-posing lessons, one student teacher said,

> I want to take guidance from Bandura because of the social cognitive theory that shows humans observing behaviors as a model. I think this is true in my family as by our teaching music in schools and community centers we always are modeling for

students in the community. When I teach children to play an instrument, I want them to not only learn to play, but also to respect the instrument.

She also took guidance from the National Organization for Music Education and their emphasis on including singing, moving, listening, performing, composing/improvising, and reading/writing. She used the organization's guidelines for creating her problem-posing activities.

She explained that the Head Start program serves low-income families and that the teachers reported to her that the children's families have many struggles and barriers in their lives. When the student teacher began her work in the classroom she talked with the children informally and asked about music in their families and whether they knew about Mariachi music.

They all did! I was shocked, but I guess I shouldn't have been. Many are really recently from Mexico. It seems even at this age (three to five years old) they are thrilled to have someone talk about an aspect of their history and culture that they know about in their families and communities.

The Head Start classroom is equipped as many preschools are with a dramatic play area, a block area, a book area, a science center, an art area, a water table, and a few other tables where children can work with manipulatives and other equipment. She noted that things all over the room are labeled in English and Spanish.

She said, "I see how the teachers encourage the kids to read." And she noted that the children often run up to one of the adults and say, "Teacher, read this to me."

The student teacher said,

I see that the children have great opportunities to discover themselves. As a future teacher, I notice them experimenting in English and in Spanish. If only those children knew how inspiring they are to me. I see them come in every morning and write their name. I see them learning so much every week. In reality, they are teachers, teaching me.

Day One: Mariachi Uniform

Listening and Dialogue:
The student teacher gathered the children on the rug and asked, "What do you know about mariachis?" After the children had a chance to say what they knew about the music and the people who make the music, she showed the children a globe. She asked whether they knew where Mexico was. Many did. Then she asked whether they knew where the United States and California are. Many did.

Then she said she was going to tell the children a quick story.

A long time ago, before people came from Spain (she showed them on the globe) to Mexico (she showed them), native people made music with rattles, drums, reed and clay flutes, and horns made from sea shells. Then when people from Spain came to Mexico they brought other instruments including violins, harps, and guitars. The groups of people mixed and the musical instruments mixed. And then many years ago, maybe before your grandparents were alive, Mariachi Bands began. And this is a type of outfit that they use.

She then showed them a mariachi outfit, or "traje de charro." She explained that the style of the outfit is very old and comes from the Mexican cowboys called "charros." She then asked a few of the children to come to the front of the group and try on the outfit, which consists of a white shirt, a jacket, tie, pants/skirts, boots, and hat.

Action:
At the literacy center, the student teacher provided simple homemade books for each child titled "How to Build a Mariachi Outfit." She drew an outline of each clothing item, one per page, with a label of each item in Spanish and English. The children could color their book in any way they chose. Each one participated with enthusiasm.

At the dramatic play center, she had added the items of the outfit that she had collected over the years from thrift shops and garage sales.

At the art center, she had materials available so that the children could create hats out of clay and foam for potato head figures.

At the felt board, she brought in figures she had made out of felt and clothing items for the children to dress the mariachis.

Day Two: Mariachi Instruments

Listening and Dialogue:
The student teacher brought in all the mariachi instruments—trumpet, violin, guitarron, vihuela, and guitar—to the class group time. She explained that the trumpet is a brass instrument and was the last instrument to join the mariachi style of music historically. She explained that the violin is used for the melody and that the guitarron is the heart and bass of the mariachi. The guitar and the vihuela are used to make the rhythm for the music. The children asked questions as she explained and demonstrated.

Action:
In the dramatic play area, the student teacher set up a Mariachi Store. She added play instruments (or old donated instruments) to the mariachi outfit clothing that was previously in the center. They had a cash register and a big mirror for trying on their purchases.

At the science table, she provided empty tissue boxes and rubber bands so the children could make guitarrones.

At the art table she made cutouts of people and outfits and instruments for the children to create paper doll mariachis.

She filled the water table (she had drained the water) with tiny rocks and bird seeds and had plastic water bottles and small containers that the children could fill and experiment with as shakers or maracas.

Day Three: Mariachi Songs

Listening:
The student teacher read *The Best Mariachi in the World/El Mejor Mariachi Del Mundo* by J. D. Smith (2008).

Dialogue:
The student teacher asked the children to talk about any time they might have seen a mariachi band play and whether or not they knew any songs that were sung traditionally. Many said they had seen a band and many did recite parts of traditional songs. She explained briefly that folk songs are old songs that are sometimes true and sometimes a combination of truth and legend or story. She explained that corridos are examples of this and were influenced by people from long ago. She said that corridos are songs that teach us about history from our great, great-grandparents. An example of a corrido is the song "De Colores." (They gasped, "I know it!")

Action:
They practiced singing a traditional folk song from Mexico, first in Spanish, then in English.

1. De colores, de colores se visten los campos en la primavera.
De colores, de colores son los pajaritos que vienen de afuera.
De colores, de colores es el arco iris que vemos lucir.

Estribillo
Y por eso los grandes amores de muchos colores me gustan a mí.
Y por eso los grandes amores de muchos colores me gustan a mí.

2. De colores, sí, de blanco y negro y rojo, y azul y castaño.
Son colores, son colores de gente que ríe, y estrecha la mano.
Son colores, son colores de gente que sabe de la libertad. Estribillo

3. De colores, de colores son esos paisajes que visten la aurora.
De colores, de colores son las maravillas que el sol atesora.
De colores, de colores es el arco iris que vemos lucir. Estribillo

1. All the colors, yes the colors we see in the springtime with all of its flowers.

All the colors, when the sunlight shines out through a rift in the cloud and it showers.
All the colors, as a rainbow appears when a storm cloud is touched by the sun.

Chorus
1. All the colors abound for the whole world around and for ev'ryone under the sun.
All the colors abound for the whole world around and for ev'ryone under the sun.

2. All the colors, yes the colors of people parading on by with their banners.
All the colors, yes the colors of pennants and streamers and plumes and bandannas.
All the colors, yes the colors of people now taking their place in the sun. Chorus

3. All the colors, yes the black and the white and the red and the brown and the yellow.
All the colors, all the colors of people who smile and shake hands and say "Hello!"
All the colors, yes the colors of people who know that their freedom is won. Chorus

In the dramatic play center, she added a few more instruments and sheet music and pencils so the children could write their own music and songs.

At the art center, she provided empty plastic water bottles and small objects such as beads and rocks that the children could make more shakers as instruments.

At the science center, she displayed different types of music shakers so the children could experiment with the sounds.

She filled the water table with water and then provided jars, cans, and water bottles and sticks so that they could experiment with more sounds.

Day Four: Family Fiesta

Listening and Dialogue:
The children and parents gathered on the rug, and the student teacher introduced her Mariachi Band. She introduced each member (including her own mother, two of her brothers, and three other musicians) and the instrument they played. The band played a song, and then the student teacher invited the children to comment and ask questions. They played another song and repeated the dialogue session.

Action:
Then the student teacher and one woman from the mariachi group left their instruments and joined the children to form small groups for the Mexican Hat Dance. The band played and the children danced and danced and danced.

After this, everyone sat down and they all sang "Cielito Lindo" together as the band played. All the children (and the parents) joined in with every lyric.

e la Sierra Morena,
Cielito lindo, vienen bajando,
Un par de ojitos negros,
Cielito lindo, de contrabando.

Estribillo:
Ay, ay, ay, ay,
Canta y no llores,
Porque cantando se alegran,
Cielito lindo, los corazones.

Pájaro que abandona,
Cielito lindo, su primer nido,
Si lo encuentra ocupado,
Cielito lindo, bien merecido.

(Estribillo)

Ese lunar que tienes,
Cielito lindo, junto a la boca,
No se lo des a nadie,
Cielito lindo, que a mí me toca.

(Estribillo)

Si tu boquita morena,
Fuera de azúcar, fuera de azúcar,
Yo me lo pasaría,
Cielito lindo, chupa que chupa.

(Estribillo)

De tu casa a la mía,
Cielito lindo, no hay más que un paso,
Antes que venga tu madre,
Cielito lindo, dame un abrazo.

(Estribillo)

Una flecha en el aire,
Cielito lindo, lanzó Cupido,
y como fue jugando,
Cielito lindo, yo fui el herido.

(Estribillo)

Through the Sierra Morena,

heavenly one, a dark pair of eyes
(that could steal a man's heart)
lower as they approach.

Refrain:
Ay, ay, ay, ay,
sing and don't cry,
for hearts are happy, heavenly one,
when singing.

If a bird abandons his nest,
heavenly one,
then finds it occupied by another,
that first bird got what he deserved.

(Refrain)

Don't give away that beauty mark
that you have next to your mouth,
heavenly one, to just anybody.
Share all your beauty with me.

(Refrain)

If your little dark mouth
were made of sugar,
I would spend my time, heavenly one,
kissing it.

(Refrain)

Your house is only steps away from mine,
heavenly one.
So before your mother shows up,
give me a hug.

(Refrain)

Cupid shot off an arrow
heavenly one.
It played through the air,
and I was the one it hit.

Then the families and children shared the lunch that had been prepared by the parents and the school. The student teacher said as we
walked out with the Mariachi Band, "Wow. I think that was the evaluation of my lesson!" I agreed.

She provided the following resources for her classmates:

http://www.mariachi.org/history.html
Marin, Cheech (2007). *Cheech the School Bus Driver*. New York: Harper Collins.
http://mariachiconnection.com/
http://casadelmariachi.com/englishframe.htm

Case Study Ten

In particular, in the case of new refugees and immigrant students, the issues of myth, legend, and history are complex. The Hmong refugees who came to the United States in the 1990s had had little or no formal education and often had not had opportunity to learn English. Some were pre-literate. The Hmong culture is historically an oral culture; this was the first generation of Hmong who were using printed materials as a way to learn.

The case study documents a lesson in a first-grade classroom in an urban school in a large city. The teacher and student teacher both believed in the importance of history, family, and community, and the importance of young children connecting their actions with these histories. The teacher is a twenty-year veteran teacher with the district, a woman of Irish American descent. The student teacher with her is a Hmong male who is from the community where the school is situated. The students in the class consisted of sixteen Hmong children, three African American children, and one child from South America.

Listening:

For this lesson, the teacher used the storybook *Whispering Cloth: A Refugee's Story* by Pegi Deitz Shea, illustrated by Anita Riggio and stitched by Youa Yang (1995). The teacher began by gathering the children around her in the classroom center area, where she unfolded several quilts. She reminded them of previous discussions and stories they had shared about quilts. Then she showed a weaving from Ireland and explained that it was from the country her family came from. Then, she held up a large, colorful "storycloth" that had been made by one of the school staff's relatives who is Hmong. The teacher asked, "Do you think a quilt could tell a story? Do you think you can hear a story from a cloth?"

Dialogue:

The children discussed briefly what they thought about the question.

Then the teacher passed the folded cloth around the circle, so that each student could "listen" to the cloth. Then, she showed the class the book and told them just a little about the book. "It is a story about a Hmong girl and her grandmother who live in a refugee camp in Thailand. Grandmother is teaching Mai how to make storycloths and Mai creates one that tells her story." Then the teacher showed the bilingual glossary in the book with

Hmong words and English translations, and explained that she would read the story in English in a few minutes, but first, the student teacher would read it in Hmong.

Action:
The story was read in Hmong. The students who did not understand Hmong appeared to be fascinated by the words in spite of not comprehending. The teacher then asked questions: Can you guess what the story was about based upon Mr. Z's intonations, the pictures, and so forth?

Then the teacher read the story in English.

During choice time, the children went to centers where they could begin drawing a storycloth and documenting the history it told. The geography center had maps and storybooks showing Laos and other Southeast Asian countries. There was a language center with a tape of a story being read in Hmong and a writing center where children could write questions to ask family and community members about their migration history.

The student teacher explained to the students that he had written a letter to their families explaining what they were learning about. The letter was written in English, Hmong, and Spanish. In the letter, the teachers ask the parents whether their child could share a storycloth, quilt, or an artifact that tells a family story. When the items were brought to school, extension activities were implemented. The students made a class storycloth with a contribution from each student's drawing and writing (native language or English or both) during the following days.

Case Study Eleven
Ms. Rafiq's first grade class in Queens, New York, was introduced in Chapter 1. In this class every child came to this country from another country, recently. Some never spoke English before kindergarten last year. Some spoke the English of Guyana and don't qualify for English language services, but the dialect is so different that it is as if the children are working with a second language. Some children are from Central America, some are from India, some are from Russia, and others are from Haiti. In a study of New York City landmarks, coming and going personal stories, dioramas set in countries around the world, the teacher began with a "Where I'm From" poetry activity. This teacher was especially interested in children connecting their learning in literacy and social studies to multiple sources of knowledge.

Listening:
She initiated the session by explaining her experience with the "Where I'm From" activity in her university class and asking children to listen to a little of her "Where I'm From" poem as part of her own story:

I am from spices and scarves,
hand-me downs and baseball cards
I am from friendly neighbors and bus stops
and a place where we walk and not drive
I am from Ahmed and Razia
who came here to give me a better life.

Dialogue:

While she wrote on a chart tablet, the teacher asked the students to give examples of

1. some items found around their homes
2. items found in their neighborhoods
3. names of relatives
4. sayings of family members
5. names of foods and dishes
6. names of places they keep treasures, music, and games they like.

Action:

During Writing Workshop, the teacher asked the students to use their lists to create their own poem.

Then, they made dioramas for a social studies project. The dioramas were set in a country where their families come from, and after a mini-lesson on voice as a part of the week's Writers Workshop, the children wrote in their own voices what the characters in the dioramas were talking about. They wrote the words, sometimes in English, sometimes in the home language of the families.

This teacher reported that after a school year in her class, all the first graders—even the two struggling students who weren't able to negotiate their new second language of English and the beginnings of reading instruction at springtime evaluations—have become successful readers (in English) and been promoted to second grade.

Case Study Twelve

A student teacher planned and implemented this lesson with a group of second graders at the beginning of the school year when it is important to establish community in the classroom. She asked the children to sit in a semicircle for the Listening and Dialogue sections to give the message that it was a learner centered environment. The story is historical, and it is also connected to personal history, multiple sources of knowledge, and transformative action.

Listening:
She asked the children to think of a symbol (a visual of some sort) that has a special meaning for them. She asked that they draw a sketch of it (on your white board or a clipboard) and write a few lines about the meaning it has. The she asked them to write about any knowledge they have about the origins of their own names.

Then she read *A Boy Called Slow: The True Story of Sitting Bull* by Joseph Bruchac (1998) to the group.

Dialogue:
The student teacher then asked whether anyone knew this story. She then asked what they had heard about American Indian naming ceremonies and traditions. She then asked, "Who chose the names of the babies in your family? How were the names chosen? Did you have any ceremony attached to the naming? What about nicknames? How did they come about? In what ways did any of your naming stories have any similarities with this story?"

Action:
The teacher then asked the children to think about inventing a name for themselves. Then they were asked to write a short paragraph about why they chose the names they did. The children were given the task of thinking of a way to present the meaning behind their names and express this to a partner. Then the pair was asked to develop an artistic way to present this for a class mural.

They were then asked to read *If Your Name Was Changed at Ellis Island* by Ellen Levine (1993). The book is a historical explanation of Ellis Island, who came there and why, and some of the procedures and policies that immigrants were exposed to when they arrived.

The teacher reflected that this activity gave students the opportunity to learn about American Indians, themselves, and each other. This was intended to encourage the students to talk, build community, and consider the meaning of the story.

Case Study Thirteen
Another student teacher, who is passionate about cultural history and travel as a way to learn more about people and the world, chose a book about Baghdad for use with her first graders.

Listening:
The multicultural storybook used was *The House of Wisdom* by Florence Parry Heide and Judith Heide Gilliland (1999). The book is about a boy, Ishaq, who seeks to become a scholar and travel the world in search of books for a

famous library in Baghdad. He travels to many countries and learns much about different cultures and languages.

The student teacher began the lesson by reading the book to the class. She had a map of the world posted adjacent to the reading area. After reading the book, she asked the students to recall the cities that Ishaq visited, making note of the cities on the map.

Dialogue:
The student teacher asked the children, in groups of four, to discuss, write, and/or draw about the countries they have traveled to or wish to travel to.

Action:
She had set up the classroom with stations that each represented different countries. Each group of four children sat at a station and looked over material on that specific country, such as maps and pictures. Later, each group spoke to the class about that country and what they found interesting or surprising.

Outside of class, each student interviewed a parent, relative, or friend who had traveled to another country or traveled to the United States from another country. They were encouraged to bring in small artifacts to illustrate information from their interviews. The students shared their interviews in class the next day.

The student teacher reflected about her problem-posing with multicultural children's literature. She said:

> When children take literature to heart, they establish a strong, meaningful connection with that poem or story or verse or whichever type of literature it may be. The content within this piece of literature is relevant to the child's life and s/he may very well carry this idea, moral or significance with her for the rest of her life. I feel that an artifact can evoke the same intense feelings of devotion, admiration or importance that literature can.
>
> We can introduce a child to a hundred books or a hundred artifacts and never get a response from that child. Sometimes adults need to refrain from dictating their opinions and let children explore among themselves, their attitudes and their strengths and skills. Much focus is on the knowledge that children portray through their writing and other communicative intents. Most children are eager to write because it helps them to convey their feelings and emotions.

Case Study Fourteen
A teacher education student was interested in ways to use critical story to facilitate her second graders' learning about slavery and the civil rights movement. She wanted the children to understand that while the events took place over a century ago, there are still personal connections students can make with the people and their struggle.

Listening:

She asked students to write about a memory that they may have of their parents or a family member helping someone who was in danger. She asked, "What do you remember about what was going on? How did you find out about this?" The students were asked to write about the events.

She also asked students whether they had any family stories, or personal experience, in which a child works to contribute to the family's livelihood. The students were also asked to write about these experiences.

Then over several days and a few weeks, she read a chapter a day from *The Lost Village of Central Park* by Hope Lourie Killcoyne (1999).

Dialogue:

During the days in which the story was read, students were given opportunity, in small groups, to discuss any of the group members' knowledge about life among different groups of people in the 1850s. They were also encouraged to discuss their examples of a family member's helping someone in a difficult situation and stories of family members working as a child.

Of course, after each chapter, they discussed the story *The Lost Village of Central Park*. What was old information? What was new information? How did the personal stories of the students' families from the discussion above relate to anything in the story?

Action:

After *The Lost Village of Central Park* was completed, the student teacher read *Aunt Harriet's Underground Railroad in the Sky* by Faith Ringgold (1995). Students compared the storybook to the information they had learned through *The Lost Village of Central Park*. The student teacher then made an appointment with the library at the school so that the students would have opportunity over a two-week time frame to research both primary and secondary source documents about Seneca Village (*The Lost Village of Central Park*). According to their particular interest area of focus, such as slave activists, children of slaves and freed former slaves, Irish families, school and work for youth in 1860s New York City, the students formed groups to compile and present their findings to the class.

Later, the student teacher obtained slave narratives that gave information about the Underground Railroad and other ways in which people gave sanctuary to runaway slaves. She shared these narratives with the children.

Then, the class researched the situation of poor families from Ireland who came to the United States and Canada. They investigated where many families settled and why. They investigated who helped them and how the families survived.

The student teacher took the class to a museum and investigated ways in which oppressed peoples' histories are documented through art. Children reported to the class using a visual medium.

Finally, this student teacher implemented a follow-up unit based on *The Watsons Go to Birmingham—1963* by Christopher Paul Curtis (1997). This story is about a family from Flint, Michigan, who travel to visit a grandmother in Birmingham, Alabama. They find themselves in the middle of some of the most chilling moments in the struggle for civil rights in the 1960s. This novel, full of history, led students to the more recent history of the civil rights movement.

The student teacher reflected on her extended problem-posing work with children about this topic so important to her own learning and living. She wrote:

> We can see the creation of new realities through the magical power of story, art, and imagination. When children are exposed to historical information that relates to their own sense of place, families, and communities they learn. There are many ways that students' ability to translate history into observation requires students to use a language that is not literal, that employs metaphor, illusion, and innuendo, and through story students recognize that problems can have multiple solutions, questions can have multiple answers.

Finally, in a book of folktales connected with indigenous peoples involved in the Zapatista movement, Ortiz (2001) explains that many indigenous cultures in Meso-America have 500 years of living a history of questions. Their history is one in which folktales and art are the ways indigenous people speak truth to power. In "The Story of Questions," the conversation between Subcomandante Marcos and the elder Antonio is about Zapata. He says, "But it is also not about Zapata. It is about what shall happen. It is about what shall be done" (Ortiz, 2001, p. 51). The folktale ends with:

> This is how the true men and women learned that questions are for walking, not for just standing around and doing nothing. And since then, when true men and women want to walk, they ask questions. When they want to arrive they take leave. And when they want to leave, they say hello. They are never still. (p. 51)

Good advice.

References

Anaya, R. (2004). *Serafina's stories*. Albuquerque, NM: University of New Mexico Press.
Bateson, Mary C. (2004). *Willing to learn: Passages of personal discovery*. New York: Steerforth.
Bateson, Mary C. (1994). *Peripheral visions: Learning along the way*. New York: Harper Collins.

Bigelow, B., & Peterson, B. (2003). *Rethinking Columbus: The next 500 years*. Milwaukee, WI: Rethinking Schools.

Brown, C. N. (1990). *Ready from within: A first person narrative: Septima Clark and the civil rights movement*. New York: African World Press.

Bruchac, J. (1998). *A boy called Slow: The true story of Sitting Bull*. New York: Scott Foresman.

Clark, S. (1962). *Echo in my soul*. New York: E. P. Dutton.

Curtis, Christopher P. (1997). *The Watsons go to Birmingham—1963*. New York: Yearling.

Green, A. (2003). Ann Green. In Elizabeth P. Quintero & Mary K. Rummel (Eds.), *Becoming a teacher in the new society: Bringing communities and classrooms together*. New York: Peter Lang.

Heide, F. P., & Gilliland, J. H. (1999). *The house of wisdom*. New York: Mulberry Books.

Killcoyne, H. L. (1999). *The lost village of Central Park*. New York: Silver Moon Press.

King, N. (2006). Interview at STAR offices in London, England. January 2006.

Kushner, T., & Sendak, M. (2003). *Brundibar*. New York: Michael Di Capua Books.

Larson, B. (2003). Bea Larson, English as a Second Language Teacher. In Elizabeth P. Quintero & Mary K. Rummel (Eds.), *Becoming a teacher in the new society: Bringing communities and classrooms together*. New York: Peter Lang.

Levine, E. (1992). *If your name was changed at Ellis Island*. New York: Scholastic.

Ortiz, S. (2001). Essays. In Subcomandante Marcos (Ed.), *Folktales of the Zapatista revolution*. El Paso, TX: Cinco Puntos Press.

Quintero, Elizabeth P. (2004). *Problem-posing with multicultural children's literature: Developing critical, early childhood curricula*. New York: Peter Lang.

Quintero, Elizabeth P. (2007). Critical pedagogy and qualitative inquiry. In J. A. Hatch (Ed.), *Early childhood qualitative research*, pp. 109–130. New York: Routledge.

Ringgold, F. (1995). *Aunt Harriet's underground railroad in the sky*. New York: Dragonfly Books.

Romo, D. (2005). *Ringside seat to a revolution: An underground cultural history of El Paso and Juarez: 1893–1923*. El Paso, TX: Cinco Puntos Press.

Rummel, Mary K. (2006). *Illuminations*. Cincinnati, OH: Cherry Grove Collections.

Shea, P. D. (1995). *Whispering cloth: A refugee's story*. Honesdale, PA: Boyds Mills Press.

Shissler, H. (2006). Tolerance is not enough: Migrants in German school textbooks. Unpublished paper presented at "Educating for Migrant Integration-Integrating Migrants into Education: European and North American Comparisons." University of Toronto, Toronto, Canada.

Smith, J D (2008). *The best mariachi in the world//El mejor mariachi del mundo*. McHenry, IL: Raven Tree Press.

Tingle, T. (2006). *Crossing Bok Chitto: A Choctaw tale of friendship and freedom*. El Paso, TX: Cinco Puntos Press.

Tolkien, J. R. R. (1977). From a letter by J. R. R. Tolkien to Milton Waldman, 1951. In C. Tolkien (Ed.), *The Silmarillion*, pp. x–xxiv. London: Harper Collins.

von Foerster, Heinz. (1993). Kybernetik einer Erkenntnistheorie und Verstehen verstehen. In Wissen und Gewissen (Eds.), *Versuch einer Brücke*, pp. 50–71 and 282–298. Frankfurt, Germany: Suhrkamp.

CHAPTER SIX
Artful Story and the Arts

"...at our best, the writer, painter, architect, actor, dancer, folksinger—we *are* the people.... What we ought to be doing is singing in the parks, talking to children, going to gatherings of parents, doing whatever it is we do—dancing, reading, poetry performing—all the time..." (Angelou, 1996, p. 23)

Complicated Conversations—Artful Story and the Arts
In his poem "En mi barrio/In My Barrio," Alarcón (2001) says that you can hear the music of life coming from the murals painted in the neighborhoods. All the meta-themes that emerged from this study have emphasized that literacy is multimodal, intertextual, and develops among particularities, among persons, and objects in families and communities. This is seen also as we looked at the ways the arts influence, inspire, tie together, and document learning.

An example of art illustrating meaning across eons can be seen through the documented history of the Armenian people. Their survival owes much to their attachment to their native language with its distinct alphabet even though the largest Armenian community in the world today is in the United States, where there is such a push for use of English over other languages. For 1,700 unbroken years the Armenians have expressed the beliefs at the heart of their identity through text illuminated with art. For hundreds of years manuscripts were illuminated, embellished with luminous color with either literal or symbolic decoration to help with the layout or reading.

Thinking about the complexities of history, the arts, learning, and living, Susan Sontag once wrote that "art is not only about something; it is something. A work of art is a thing in the world, not just a text or commentary on the world" (White, 2006, p. 13). This quote by Sontag was used by White to discuss art in the context of a play that was written by Thomas More and others. The play was about the social and political issues of the day in England in the second half of the 16th century. Times were turbulent surrounding issues of religious belief, succession to the throne of England, economic crises, colonization, social mobility, civil disorder and threats of invasion, and the conflicts brought by people migrating from one region to another. White said that this form of art in theater was prevalent in semi-literate cultures, as London was in the 16th century. The words spoken in a playhouse were a major way by which men and women formed their beliefs and conceived of their actions. This is true for adults making theater today, and it is true as young children make theater everyday in the contexts of their classrooms.

Poets use words and language to reflect our hearts, souls, visual images, and dreams. Isabel Campoy and Alma Flor Ada have written close to one hundred bilingual children's books, picture books, and books for young adults. While both authors are completely balanced bilinguals themselves, they have learned a very telling lesson over the years as they have struggled with the authenticity of translations of a story from one language to another. They began to employ the talents of poets as translators. They learned that poets are extremely effective at interpreting intention that is more complex than mere translation (Campoy, 2005).

This complex thought about the importance of art in itself and as a means of communication and transmission of ideas is a challenge to us as learners, educators, and the creators of our lives. None of us lives or works in isolation, and we draw our inspiration from a global community. James Baldwin wrote in 1962, "The purpose of art is to lay bare the questions which have been hidden by the answers" (p. 17). Painter and teacher Ali Raza, a native of Pakistan who currently resides in the United States, illuminates Baldwin's statement by telling how he paints with many active questions in mind, including:

> What is the relationship between the practice of art across global and regional boundaries? What happens to an image's significance when it crosses cultural boundaries? What has been filtered and lost in art forms during the post-colonial era in South Asia? What form of values in art can be studied to revive and modernize? While living in a multicultural, post-capitalist society, to whom am I addressing my work? (2002, n.p.)

Raza believes that teaching and participating with critical learners are closely related to his work as an artist because it provides access to the critical thinking that gives rise to these questions. His process is like that of many teachers who create curriculum and teach with active questions in mind. The arts are important as a way of connecting the global with the particular. The arts have often been the carriers of history, bringing us the stories of those who have not appeared in history texts.

In modern times this oneness of the written with the visual was lost except in books for children or more recently in conceptual art. The written and visual are moving together again in this new graphic age and hence literacy has to be intertextual. A literate person must be able to read between and within these different texts. Writing is central to this intertextual literacy. "Writing is not just a mopping up activity at the end of a research project…(it) is also a way of knowing…a method of inquiry" (Richardson, 1994, p. 516).

What We Know about the Arts and Learning

Elliott Eisner (1998) reflects on a lifetime of scholarly work which demonstrates that in the arts nothing stands alone. He maintains that in music, theater, pottery, or painting, every aspect of the work affects every other aspect and that attention to community relationships is a fundamental mode of thinking that the arts require. He documents in much detail in many venues that students' ability to translate creation into observation requires students to use a language that is not literal, that employs metaphor, illusion, and innuendo and through the arts students recognize that problems can have multiple solutions, questions can have multiple answers. Imagination and metaphor are essential to classes in literacy education.

Eisner's (1998) beliefs are grounded in the philosophies of Dewey and he maintains that there are some important goals of education such as appreciation of art and an open-minded skepticism of science that are not easily broken down into small bits of manageable data that can be taught and reinforced. Eisner says:

> The problems of life are much more like the problems encountered in the arts. They are problems that seldom have a single correct solution; they are problems that are often subtle, occasionally ambiguous, and sometimes dilemma-like. One would think that schools that wanted to prepare students for life would employ tasks and problems similar to those found outside of schools. This is hardly the case. Life outside of school is seldom like school assignments—and hardly ever like a multiple-choice test. (1998, p. 4)

Eisner (2002) has become known not only for criticisms about the current tide of education, but also for the positive constructive ways he believes educators can use the arts. He has identified ten "things the arts can teach":

1. The arts teach children to make good judgments about qualitative relationships.
2. The arts teach children that problems can have more than one solution and that questions can have more than one answer.
3. The arts celebrate multiple perspectives.
4. The arts teach children complex forms of problem solving.
5. The arts make vivid the fact that neither words in their literal form nor number exhaust what we can know. The limits of our language do not define the limits of our cognition.
6. The arts teach students that small differences can have large effects.
7. The arts teach students to think through and within a material.
8. The arts help children learn to say what cannot be said.

9. The arts enable us to have experience we can have from no other source and through such experience to discover the range and variety of what we are capable of feeling.

10. The arts' position in the school curriculum symbolizes to the young what adults believe is important. (Eisner, 2002, pp. 70–72).

Critical literacy supports the creation of new realities through the power of art and imagination and has a definite role in creating a sense of place, a community. This relates to the rethinking of the narrative of neighborhood and construction of the "poetry of neighborhood" discussed by Crichlow (1995), who describes different maps of a neighborhood drawn by parents and children. Arts and ceremony are arenas for cultural transmission in neighborhoods.

A student teacher just beginning her career as a teacher (to combine her interests in art and teaching) wrote at length about why she considers art so important for children. She said, "When it comes to education, art has so much value. Art is viewed as a building block for the basic knowledge in key skills used for reading, writing, representing, and symbolizing."

Banner (2006), an arts advocacy historian associated with the California Art Education Association, notes the importance of art in the classroom. She maintains that education through art provides an avenue of understanding in children through the representation of their work. She documents the universal language of visual arts as a symbolic way to represent the world, a way to construct meaning that enhances cognitive learning, emotional expression, perception, cultural awareness, and aesthetics.

The student teacher noted all the ways that art enhances the education of children.

1. Through art children gain a sense of visual discrimination and problem solving skills.

2. Children are exposed to quantitative concepts. How many objects do I have? How many do I need? Can I create this picture using fewer or more objects?

3. Children learn social skills by working on group projects.

4. In working in these groups, children improve their language and communication skills.

5. Children learn how to follow directions and to pay attention when they are being given instructions.

6. They also learn that it is okay to ask their peers or their teacher for help when something is difficult to them.

7. Through art children learn fine motor skills and eye-hand coordination.

While this student was hesitant to "give up" (as she first saw it) her focus of art education to take part in problem-posing curriculum, she quickly saw that problem-posing curriculum allows for and encourages much of the same methods as good art education. The possibilities in tying art (and problem-posing) into a variety of subjects are endless. This allows visual learners to shine in environments where they normally would "get by."

It has been reported that some students who are not excelling in traditional academic activities do excel in art (Studio, 2001). Through art and problem-posing, children value their personal uniqueness, and they gain a sense of self-achievement. They understand their relationship to the class as a part of the whole, and this helps them relate to themselves in the wider world. Students learn to become sustained and self-directed learners (Banner, 2006).

So why have the arts been almost eliminated from many schools' curricula? Much of the problem associated with support for art in the classroom is lack of funding. In the mid-1970s, because of the financial crises, New York City eliminated their budget for art education in public schools. In response to public outcry, a few programs were founded for the inclusion of art in the classrooms. One such program was Studio in a School, founded by philanthropist and president of the Museum of Modern Art Agnes Gund. She set up a program in which administrators, artists, as well as members of the New York City board of education met to discuss ways to provide schools with a visual arts experience. Their goal was to develop age appropriate programs as well as offer guidance through the arts for teachers and administrators (www.studioinaschool.org). In 2004, Studio in a School established a partnership with the Department of Education to work on the art curriculum in their public schools. They established a blueprint for teaching and learning arts catering to students from kindergarten through twelfth grade.

With the *No Child Left Behind* legislation enacted by Congress in 2001, teachers and administrators have shifted most attention, practically and fiscally, to remediation in math, reading, and writing, leaving little support for the arts (Goldman, 2005). The tragedy is that the arts actually aid the development of skills needed to excel in the other core subjects. Goldman (2005) goes on to say:

> There is national data that show the arts help students gain deeper understanding in all the content areas. When kids study the arts, they are more engaged in their learning. When kids acted stories out, or drew pictures about them, they understood and remembered the stories better, they had made a personal connection. Children learn all different kinds of ways, so the more modalities you see—the more kids you'll reach, and the better the learning will be. (p. 25)

Yet, in spite of this research, some student teachers in my study were critical about what was happening in the classrooms where they were working. They felt that what was being implemented (in art) negated what we know about children's creativity and learning. One student teacher said of the learning opportunities relating to art:

> I was very disappointed by their art lesson this week. They were given such specific instructions on how to draw a leaf that there was very little creativity left in the process. When a child produced a leaf that was not according to the model, the art teacher basically told him it wasn't correct, even though it was a beautiful leaf. He tried to tell her that he had seen leaves like that, and she essentially told him that only HER version of a leaf was correct for this project. I felt that creating a project with such a specific product expected forbids creativity and sets the children up for frustration when they are unable to replicate the exact leaf! I would have liked to see a more open-ended project—the assignment still could have been to create fall leaves, but they could have been given a little more freedom to express how they saw leaves, or what they wanted their leaves to look like.

Artful Story and Visual Arts

Presently many teachers in the United States are beginning to realize the importance of art in the classroom and its impact on their students. These teachers have started to implement some of the techniques of Reggio Emilia into their curriculum, particularly as the approach relates to the visual arts.

The "Reggio Emilia" approach originated at a city in northern Italy called Reggio Emilia. The "Reggio" approach was developed for municipal child care and education programs serving children six years of age and younger. The approach assumes children to be seen as competent, resourceful, curious, imaginative, inventive with a desire to interact and communicate with others. The "Reggio" vision of the child as a competent learner has produced a strong child-directed curriculum model. Teachers follow the children's interests and do not provide focused instruction in reading and writing. The Reggio approach has a strong belief that children learn through interaction with others, including parents, staff, and peers in a friendly learning environment.

The Reggio Emilia technique values art in the classroom with the beliefs that artistic expression is more than just a way to express one's feelings. There are five main characteristics of the Reggio method that teachers adhere to. Art is used as a representation of learning and it is combined as part of the curriculum. By combining art into the curriculum it serves as an aid to other subjects being discussed in the classroom. Art and all other learning experiences are collaborative. There is emphasis on group activities, and learning is viewed as a hands-on experience. In the Reggio Emilia practices, time and space are devoted to artistic representation. There is a separate "art studio" set up in the classroom, and the children are encouraged to spend time there. Also, there is a visual arts teacher in the classroom to guide the children in their works of art. The visual arts teacher also works alongside the teacher to come up with ways to integrate art into all subject matter. The Reggio Emilia technique displays the learning experiences in the classroom using documentation panels. These walls displaying the children's work allow the children to feel a sense of pride and accomplishment and give the parents a chance to view their children's development (Trawick-Smith, 2006). The Reggio Emilia way "supports children to communicate their ideas visually, helps promote learning experiences, and design environments that enhance children's perceptual awareness and provide places for wonder, curiosity and the expression of ideas" (Tarr, 2001, p.9).

A student teacher who was interested in community visual arts planned activities focused on the storybook *Historias de mi barrio: El San José de ayer (Barrio:Jose's Neighborhood)* by G. Ancona (1998). This is a book about the Mission District in San Francisco. It contains photographs and text that discuss the traditions, customs, art, and food of, what the locals call El Barrio. The book does this by following the goings-on of El Barrio through the life of one boy, Jose, and his elementary school. After reading and discussing the story, the adults and children went for a walk around their neighborhood and drew/wrote some of the environmental print (signs and murals, and other scripts), including those in different languages. Some of the children then wrote, drew, and audiotaped a short report answering the following questions: What can you say about the neighborhood that these photos were taken in? What stories do these murals tell?

The student teacher documented her beliefs related to the importance of the arts, especially for certain children, with evidence:

> There was this one boy in my class that was a little different than the other children. He would have days where he would get along with everyone and be the most charming little boy and then, he would have days where he seemed as if he was mad at the world. Towards the end of the year the class was preparing for a simulation of Ellis Island. As they were getting ready they were doing various activities in the classroom, making signs, writing letters and setting up the different areas. This one boy was sitting at his desk with his arms folded showing his disinterest in the group activity. I approached him, wanting to get him involved in some way. I brought over a piece of oak tag and asked him if he wanted to color in some of the letters on the poster. His eyes lit up with excitement. He sat there and colored in these posters so carefully and beautifully as I observed so much in him that day. Art was a way of releasing his frustrations in a quiet way and it allowed him to still be a part of the group. Through his involvement, he came to realize his importance in the group activity.

She then began to notice his strengths.

From that day on I took greater notice in the way he completed classroom assignments. His writing notebook had minimal writing but always had a detailed picture to go along with it. Through his drawings he was able to express himself in his own way and he taught me so much about him through his markings on his papers.

Artful Story and Content Learning through Song and Dance

Examples of children learning social studies content in the form of geography, history, and sociology through song are everywhere. One such example can be seen in a kindergarten class where the teacher brought in and played the music and song by Rafi, "All Around the World." She began the lesson by asking the children to talk about where they and their families come from. She then played the song a second time and asked the children to think in their heads how they could change the song by using the names of their peers instead of the ones used in the song. Then, the class actually did this as a whole group. For example, Yuki is from Japan, so substitute one of the names and countries sung in the song with "Yuki is from Japan." She ensured that all the nationalities that were represented in the classroom. To fill in the remainder of the song, she asked children about people they know who came from another country. They used these names to fill in the rest of the song.

Then she showed an enlarged world map to the children. She pointed out where the United States of America is, and then briefly described the other parts of the world. Then, she asked each child to write the name and part of the world that they contributed to the song on a piece of post-it paper. The children went up one at a time to stick their post-it paper on the correct part of the map.

The connection of children's dance with children's literature provides in a problem-posing format both aesthetic and transformative action opportunities for children. They can express their understanding of a literary experience (Cone, 2003) and relate the story to their personal lives (Quintero, 2004). Together the dance and the story give children the opportunity to enhance their critical thinking and analytical skills, cooperation, self-expression and self-esteem, organizational and problem solving skills, cultural literacy, and communication skills (Overby, 1992).

Pairing dance and literature provides a context for studying cultural pluralism. "The arts have always defined and celebrated diversity in a nonviolent way, while giving us the opportunity to feel, smile, and hurt" (Gilbert, 2005, p. 27). Much of modern dance draws upon dances of other cultures, and through a study of folk dance, an appreciation of the similarities and distinctions of various cultures is also gained. Children's multicultural literature based on folktales, history, religions, and customs can be an aid to a dance teacher in the classroom, but studying the movements customary to specific cultures, religions, and folktales enhances the students' understanding of the stories.

Wei (2005) reports that folk arts challenge the notion that knowledge is a commodity.

> Folk arts are the way we have passed knowledge and values from generation to generation in our community. The values that are embedded in a lot of the folk arts our elders practice are counter-materialist. When we do this art, students learn outside of institutions. (Wei, 2005).

Wei (2005) gave the following description of a new small school that Asian Americans United was opening in Philadelphia:

> We decided that if we were to build a school, it had to be a school that was consciously a school for democracy, a school for self-governance, a school for creation of community. We needed to build a school that was consciously anti-individualistic, anti-racist, anti-isolationist, and anti-materialist. We wanted the school to be a place where children can reclaim a sense of community. And we wanted children to have an alternative way to measure their sense of worth... (Wei, 2005)

She described Sifu, who teaches kung fu and does lion dance and dragon dance in the community, and she emphasized the importance of the lion dancers in the community. She noted that some of Sifu's students have been with him for twenty years. She stressed that these traditional art forms are about persistence, patience, and respect (Wei, 2005).

Negri-Pool (2005) documents the transformation that music and dance made in her classroom for a child from the Marshall Islands. The girl had brought some of "her music" to class. At first they listened to the music as background music while the students played. Later the girl went to the large rug area. Negri-Pool (2005) explained:

> I began to move to the music and told her how much I liked it. Then she began to dance. As she danced, a magnificent smile appeared on her face. She clearly had a specific routine that she'd learned for that particular song. I began to mimic her movements. When the song ended, I rewound the tape and started it again. She began to teach me the moves. We laughed and moved, reveling in our intimate shared enjoyment. The other children watched, pausing in their own play to see our scene unfold. Later, some came and joined us. Kalenna's delight was evident as our dance continued. I had finally touched her where she lived. (Negri-Pool, 2005)

Critical Literacy in Action—Artful Story and the Arts

Case Study Fifteen

The underlying theme of the series of problem-posing activities presented in this assignment is art. The problem-posing activity offers a combination of literature, math, science, music, art with a social-emotional emphasis. The National Association for Education of Young Children's position statement recommendation regarding curriculum is:

> Implement curriculum that is thoughtfully planned, challenging, engaging, developmentally appropriate, culturally and linguistically responsive, comprehensive, and likely to promote positive outcomes for all young children.

This stance provides support, framework, and guidance for the following problem-posing activities.

The concept of learning and curriculum in our daily lives motivated my desire to promote a similar learning experience in my classroom. From the three books *Abuela* by Arthur Dorros (1997), illustrated by Elisa Kleven; *Life Doesn't Frighten Me* poem by Maya Angelou (1996), paintings by Jean-Michel Basquiat; and *Manuelo, the Playing Mantis* by Don Freeman (2004), the gathered common theme is art. Through the problem-posing activities, the student teacher intended that the students involved would achieve a greater insight into the theory of art and incorporate a vision of art into their daily existence.

To begin the series she began with gathering information regarding the children's knowledge of art.

Day One

Dialogue:

The student teacher asked the class to turn and talk to a partner about "What is art?" After talking with a partner, the children shared with the class what they had discussed.

Listening:

Then the student teacher read aloud *Manuelo, the Playing Mantis* by Don Freeman (2004).

Dialogue:

She then discussed with the children the issue of what could be considered art in this book and had a display of musical instruments available for the children to explore. Then they discussed how music is a form of art.

Listening:

The class then listened to instrumental music (pre-recorded and/or with the instruments on display).

Action:

In the book, the character of the mantis is searching for the perfect instrument, which suited him. In small groups, she asked the children to select from the variety of musical instruments, which were displayed in the previous dialogue portion. The children had a choice in writing topics regarding the instruments. The writing topics were as follows: if you were an instrument, which instruments would you be and why; write an imaginative story incorporating an instrument; or write about your past experience with music or instruments.

An extension action with this book would include the curriculum of science by initiating a study on insects. A potential action activity could be a cooking lesson, where the children would create different insects out of food. Through cooking, the children would also be learning math. Lastly, to further the study of music, a field trip to a concert or even a multitude of concerts where the children would compare different types of music would provide more listening, dialogue, and action activities.

Day Two

Listening:

To continue with the problem-posing activity, the second day began with the reading aloud of the book *Abuela* by Arthur Dorros (1997), illustrated by Elisa Kleven.

Dialogue:

After reading the book, the student teacher explained that Abuela means "grandmother" in Spanish. The teacher asked each child to think of their grandmother or someone who is extremely special to them. Once the children had been given a moment to think of their grandmother or a special individual, the student teacher explained that everyone calls their grandmother/special someone something different. The children were asked to share what they call their grandmother/special someone. The children were asked to share why they call their grandmother/special someone what they call them.

The teacher made a list of the names given.

The teacher will again have the class look at the book where the illustrations will be the focus. The illustrations are of note because they are muralistic in nature.

Action:

The children were invited to draw their grandmother or someone special in a painting. They could either draw a portrait of their grandmother/special someone or draw something that represents them. The pictures must somewhere include what they call this special person. Upon conclusion, the class assembled each of their pictures into a large mural to be displayed in the classroom.

Dialogue:

After looking at the mural, the children discussed the similarities and differences in the artwork. The differences encouraged discussion regarding the diverse names and the diverse cultural connections regarding those names.

An extension action with this book, which included the curriculum of math, was to develop data regarding grandmother/special individuals. For instance, data was collected regarding where each child's grandmother/special someone is from and a graph was made.

Day Three

Action:

Each child initially was given a print of Jean-Michel Basquiat's artwork. The children were asked to merely look at the artwork to notice anything and everything about their specific print. Then the children were asked to turn and talk to a partner where they will show each other their prints and discuss each print with one another. Last, the partners shared with the entire class, so the diverse conversations can be heard.

Listening:

Read aloud *Life Doesn't Frighten Me*, poem by Maya Angelou (1996), and viewed paintings by Jean-Michel Basquiat.

Dialogue:

Then they discussed as a group how individuals express emotions. What means do people use to express themselves? In addition, they discussed the concept of poetry and art not only as a method of expression, but also as a means of invoking emotion. Specifically, they discussed the poem and artwork in the book *Life Doesn't Frighten Me* and related it with the emotions of being frightened.

Action:

The student teacher asked each child to write a poem regarding emotions whether it be their own, emotions in general, or in reaction to the book. The children had freedom regarding this assignment, so the results of the writing were individual.

Dialogue:

They shared the poems at the conclusion of this activity. The children's thoughts and emotions while writing these poems were discussed. Also, they discussed the reaction of the reader after listening to each poem.

An extension activity was a class trip to the Museum of Modern Art (or any other museum where Jean-Michel Basquiat's artwork is showcased). While observing the artwork, the children wrote down describing words or phrases in response to the artwork. After the field trip, the reactive adjectives were then collectively used to form a poem. Each child contributed to the poem forming a group class poem. In addition, further investigations of the works of Maya Angelou were implemented.

The student teacher reflected on her experience with this extended problem-posing activity:

> I realized that each time I put the lesson into practice it could potentially be implemented differently dependent upon my students. I also learned in developing my lesson the needs of diverse learners and their abilities needed to be considered while developing the lesson. Throughout the lesson I planned expansion activities for older learners, simplifications or alternatives for diverse learners or learners with specific needs. These adjustments helped me to think of individual students as well as the whole class. I learned that while you are responsible to ensure the learning of the entire class, the individual child's learning is of the most importance. The individual must be considered and their learning must be regarded in terms of the whole child. Through developing a problem-posing lesson using integrated curriculum I was able to consider the individual student, use a variety of curriculum addressing specific aspects of the whole child, and recognize the evolution of my own lesson of integrated curriculum.

Case Study Sixteen

With the aim of educating young children about the vast array of arts in cultures around the world, this teacher found the four-year-old children receptive to new learning experiences.

Listening:

The problem-posing series began with the story *The Caravan* by Margo Fallis (2004). The story is about a camel and is set in the Middle East.

Dialogue:

The story led the students to discussion and activities about learning new skills and information.

Action:

Then a series of activities was implemented surrounding the *Lights of Winter: Winter Celebrations around the World* by Heather Conrad (2001). The children discussed their own family celebrations in winter, and then in small groups they studied celebrations in different cultures. Then a problem-posing activity was framed around the CD *World Party* (www.musicforlittlepeople.com) with traditional children's songs from all over the world, from Morocco to New Zealand to Venezuela. The series of activities included experimenting with instruments, rhythm activities, and dancing. The children began their dialogue by discussing the songs and music they had heard before. (On this CD there are songs such as "The Lion Sleeps Tonight" from Africa that they may have heard before.) Did they hear different types of singing? Did they hear different instruments? Finally, a series of problem-posing activities beginning with *Houses and Homes* by Ann Morris (1995) focused on diverse forms of shelter around the world. There was a component underlying this series of activities that addressed the art in architecture and the art of nature, particularly as this art is seen in shelters of various cultures, from the Taj Mahal to Machu Picchu.

The student teacher reported:

> I was so happy that the children were so interested and involved in the activities. And I was glad you pushed me to document them with photos, journal notes, and work samples, in part, because while my cooperating teacher permitted me to plan and implement the activities, she thought the students wouldn't be interested. Well, they were! Now, it has been a month since we did the activities, and some of the children are bringing in library books about Matcu Pitchu and the Taj Mahal. One child brought in a CD of Middle Eastern music she'd asked for as a birthday gift from her parents.

Case Study Seventeen

This problem-posing case took place at the beginning of the school year as a tool to learn more about what the students enjoy doing outside of school. The teacher used as a focus for the first graders the storybook *Frida* by Jonah Winter (2002).

Listening:

The student teacher began by showing students various works of art by Frida Kahlo (not telling them who the artist is) and asking them what their opinions are regarding the works. She then read a version of the story in English and/or Spanish out loud to the class.

Dialogue:

Then they discussed the artwork shown previously and the story. The students were asked to describe and discuss what they enjoy doing when they have free time.

Action:

Students researched ways they could improve their craft. After about a month, students presented their craft to the class in the form of a "timeline" describing how they have improved and what their work looked like in the beginning and how it looks now. Outside the classroom, students kept a journal about how they are improving their craft/hobby/activity.

Case Study Eighteen

This case documents problem-posing in kindergarten with Van Gogh's *The Bedroom in Arles* (or *Vincent's Bedroom in Arles* or *The Bedroom at Arles*). The student brought to the classroom a print that she had bought from the Vincent Van Gogh Museum in Amsterdam.

Listening:

She sat in a rocking chair on the rug with the print rolled up in a cardboard case as the children gathered. Some of the children were able to notice the word "museum" on the case and predicted that is was a painting. She took out the painting and showed the class *The Bedroom in Arles* (or *Vincent's Bedroom in Arles* or *The Bedroom at Arles*).

She then shared with the children a letter Van Gogh had written to his brother that she had found on the museum's website. The letter said,

> My eyes are still tired by then I had a new idea in my head and here is the sketch of it. Another size 20 canvas. This time it's just simply my bedroom, only here colour is to do everything, and giving by its simplification a grander style to things, is to be suggestive here of rest or of sleep in general. In a word, looking at the picture ought to rest the brain, or rather the imagination. (retrieved May 19, 2003)

She put the print of the painting on an easel and asked the children to look at it for a few minutes. She asked them to think about how they would draw or write a response to the painting.

Dialogue:

Before they began their creations, the student teacher shared her response, which was a poem she had written titled "My Bed."

Action:

Then she gave out pencils and blank pieces of paper to go wherever they wanted to go in the classroom with their writing tool and create a response and asked them to create a response to the painting.

Most of the children drew pictures of their own bedrooms and wrote about the things that are in them or what they do there. Many children wrote a question that they had about the painting: "Who's room is this?" Some of the comments they wrote were:

> "BEDS R SAOFT AND RWOM" (Beds are soft and warm.)
> "MY LAME IS CIDE. I SLIP WITH HR AVR NIT." (My lamie is cuddly.
> I sleep with her every night.)
>   "I LOVE MY BED I SLEEP WITH MY DOLL SARAH. MY
> MOMSINGS SONGS. I LOVE MY BED."

One child drew a picture of himself in his room and explained to me the items in it. He showed me the blanket all around him, his apple, reading lamp and ladder.

One child was compelled to write a heartfelt song filled with well wishes. "I WISH, I MAY, I WISH, I MIT (might), HAVE THE WISH TONIT (tonight), I WISH, YOU SEEP (sleep) WEL AND HOPE I DO TO (too).

She commented "that seeing and hearing them problem-pose and critically think about art culminated the activity."

Case Study Nineteen

Another student teacher working with kindergarten and first-grade students in the same classroom reported her experience using problem-posing with multicultural literature. Her write-up of the experience combined her plan and what actually happened when she tried out her plan with a mixed group of kindergarten and first-grade students:

> The multicultural book I chose for this assignment was *Yoko's Paper Cranes* by Rosemary Wells (2001). The book is about a Japanese girl (personified as a cat) who learns how to make paper cranes from her grandparents. Later, Yoko moves to America and misses her grandparents. Then, for her grandfather's birthday, she mails him a birthday card with three paper cranes. The grandparents hang the cranes by the windows during winter and think of Yoko every time they see them. I chose four students from my K-1 student teaching placement to participate in this activity.

Listening:

The student teacher reminded the children of another Rosemary Wells book they had read called *Yoko*. She reminded them of the plot of the book, and then asked whether they remembered the book, and liked it. They made brief comments that they remembered it and liked it "a little."

She then read *Yoko's Paper Cranes*.

Dialogue:

The children became more enthusiastic during the reading of the book, mostly because of the illustrations. The illustrations are very colorful and remind one of a collage made of paper of different patterns. The illustrations of Yoko's new home in California are surrounded by a border of American symbols like an American flag, watermelon, and ice cream cones. The student teacher said:

> The children loved these illustrations. They asked me to stop reading so they could remark on how warm California looked, and how yummy the watermelon and ice cream looked. They also loved that some of the illustrations were shiny. They all wanted a chance to touch the book. One illustration shows a calendar with the date of Yoko's grandfather's birthday circled. They all then talked about when their birthdays were.

After she finished the story, the student teacher asked the children whether they had friends or relatives who lived far away. A first-grade girl spoke about her grandparents and cousins but couldn't remember where they lived. A kindergarten girl mentioned her grandparents, whom she says she has never met and who live in Michigan. A first-grade boy had friends in California, and he described in detail the plane trip he took when he visited them. A kindergarten boy spoke about his grandmother who lived in another country, but he forgot which one. The student teacher then told the children that they would be writing letters to friends and family who lived far away.

Action:

Over the next week, she gave several mini-lessons on how to write a letter and how to address an envelope. The children then wrote their letters and decorated them using origami paper, like the illustrations in *Yoko's Paper Cranes*. The student teacher had sent a letter home to the children's parents asking them to help the children choose somebody to write to. Three of the children wrote to their grandparents, and one child wrote to her cousin. Three of the children wrote in their letters messages like "I love you," "I hope you are doing well," and "I hope to see you soon." One first grader wrote to his grandmother about how much fun he had over vacation when he was at her house. While they were decorating their letters, students made pictures of things that were special to them or to the person they were writing to.

After the series of activities, the student teacher reflected on the experience:

> Doing the activity in a small group was very important for these children. At their age and stage of development, it is important that they talk out loud to other children about what they are doing. It helps to clarify things for themselves. One kindergarten boy in the group is usually very quiet during class. However, a first-grade

boy helped to draw him into the conversation. The first grader was talking to the children about how his grandmother had a lot of pets and how her parrot was named Taco. This made the kindergarten boy (who loves animals) laugh, and then he started talking more about his own letter.

Regarding the dissonance between the push for subject-area content knowledge and the need for the teacher to follow the interests, needs, and developmental contexts of individual children, this teacher education student wrote:

> I've learned of the possibility of many students being pushed too hard in kindergarten, and as a result they experience a developmental lapse in first grade. I've learned that literacy is a much bigger force than I ever imagined and, at least in my classroom, takes precedence over all else, and that although developmental differences are huge and students can experience spurts and stalls of gigantic lengths, the average kindergartner can blow you away with their breadth of knowledge, even if they don't express it.

Case Study Twenty

Excerpts from the next case study reflect work of an experienced teacher of infants and toddlers. Yes, artful story and integrated curriculum that focus on the arts are appropriate for very young learners. First she describes the setting:

> This is an alternative school setting that serves teen parents and a small percentage of families who pay tuition from the community. Child care, food, and formula are free of charge for minor parents. The teen parents have the benefit of enrollment priority. Some of the minor parents chose to return to their comprehensive high school. Although they are off of our campus they utilize our child development center.
>
> The program is licensed to serve a total of twenty-four infants and toddlers. The infants and toddlers are grouped by age. Children under the age of two remain in the infant room until they are developmentally ready to transition into the toddler room. Children may transition from the infant room as early as eighteen months of age and remain in the toddler environment until the age of three. Our adult/child ratio in the infant room is one to three and one to six in the toddler room.
>
> The children enrolled in our program are between the ages of six weeks to three years old. The majority of families served are of Mexican decent. One child is of dual ethnic heritage and six children are Euro-Americans. Most of our parents are minors who live with their parents. As a result their children are raised with the help and support of their extended family. Some of the children have both parents and their grandparents involved in their lives. However due to the parents' age most of our children come from single parent families.
>
> All of the children have varied needs and abilities. For that reason we provide individualized care and curriculum. Bonding between the children and teachers is encouraged by providing primary caregivers. Each teacher is assigned a group of children. The primary caregiver is responsible for ensuring that their entire group of

children's needs are met. They make sure the child's feeding, diapering, and rest routines are taken care of. This enables the child to build trust and attachment. In addition the teacher is responsible for creating problem-posing activities that supports the child's growth and development.

The teacher goes on to discuss the program's general curriculum and then her specific problem-posing lessons that she focuses on literacy and nutrition. We have included her lesson examples in this chapter category of Artful Story and the Arts because this is the way that this teacher uses the Arts to maintain the integrity of her philosophy about working with infants and toddlers—the three aspects of critical literacy of participation by learners, multiple sources of knowledge, and transformative action—and to address her goals of literacy and nutrition.

Much of our curriculum is incorporated into meeting the children's needs. As we learn about the child we are better able to meet their individual needs. We utilize one-on-one time to interact, build relationships, and stimulate the child's cognitive development. As a result we gain an understanding about the child's and become skilled at following the child cues.

Our environment is set up to encourage development in the areas of social, cognitive, motor, cultural, and linguistic skills. The infant's needs are met on demand and the toddlers have a very flexible schedule of daily routines. Our classroom environment is center based. Mobile children have large blocks of free play. This enables them the time they need to choose the centers they are interested in exploring. They also have the option of participating in the teacher-directed activity. The younger infants have the opportunity to play independently, practice moving their body and manipulate smaller hand toys and books. The caregiver stays close to talk and responds to the children.

Our curriculum supports the development of the whole child. The daily routines include activities that encourage growth in all areas. Busy play and imagination occurs in the dramatic play and block center. Our reading center provides the children quiet time and encourages print awareness. The climbing structures, outdoor environment, puzzles, self-feeding, and other manipulatives support motor development. Interactions with adults as well as their peers promote social development. Exploring the environment and participating in the other activities and interactions encourage cognitive development. Their learning experience is encouraged with a balance of teacher-directed and child-initiated activities.

Language learning takes place all throughout the day both indoors and outdoors. The teachers talk, sing, and read with the children. The children have easy access to books and we label objects in our environment. Through observations we become aware of each child's interest, likes and dislikes, areas of strength, and areas they are working on. Our observations enable us to develop individualized curriculum and plan for meaningful experiences.

When discussing the most influential theorist who had influenced her work with infants and toddlers she immediately identified Maslow:

I embrace Abraham Maslow's theory on the Hierarchy of Needs. His theory suggests that humans are motivated to reach their fullest potential when their needs are fully met. Maslow's pyramid begins with the very basic needs on the bottom. When the needs are met at one level we move upwards on the pyramid. Maslow's pyramid illustrates our needs starting with physiological needs at the bottom. After the physiological needs are met, we seek safety, love/belonging, esteem, and self-actualization. Therefore, building relationships based on trust and respect in a safe and nurturing environment is crucial for learning to take place.

She then connects these principles to the guidelines from the National Association for the Education of Young Children (NAEYC) and her interest in early literacy learning and health. These NAEYC Guidelines emphasize children's need for meaningful literacy experiences. She wrote:

Infants and toddlers should be involved in one-on-one interaction that encourages literacy development. For example, children need an adult to talk with, sing with, and do finger plays with. At our program we nurture this development during one-on-one play and in small group activities. Additionally we promote language learning through dialogue during our meal time, diaper changing routines, and prior to nap.

To further encourage language development we expose the children to print. The children are read to on a daily basis. They also have access to a diverse collection of age appropriate books and other learning materials. We provide board books and cloth books because they are durable and easy for young children to handle. The NAEYC Guidelines state that when children are read to and have the ability to handle books they are engaged in pre-reading activities. They learn to hold the book upright, turn the pages from right to left, as well as become familiar with the cover of the book, title, and author. These skills emerge when children have repeated experience with age appropriate literature. As the child continues to mature they develop a further understanding about books and print.

She then talks about ways she builds in nutrition information into her problem-posing:

In my problem posing activities I have also built nutrition into the curriculum. The NAEYC suggests that early experiences with food have a lasting impact on future eating habits. Therefore they encourage teachers to integrate healthful foods into their learning activities. I believe that it is important to introduce children to a variety of nutritious foods. Through food activities children can learn about self help skills, science, culture, math, and proper use of utensils. Most importantly introduction to nutritious snacks helps to build interest in and desire for healthy foods.

And now, notice the arts.

Spilt Milk Problem-Posing Activity

Materials:

It Looked Like Spilt Milk by Charles G. Shaw (1988), flannel board, flannel board story pieces, white paint, blue construction paper, shaving cream, zip lock bags, tape, milk, fruit, emersion blender, dull butter knives, small pouring pitchers and a large pitcher to blend smoothie, graph, picture of the fruits used in the smoothie, name tags for each child in the class or a picture of each child with their name written next to it, sentence strips, bubble recipe, Dawn dishwashing detergent, water, sugar, bubble wands or pipe cleaners.

Listening:
During outdoor play the teacher asked children to look for clouds. When the children returned to the class she asked each child to pick out a flannel board story piece to the story. Then she asked them to find a place to sit down. Before reading the story she talked to the children about the title, author, and illustrator of the book.

Then she read *It Looked Like Spilt Milk* (Shaw, 1988).

Dialogue:
She asked the children about things they saw in the sky when they were outside. Did you see any clouds? What other things did we see in the sky (birds, airplanes, sun, moon)? The teacher followed this up by asking open-ended questions during center time. Children who did not have the language skills were asked Did you see a bird, airplane, blimp, sun, kite, bubbles? (Name one or two objects.)

Action:
At the music center, the teacher sang the song "Floating Cloud up in the Sky" to the tune of "Twinkle, Twinkle, Little Star."

> Floating clouds up in the sky,
> Changing shapes as you pass by
> Angel, flower and mitten forms
> Moving, drifting before the storm
> Floating clouds up in the sky
> Changing shapes as you pass by

At the art center, each child had the opportunity to finger paint or use brushes to apply white paint onto navy blue paper. (For different experiences, children could tear white paper into shapes and then glue them onto paper, or the teacher could put out glue and cotton balls for the children to put onto the blue paper.) She asked open-ended questions and gave the child words that described cotton (soft, fluffy, white) and glue (sticky, white, liquid) during art activities.

At the science center, the children had the opportunity to explore shaving cream enclosed in a plastic bag. The teacher secured the zip lock bags with tape at the opening. Then she taped the bags onto the table in the science area. During science exploration she asked open-ended questions such as, How does the shaving cream feel? She gave words that describe how shaving cream looks, feels, and smells to children who have limited language development.

For nutrition, health, math, and science, the teacher implemented a cooking activity. The children washed their hands, then sat at the table to help cut fruit or break bananas to put into the smoothie. They poured milk from small measuring cups into the pitcher and blended the fruit and milk together. During the activity she asked open-ended questions such as What is your favorite fruit? What is the name of this fruit? What color is the banana?

After the children were done with their smoothies, the teacher asked them to find their name tags. She asked them to place their name/picture tag next to their favorite fruit on the chart. As a group, they counted the number of children's names that are next to each fruit.

At the writing center, after each child was done with their artwork, the teacher asked them about what their cloud looks like. She filled in the blanks to the sentence strips: Sometimes it looked like a _____ but it wasn't a _____.

In evaluation of her experience with this activity, this teacher wrote:

> When I did this activity with the infants they did not make the connection of the book to the art activity. Most of the toddlers made the connection. When I did the flannel board I paused before I named the shape of the flannel and one of the toddlers named all of the flannel pieces prior to me saying it. When we did the paint activity one of our children who speaks Spanish smiled as the teacher said sometimes it looked like spilt milk when the white paint was put on his dark blue paper.

Busy Spider Problem-Posing Activity

Materials:
"The Very Busy Spider" (English and Spanish), lyrics to "Old MacDonald Had a Farm," farm animals and barn, dream catcher, eggs, cheese, fruit, milk and toast, graph chart (horse, cow, sheep), name/picture tags, live spider and jar, white paper, pencils, glitter, glue, and construction paper.

Listening:
The teacher introduced the children to the book by reading the title and naming the author and illustrator. She asked the children to guess what this book may be about. She gave them the opportunity to answer and support them if they don't respond. Then she read *The Very Busy Spider* by Eric Carle (2006). To encourage participation of the older children, the teacher paused and allowed them the opportunity to name the animals or make the animal sounds during the reading experience.

Dialogue:

The teacher then asked the children to talk about their favorite animal. During center time (Action), the teacher asked open-ended questions. For example, what can you tell me about that animal you are holding? During nutrition activities, the teacher talked about foods that come from farm animals (eggs, milk, cheese, yogurt, meat).

Action:

At the math center, children graphed their favorite animal on the graphing chart. After the story, the children had the opportunity to put their name under their favorite animal from the story.

At the science/discovery center, during center time, the children had the opportunity to play with the farm animals and barn. The teacher also placed a harmless spider into a large see-through jar for observing. The children, with supervision, fed the spider flies.

For the nutrition activity, the teacher and children prepared egg and cheese omelets with milk and fruit. Older children set up the table for breakfast. Toddlers poured the milk from a small measuring cup into their cup. Meals were served family style. (Children under one were given an alternative snack, such as fruit, yogurt, or toast.)

For music and movement, the teacher led the song, "Old MacDonald Had a Farm." She then led a movement activity, in which the children were asked to walk like a spider, gallop like a horse, and fly like an owl.

At the art center, the children were given glue to squirt from the bottle onto paper, and then they sprinkled glitter onto the glue to create a spider web.

In the block area the teacher made available many toy farm animals.

Dos Años Problem-Posing Activity

Materials:

Dos Años by Anastasia Suen (2002), Orozco's CD, Greg and Steve's CD, tunnel, large climbing blocks and ramp, paint and construction paper, masa mix, tortilla press, and an electric skillet.

Listening:

During the diaper changing routine, the teachers talked to the children about their body parts. For example, you are putting your leg into your pants, arm into your sleeve, foot into your shoe.

The teacher introduced the children to the book by reading the title and naming the author and illustrator. She asked the children what they thought this book might be about. She gave them the opportunity to answer and supported them if they didn't respond. During circle time and at one-on-one time, she read *Dos Años*.

Dialogue:
After the story she asked the children what they use their hands (arms, feet, legs).

Action:
For music and movement the teacher led the songs "Dos Manitas," "Diaz Deditos" by Jose Louis Orozco, and "Put Your Right Hand In," *Gallop* by Greg and Steve.

During outdoor play, the teacher created an obstacle course out of the climbing blocks and tunnel for the children to explore. They also had the parachute out for a group of children to play with.

For math and science, the children assisted with making tortillas.

At the art center, the children had the opportunity to dip their feet into paint and walk on paper to create footprints.

For nutrition, the children helped make tortillas. They had the opportunity to listen to instructions, measure the ingredients, roll the masa into balls, and flatten the masa on the tortilla press.

In the block area, diversity figures (people in wheelchairs, people with walkers, diverse ethnic figures, and diverse career figures) were added to the available toys.

In the dramatic play area, mirrors, diversity foods, and empty food containers or boxes that had come from the homes of the children and teachers were available for the children to play with.

Art allows for development of the infants and toddlers to flourish and express themselves.

References

Alarcón, F. X. (2001). *Iguanas in the snow and other winter poems/Iguanas en la nieve y otras poemas de Invierno*. San Francisco: Children's Book Press.

Ancona, G. (1998). *Barrio: Jose's neighborhood*. New York: Harcourt Brace. Spanish language edition, Barrio: El barrio de José New York: Harcourt Brace.

Angelou, M. (1996). *Life doesn't frighten me*. New York: Stewart, Tabori and Chang.

Baldwin, J. (1962). *Creative process*. New York: Ridge Press.

Banner, D. (July, 2006). Personal Interview. San Diego, California.

Campoy, I. (2005). Personal communication. San Antonio, Texas.

Carle, E. (2006). *The very busy spider*. New York: Grosset & Dunlap.

Cone, Theresa P. (2003). Off the page: Children's creative dance as a response to children's literature. *Research Quarterly for Exercise and Sport 74*(1): A-2

Conrad, H. (2001). *Lights of winter: Winter celebrations around the world*. New York: Lightport Books.

Crichlow, W. (1995). Rethinking the narrative of urban neighborhood: Perspectives on the social context and processes of identity formation among African American youth. Unpublished paper. American Educational Research Association, San Francisco, CA.

Dorros, A. (1997). *Abuela*. New York: Puffin.

Eisner, Elliot W. (1998) *The enlightened eye: qualitative inquiry and the enhancement of educational practice*. Upper Saddle River, NJ: Merrill.

Eisner, E. (2002). The Arts and the Creation of Mind. In Chapter 4, What the arts teach and how it shows, pp. 70–92. Yale University Press. Available from NAEA Publications.

Fallis, M. (2004). *The Caravan*.
http://www.electricscotland.com/kids/stories/middleeast25.htm, retrieved February 20, 2003.

Freeman, D. (2004). *Manuelo, the playing mantis*. New York: Viking Juvenile.

Gilbert, A. G. (2005). Dance education in the 21st Century. Jopard, VA: AAHPERD. 76(5) May/June: 26–35.

Goldman, R. (2005). No arts left behind. Maui arts and cultural center: *Centerpiece Magazine*.

Morris, A. (1995). *Houses and homes*. New York: HarperCollins.

Negri-Pool, L. L. (2005, Spring). Welcoming Kalenna, *Rethinking Schools*. http://www.rethinkingschools.org/archive/19_04/chin194.shtml, retrieved 4-6-2008.

Overby, L. Y. (1992). Status of dance in education. ERIC Clearinghouse on Teacher Education, Washington, D.C. http://www.ericdigests.org/1992-3/dance.htm

Quintero, E. P. (2004). *Problem-posing with multicultural children's literature: Developing critical, early childhood curricula*. New York: Peter Lang.

Raza, A. (2002). Idea into image: An exhibition of five Pakistani painters at the Indo Center of Art and Culture, New York.

Richardson, L. (1994). Writing, a method of inquiry. In N. Denzin & Y. Lincoln (Eds.), *Handbook of qualitative research*, pp. 516–529. Thousand Oaks, CA: Sage.

Shaw, C. G. (1988). *It looked like spilt milk*. New York: Harper Trophy.

Studio in a School website. (2001) [online] Available at: www.studioinaschool.org.

Suen, A. (2002). *Dos años*. New York: Lee & Low Books.

Tarr, P. (2001, May). What art educators can learn from Reggio Emilia. Art Education. National Art Association, New York.

Trawick-Smith, J. (2006). *Early childhood development* (fourth edition). Upper Saddle River, NJ: Pearson Education.

Wei, D. (2005). A Little School in a Little Chinatown, Rethinking Schools. http://www.rethinkingschools.org/archive/19_04/chin194.shtml, retrieved 4-6-2008.

Wells, R. (2001). *Yoko's paper cranes*. New York: Hyperion.

White, E. (2006). *Thomas More*. London: Trafalgar Studio Whitehall Theater Program.

Winter, J. (2002). *Frida*. New York: Levine.

CHAPTER SEVEN

Artful Story as a Frame for Activist Work

A lot of people that we work with in a place like ours have not exercised choice. They are bound by other people's choices, by circumstances. A good education will give them more choice. (Rosen, 2006)

Complicated Conversations—Artful Story as a Frame for Activist Work
In a study of cases of activist teachers, Casey (1993) found that teaching is much more than being employed in a school. Teachers, both in- and outside the classroom, have the power to change their students' lives. And these teachers understand that children have the power to change their own lives. Through my research I have strengthened my belief that teaching practice of effective educators is an interrelationship of life's activities and priorities both inside and outside the classroom. Furthermore, children—regardless of age—when given an environment of support and acceptance become experts at activism in their own worlds inside and outside the classroom.

In a study of effective literacy teachers mentioned earlier (Rummel & Quintero, 1997) we found that teachers bring past experiences and present values and priorities to the schools. Teachers' beliefs and their life experiences cannot be separated from what they do in the classroom. These teachers reflect the observations of Daniel Berrigan (1999): "If we are in one aspect of human struggle we are in the whole thing. Touching human life in one way, we touch all of life" (p. 37).

A director in a Head Start program in Southern California that serves one of the most economically challenged neighborhoods in the state continually works, along with the teachers in her program, to observe and build relationships with families and children in order to continually make the program more responsive to the needs of the children. For example, she told the story of a particular child in the program the previous year who came to the program in September shortly after his family had come to the area from Mexico. In spite of the supportive, flexible, and child-friendly environment, the boy just couldn't acclimate. She said he just couldn't sit or stay still for any reason—not even to play with blocks or toy cars, or to paint, or to play with the water in the water table. He only seemed calm and only played with the other children when he was outdoors.

So, after a few days of this mutual struggle, the director and teachers decided to experiment with moving many of the classroom activities outside (she smiled and said, "an advantage to being in Southern California"). She said the change in the child was immediate and profound. He was calm and apparently happy. He experimented with virtually every type of activity provided, and he began to make friends and collaborate with other children on work and in play.

The director then explained that they continued this setup for a few weeks and then gradually moved a few activities back inside, little by little, and the child adjusted to the indoor classroom. In the meantime, she made a home visit (a vital component of Head Start programs) to talk with the family to get to know them and to explore other needed support. What she learned there explained the probable reason for the child's inability to stay indoors at first. His family had recently moved from Mexico and had joined two other families who all lived in a one-room apartment that had not one window.

He needed to be outdoors. He needed his activist teachers who through observation, trust in the children and themselves, and risk-taking confidence changed their program to accommodate him. Activism.

Transformative Action by Preschool Children and Their Teachers

A group of pre-K student teachers, working with three- to five-year-olds (many of whom are Spanish-speaking English Learners) in Southern California and studying in a university class focusing on young children's learning and multilingual language acquisition and English language development in the classroom, created groundbreaking learning situations. These experienced student teachers engaged in critical literacy work that supports children's play, fantasy, and learning through story. They worked on the difficult but effective task of creating participatory curriculum that leads to learners' transformative actions. Embedded in the few examples here are illustrations of the teachers' transformative action as well as the young children's transformative action.

One student teacher working with three- and four-year-olds explained, "It all began with Book 20 from Ada and Campoy's (2003) *Authors in the Classroom*. This is the activity called "How It Is and How It Could Be" (Quintero, 2009, p. 7). The activity encourages teachers to think first about something that one would like to change or make a difference in, and then encourages them to use this idea as a beginning or a catalyst for making change on a personal level. Then, the authors of the book and teachers in the class worked on transferring this idea to the teachers' work with children.

This particular student teacher thought about her membership in the Union of Concerned Scientists that lobbies for environmental issues. She wanted to do something that deals with being proactive in preventing water pollution. So she planned a thematic lesson that centered on their class pet fish and its water conditions. She and the children did observations dictation, oral discussions, writings, drawings, and finger plays. She used visuals and activities to demonstrate how we could make a change in how we care for and conserve our water sources.

They practiced conserving water when washing their hands and picked up trash on their playground. Over the course of three weeks, the children were given a variety of activities and opportunities in English and Spanish with a great deal of consideration given to the conversational and contextual learning surrounding the clean water theme.

Finally, using a digital camera to take pictures of the pet fish and his water, both clean and unclean and by group dictation, the student teacher and her class created a class book in English and Spanish that told the story of Jack the fish that she had invented. The book documented the original clean water Jack had, how his water became dirty (unintentionally), how they cleaned the water, and then quickly learned to use dip sticks to check the water for safety for Jack. The book then addressed the "bigger problem" of dirty water and pollution in our communities, oceans, and world.

> We can test our water and even add special drops to clean our water. But remember that even clean looking water can still be dirty. The water cycle cannot clean all of the Earth's water so we have to help keep our oceans, lakes and rivers clean. (Quintero, 2009, p. 9)

The last page of the book is a list of brainstorming ideas that the preschool children came up with which showed that they understood the small steps (and big responsibility) each person has in preventing pollution. The student teacher explained,

> During my group instruction and throughout the implementation of the clean water theme, there was always a balance of English and English Learner students. While I do not have a bilingual program (officially) at work in my classroom, students do receive much of their instruction during the day in both Spanish and English. I provide the students instruction in fluent Spanish with the use of Spanish-speaking parents or my Americorp assistant. Otherwise, I incorporate as much Spanish as I can speak during the day. I read books in Spanish and encourage the students to speak in whatever language that is most comfortable for them.

She goes on to explain:

> I work in a preschool classroom on an elementary school campus with a population of 90% Latino children. My personal goals are to further incorporate optimizing language input that is comprehensible, interesting, and of sufficient quantity, as well as providing opportunities for output, to use languages other than English (Spanish,

in my case) 50% to 90% of the time, and to create a bilingual environment where development of the native language is encouraged. All children deserve to become bilingual and biliterate without the legislation prohibiting this fundamental right to a fair and adequate education.

By implementing lessons based on a theme, I was able to facilitate content learning. I began with a preview in their native language, a continuation in the target language (English), and then a review in the primary language again. I provided opportunities for language development, interaction with print-rich materials such as books, dictation, children's drawings, maps. We practiced expressive language skills via open discussions.

Culturally, many of the children live with other families in small, one bedroom apartments; most of the apartments do not have a community swimming pool. When we discussed uses of water, I found that most of the children would describe the small, round plastic pools as their swimming pool. Also some of the children were able to describe trips to the beach. Some children described a small patio of plants and chairs, while others do have a front yard and a backyard. This was an awesome conversation for me and the children had a lot to say. I think that they all got the idea that the places that they live are all very similar and maybe they even connected with a sense of community.

Through the means of my clean water theme, I focused on giving the three-year-olds as much instruction in Spanish as possible. My focus shifted from what I needed them to do (speak English) to trying to meet their needs of gaining a better foundation in their primary language.

Further reflecting on her own transformative action she said,

I did take Spanish courses at the Community College and here at the university. I am just beginning to grasp the language, and even though I have a long way to go, I can effectively communicate with Spanish speakers. Not having those skills the first year I taught was difficult, and I was focused on my own learning of a second language. This gave me insight into what the children were experiencing, and I connected with them on that level.

My future hopes on a large scale are to continue to try and learn Spanish by taking Spanish classes at the university, create bilingual and biliteracy activities, while strengthening my skills as an early childhood teacher. I know that I will continue to cultivate the ideologies of cross-cultural awareness among students, parents, and co-workers in my future work with bilingual children. Last but not least, I myself will defend the rights of all children and their right to an above standard education.

The Fat Boy and His Activism

In one university class, as we were discussing transformative action, a teacher reported a crisis in her preschool class. A four-year-old girl came running over to the her. The girl was visibly upset, her face tense and fists clenched. "The fat boy took the truck from me!" Within seconds, the boy, dragging the truck, rushed over to where they were talking, and through his sobs, began trying to explain. The student teacher asked, "What happened?" (She reported being a little surprised that *he* was so upset because he did have the coveted truck.) The boy stammered, "She c...ca ... called me ... The Fat Boy!" The student teacher turned to the girl and asked, "Is that what you called him?" "Yes," she said. "Why?" "I don't know his name."

The student teacher focused on both children and asked, "What do you think we could do about this?" The girl immediately said, "Make a book." "Yes?" The teacher wasn't sure what she was planning. "Yes, we'll take pictures of everybody and put names on the pictures."

So, the girl and boy together set off with the class digital camera and took pictures of each child in the class. The teacher printed the photos and then the bookmakers asked each child to write her/his name under his/her picture. Then, after a trip to the processing shop to laminate the pages and bind the book, the class had a book so no one had to use derogatory names for children because they didn't know their real names (Quintero, 2009).

A teacher wrote to me about how her using this methodology of critical literacy with preschoolers in her program promoted important transformative action for one of the children.

> When I was in your curriculum class I was teaching at a Head Start in Harlem. I'm still there and have been using the problem posing approach with the children. The interaction is so dynamic and meaningful for the children and myself (it's great).
>
> Anyway, I wanted to share with you how the problem-posing approach (adapted for preschoolers, of course) has affected one of my students. This child is four years old. She is an English Language Learner who was diagnosed at the age of three as a selective mute. When classes began in September she barely used language. She didn't say good morning, didn't participate in activities or engage with students.
>
> The problem-posing approach with books she can relate to like *Dora*, for example, have been a vehicle in allowing her to express herself verbally. She has blossomed! I'm amazed. (Quintero, 2009, p. 8)

Writing and reading are transforming. As children read and write, they change. A child's writing can tell us much about her/his personal, family, and community contexts. It is a way of nurturing the ability to summon up an "as if," as Maxine Greene (1992) calls it, a sense of "what is out there, what I can reach if I try." It is a way of doing what Maxine Greene suggests, "helping students find language to bring dreams into being, language that introduces them to the experience of going beyond." Education must support students to become effective writers, readers, and participants in literacy.

Deep understanding of the assumption that words, deeds, policy, practice, and theoretical application are inseparably linked in our world today underlies this book. We cannot pretend that teaching is neutral, nor can the practice be done in isolation. Freire (1998) states in his last published work,

There are times when I fear that someone reading this…may think that there is now no place among us for the dreamer and the believer in utopia. Yet, what I have been saying up to now is now the stuff of inconsequential dreamers. It has to do with the very nature of men and women as makers and dreamers of history and not simply as casualties of an a priori vision of the world. (p. 121)

Children and Activism through Critical Literacy

Other teachers and student teachers are quickly able to see the power of young children's imaginations and fantasy play encouraged by using critical literacy in the curriculum. One student teacher built upon children's interests by asking them first to draw a picture of a scene from one of their favorite storybooks. She then read the classic the fairytale *The Three Little Pigs.*

After the story she explained to the children that sometimes stories have special messages to teach to people. She led a brainstorming session with her group of children about what messages they thought *The Three Little Pigs* might have. Then she asked the students to show the pictures they had just drawn. She and the children briefly discussed the stories, why they were favorites and what, if any, messages could be found within the stories. After some play time, she brought the group together to investigate the class rules (posted on the walls where the students could see them). Why do we have them? What is the meaning behind each rule? As a class, they voted on one rule. Then, together on a large piece of paper, they weaved this rule into a short story they wrote as a class.

Later in the day, she explained to the children that families, like classes, may have their own special rules and beliefs. She asked them to share a rule or belief from their own family (e.g., in my family, we always take our shoes off when we enter the front door) and explain the meaning behind this rule or belief. She asked the students to reflect on this concept and interview their parents and siblings about what they perceive are important family rules. They shared their interview results with the class the following day.

She wrote an evaluation of her lessons:

It was really exciting for the students to hear *The Three Little Pigs* in class. I think it was especially exciting because most of the students were familiar with this book and could be "experts" in predicting and discussing the unfolding of events. It provided a comfortable foundation for the students to explore and discuss morals and school and family rules in depth. Because the students were discussing THEIR favorite storybooks and THEIR family's rules, every one was the teacher and had something to share with the class. This was particularly relevant and confidence-boosting for my students. So many students came to kindergarten with varying degrees of classroom experience. Some students knew all their ABCs. Some are still learning how to hold pencils. This activity, where all the students were "experts" "leveled the playing field" and consequently was a great classroom bonding, esteem building activity.

Another student teacher was inspired to address a series of complex classroom, school, and community issues with kindergarteners. She worked in a "high need" pre-K through grade 6 school located in Spanish Harlem. Eighty-six percent of the students were of Hispanic/Latino background. Of the students, 6.8% immigrated to the United States within the past three years. Of the students, 93.8% received free lunch and in 2002, a staggering 55.6% of the student population was suspended at some time during the school year.

The kindergarteners that she worked with were a group of happy, polite five-year-olds. They deferred to their teachers for instructions and rarely questioned what was asked of them. In a parent-teacher conference she observed that the children's parents were similarly amicable and polite. They asked few questions and agreed with the teacher on all accounts. The student teacher acknowledged that there were language and cultural barriers present but also could not help wondering to what extent the parents felt their input was relevant. In her journal reflections other questions that arose from this parent conference included:

> How often and in what ways does the community use their "voice"? Is there a belief that a person can make a difference within the larger community? What sort of beliefs about "voice" and social empowerment are passed on from parents in this community to their children?

The student teacher decided that she wanted to create lesson plans designed to empower students by giving them a voice and by helping them realize how their input can impact the larger community. Curriculum goals targeted in these lesson plans included those of the Association for Childhood Education International and the National Council of Teachers of English.

In essence, the goals of her lesson plans were to be interdisciplinary in nature, integrating critical literacy, mathematical problems, art, and social studies. The lesson plans also provided opportunities for learning and the development of real-life skills within a context that is relevant to the lives of the student. Such real-life skills included learning to work together as a team, resolve conflicts, problem solve, organize and meet time lines, compromise, manage money, and debate ideas.

The student teacher asked the students to listen to a story that has the issue of teamwork as an underlying theme. For the kindergarten students, she used *Mouse Count* by Ellen Stoll Walsh (1995), a story appropriate for children of ages two to six. Ten mice work together to escape from a hungry snake who has trapped them in a jar. A few days later she read *Arthur Makes the Team* by Marc Brown (1998), a story appropriate for children of ages four to eight. Arthur makes the baseball team but has difficulties catching base-balls! His friend, Francine, gives him a hard time until the two friends realize they must work together in order for their team to win. She then discussed with students why the characters in the story were successful in accomplishing their goal.

She then asked the students to break up into groups of three and discuss the last time they worked with others. She provided students with a chart of questions to guide their discussion. Questions included: Was the group work a good experience? Why or why not? What did you accomplish as a group? How could the group work have been better?

Then, she asked the different groups to summarize what they discussed. As a class, they agreed upon some guidelines for effectively working as a group. They then recorded the guidelines on chart paper.

The next phase of this student teacher's work involved taking the children for a walk around their school. Using clipboards, they recorded their observations and noted the community's strengths and its weaknesses. Students could write or draw to record their information.

When they returned to their classroom, the students discussed their findings with the class. The teacher listed the areas of strengths on the board (e.g., a caring, active PTA, a library with lots of resources) and weaknesses (e.g., a need for computers, an unattractive school environment). The large group agreed upon the two most relevant issues and then generated a debate by splitting the class into two teams. One team supported remedying one issue and the other team the other issue. Teams stated the pros and cons of selecting one issue over the other for the duration of ten minutes. The teacher recorded the comments on a T-chart on the board. At the end of the ten minutes, an idea got one point for each pro listed beneath it with one point subtracted for each con listed. The issue with the most points becomes the targeted issue for the class to work on.

Then the kindergarten students broke into committee groups and brain-stormed different ways of resolving the problem. One student was the re-corder. One student presented the groups' ideas when the class reconvened. Then students voted on the best solution for the identified problem. Students placed three different votes for what they thought were the three best ideas. As a group, they identified the solution most people were in favor of. Then students were charged with the task of determining the budget needed to carry out the project. For the problem of the need to beautify the school, the students went online to determine the approximate amount and cost of paint needed to revitalize the school walls.

Finally, for homework, students brainstormed and researched ways to raise money to remedy the identified problem. For the problem identified as the need to beautify the school, students researched ways of raising the funds to have the walls repainted.

Another student teacher reflected about critical literacy and what children's activism might look like for young children:

> I am still becoming familiar with the terms and meanings behind problem-posing and critical literacy, however I think I am beginning to understand how to utilize these methods in an educational setting. The notion of using literacy to bring together academics and a child's own personal experience is so helpful when considering how both children and adults learn. Typically, it is much easier to grasp ideas when they are linked to things that one is already familiar with. I feel that critical literacy also has the ability to bring students together when they realize that they share experiences and I have an example of just that to share.
>
> I am currently student teaching in a kindergarten class and was able to attend school on the first day. One little boy T. came into class crying due to the intense nerves of leaving his parents and beginning something very unfamiliar to him. He cried for a while and eventually my cooperating teacher asked some children who appeared to be more comfortable to be T.'s "special friend" for the day. The next day my cooperating teacher read a story called *First Day Jitters* (Danneberg, 2000) to the class. She prefaced the book with a short discussion on feeling nervous to begin kindergarten as well as asking the children what they thought the character was nervous about. After she completed the story she asked the children to give a thumbs up if they felt nervous and T. along with many others raised their thumbs. I noticed the children looking around to see who had their thumb up and the number of raised thumbs grew as each new child felt more comfortable revealing that they too were nervous. She then had the class draw a picture of themselves on the first day of school.

Another student teacher wrote about a child exemplifying transformative action in her literacy development process:

> At my student teaching placement, there is a girl (S.) who is significantly younger than her kindergarten peers; she will turn five at the end of November. On their first full day of school, my cooperating teacher (T.) began reading and writing assessments. During choice time, T. asked S. to write her name. S. slowly picked up her pencil and held it over the paper, but didn't move. She looked up and quietly said, "I can't do it." T. gave S. her name tag to look at and assured her she would help. First, T. asked her to sound out her own name: "What sound does your name begin with?" Together T. and S. sounded out "sssss." Then S. looked at her name tag and then wrote a backward "S" on her paper. As they sounded out each letter, T. pointed to the corresponding letter. They continued in this fashion until S. finished writing her entire name.
>
> A week later, the children were doing a drawing activity and T. also asked them to write their names on their papers when they were done. As I walked around

the classroom observing, I noticed S. was telling another girl, "Stop! I *can* do it. Just let *me* do it!" She was indignant and determined, as she grabbed her pencil back. I asked what was wrong, and E., the other girl, pointed to the half-erased "S" on S.'s paper and told me, "She's not writing that right! It's backwards!" I told E. to join the rest of the class, who was already seated on the rug for group reading time. I told S. to work with me at another table. S. followed and went right to work. She quietly mumbled to herself, "sssss" and wrote a backwards "S." Then "aaahhh" and wrote an "A." I asked if she needed help. She told me, "No. I can do it." When she was done, she looked at me and beamed. Her expression was of pride and satisfaction. I couldn't be more delighted myself!

Children's Writing as Activism

Much research from many sources documents different strategies for teaching writing and the varying effects of the different approaches. Before strategies and skills can be addressed, especially considering the perspective of critical literacy, research about the writing that "real" writers do must first be considered. How do "real" writers exert their agency? How, through writing, can young children be supported in their agency? This information about poets and authors relates to the potential of young learners, the environments we create for them to work in, and the ways we teach.

It is voice that tells us the self is present in writing. Each writer, child or adult, has a unique voice that she or he opens to, listens to, and speaks from. Elbow (1998) describes writing with voice as writing into which someone has breathed. Voice, for him, has nothing to do with the words on the page, only with the relationship of the words to the writer. The words contain not just an explicit message, "the sun glints down a pathway of ripples," but also some kind of implicit message about the condition of the writer (p. 299).

More than speech, a creative writer's voice is distinct, definable, the combination of what you say and how you say it. Voice has as much to do with individual consciousness as it does with the subject of the writing. Who we are determines what we notice, and these things, patterns, ideas, sounds will be apparent in our writing, whether we are conscious of this or not.

Even when the subject is not the self, the self continues to draw individual reality by its perceptions. We write what we notice, and in the process of writing, notice more, discover more. Our own voices become stronger the closer we come to what's critically important to us and what unleashes our own emotions. Voice is strong when images are crystal clear. It becomes weaker the farther we are from the subject, or the more we intellectualize or interpret the subject for ourselves or the reader. Voice also has to do with acts of mind—the questioning, sifting, and connecting process of thought. This is different from experience because it has to do with the process of thinking.

Student teachers, once they start reflecting on personal history, demonstrate use of the two related senses of voice, the naming of oneself and the naming of the world. This prepares them to work with young learners to do the same. For example, one student teacher wrote:

> I think family is really important. I have always felt a kind of responsibility, as the oldest ... My parents are really reasonable people. My dad lets me explore my aspirations. He has given me everything. He has been so selfless my whole life, raising us, just being there for us, facilitating our education, letting us do things we wanted to do, and letting me travel. I feel like I have to give back and show that to my siblings. So, it's not only to my parents but also to be respectful to [my siblings]. I really believe that they are individuals and even though they are my little brothers and sisters, I don't have authority over them. I think I do have a little bit of authority. There's an exchange. Just like a teacher has authority. It's not something you use to your advantage. It's there so, hopefully, you are a role model and you a mode of support. You give advice when they need it and vice versa ...

On the other hand, she noted that there can be huge variations in the type of family lives and experiences of new refugee and immigrant students.

> I worked with Somalian refugee children when I was in high school. They had very little support and their lives were very difficult. They had post traumatic stress from the war. I mean, that's a lot and I can't imagine how loaded that must be for them.

Connecting to and writing from one's own voice requires an environment that nurtures the self. A writer must be able to listen and write without immediate judgment, and then afterward bring her or his knowledge of craft to bear on the material. The feedback of others is necessary in this endeavor. Literary friendship and support in the classroom create a kind of "free space" necessary for risk-taking writing in one's true voice.

It has been found that children, with encouragement and acceptance, do gain self-confidence to do their own reading and writing. They will voice their own reality in terms of culture, social issues, and cognitive development when it is valued as a sharing of knowledge (Quintero, 2004). Teachers can create classroom contexts in which all students can use their voices to affirm their social contexts and to create new situations for themselves through writing. The work of Donald Graves (1994) and his colleagues suggests that three conditions are necessary for children to make progress as writers. First, they must be allowed and encouraged to write on topics they really care about, with the expectation that their work will be read seriously for its content. After all, why should they sustain the effort of writing and revising if they are not personally involved with their topics or do not expect to be read? Second, there is a developmental aspect to writing growth. Children need time and frequent practice to get better at writing. Third, children need sensitive guidance from adults to become good writers.

In cases with young children, a problem-posing approach can enrich and keep the student-centered integrity and provide the scaffolding needed for younger learners. This methodology, with its strong theoretical and philosophical underpinnings, encourages teachers not to limit their teaching to units and lesson plans. It encourages teachers to use as a point of departure the background funds of knowledge the children bring from their lived experience rather than from a written form of normalization. The method encourages integration of the community funds of knowledge, language, and culture with the standard school curricula.

Of course, in order to write, children must read. It is from literature that children can learn how to write, but only if the thinking implicit in the literature and the language strategies used are made clear to them by an insightful teacher. The thinking encouraged by the literature must be related to the children's lives, cultural contexts of their communities, and to the lives of other students around the globe. It is from the words of others that children can learn about the possible worlds they can construct through writing. It is the combination of reading, writing, and personal choice that makes problem-posing effective.

The literacy endeavor in children's writing involves both individual transformations and transformations in context of various groups of people. If we want to encourage children to use language to create new images for themselves in cultural contexts, we need to know how to guide children's voices through reading and writing in expressive genres like fiction, poetry, and creative non-fiction. We can teach children to be attuned to the voices of the writers they read and to listen with new ears to their own lives.

Critical Literacy with Two- and Three-Year-Olds: Activism?

A student teacher, experienced in working with young children and herself a member of an ethnic minority group, had a full slate of learnings from a placement in an Early Head Start program. She wrote:

> Throughout the course of the term I have realized the power of observation as a pre-service teacher whose ultimate goals are to become an autobiographer, citizen, researcher, and educator like of Lucy Sprague Mitchell. A poignant moment during my new found commitment occurred about three weeks ago downtown. Below is an entry from my journal describing that day.
>
> The Early Head Start is located deep in the government housing projects of the Lower East Side and just steps away from tenement houses of the densely populated sub-culture of Chinatown. When I walked into the classroom there were ten Asian toddlers, one African American, two Hispanics (one was the teacher), and one White. What did I discover about schools' environments? They are a microcosm of the neighborhood. These systems make up the society in which children must live and learn.

This environment caused her to immediately reflect upon her own background:

Unfortunately [sic], I have received my education in highly different settings. At my boarding school in Princeton, we were accused of being in a utopian society. Children were handpicked and selected for reasons of alumni legacy, ability to privately pay for the exorbitant cost of tuition, and, for minorities like me, to diversify the elite setting and become symbols of tokenism in a way. We were isolated from the rest of the world while delving into Physics, Art Foundations, and British Novels. Our Headmaster, Board of Trustees, and developers of the Alumni Support System (purely financial) would have argued that education was the equalizing factor in this setting and what is more real than a white upper class girl from Berkeley and an inner-city kid from Brooklyn (me) sitting around a table?

In observing this Early Head Start program, I realized that my high school did not reflect the tensions and struggles of managing a classroom where the kids are closely tied to and are products of their neighborhoods. Although trite: To understand the students one must understand almost every aspect of where they are coming from. Additionally, to sustain copasetic race and race relations, they cannot be taboo in the classroom.

The first day I arrived, the classroom was divided. All of the Asian children were playing with dough at a table with an Asian grandfather volunteer. The other three children were scattered around the room participating in singular activities. When O., the African American, came over to the table and started to take some dough, one Asian child, N., pushed his hand back and said "NO! DON'T LIKE IT! O. hit him back then slumped away in what seemed to be an ongoing frustration with not understanding N.'s negative response to him participating in the same activity.

I talked to the director of the program later in the day; she revealed that there is an issue with the parents and thus the children of Asian descent with using the same exact phrase. For some reason it has become part of their English vernacular, and has been disruptive in the classroom particularly surrounding race relations.

With children of this age (two and three), they already notice differences between themselves and others and associate whatever negative attachments their parents have with those different people from themselves and bring these ideas into the classroom. What puzzled me was the teacher's inadequate response. She put both O. and N. in separate corners, a metaphor for what happens downtown.

In my opinion, there should be something done in and about the classroom. Of course, I am not promoting the creation of a utopian society. From experience and readings of Beverly Tatum, I know that this does not work. The classroom should reflect the neighborhoods in which the children come from and live. However, it should be in the form of learning, exploring, and creating a dialogue surrounding these issues and not confirming them. I realized that education is an easier concrete form for social change in the midst of political and economic inequalities.

The story of N. and O. raised a significant question to me as I embark on teaching. What kind of framework could be employed in the classroom (and learning environments of a larger variety) to equalize, engage, and then create a democratic setting to promote critical thinkers and life long learners as to sustain individual, familial, and social awareness? (citizen).

My answer came at ten o'clock that morning, the start time of the music circle. Although, the teacher played generic songs like "Twinkle, Twinkle, Little Star" and "The Wheels on the Bus," the music brought N. and O. out of the corners and onto the rug to actively participate together in listening, singing, and dancing to the tunes. I thought about what music could mean in teaching children about deeper issues at such a critical juncture in their life.

Much research has shown that children under the age of six are more open, accepting, and sensitive to the differences of themselves and others if positively reinforced. If children are exposed to an active understanding of their own identity, family identity, and their place in the classroom, they can appreciate this same phenomenon in others and their found "whole" knowledge can transcend time and be translated to their adult social/societal perceptions. In simply observing, I stumbled across the significance in early childhood education to learn about culture—to combat against cultural ignorance and civic apathy—and, on music as an active framework in which to do it.

Consequently, this student teacher embarked on research for her problem-posing curriculum assignment so that she could use critical literacy and promote agency among the children. She found that some programs in Hawaii are bringing together issues of advocacy, culture, and language under an umbrella of music education. Her study of programs in Hawaii confirmed that teachers can provide diverse learning experiences to children through the unique and positive experience of music. But the teachers cannot and should not do this alone. Cooperation between parents, students, and teachers is needed to understand the complex history of culture. Culture involves the way people dress, the language they speak, the foods they eat, and the music they listen to. On a deeper level, however, culture also includes such things as patterns of emotions, ways of interacting with others, conceptions of time and space, gender roles, and childrearing practices.

Critical Literacy in Action—Artful Story as a Frame for Activist Work

Case Study Twenty-One

A student teacher led first graders in a study of famous people from a historical, artistic, and human rights standpoint, while focusing on all aspects of balanced literacy. The children were learning about historically important activists while being activists in their own participation of balanced literacy. The lesson began with the storybook *Diego* by Jeanette Winter.

Listening:

The student teacher asked the children to think about something they really like to do and do well. She asked questions such as When do you do this activity and how did you learn to do it? Then she read the book *Diego* (Winter, 1994).

Dialogue:

They then discussed the activities that Diego did and how he expressed himself through art. The student teacher then asked children what ways do they prefer to express themselves?

Action:

The student teacher and the children created a Diego Bulletin Board. On this bulletin board the children constantly contributed ideas (mirroring the chalkboard walls in the story). During Writing Workshop the children wrote about what they had drawn. They had a poetry writing activity, "Where Am I From?/Where's My Family From?" which involved the children in writing list poems based upon their own lives.

Encyclopedias, magazines, and websites were provided so that the children could investigate art history and history books to learn about context in which Diego Rivera lived and worked. Two of the class's research questions were Why was his hero Zapata? Why are his murals in various national buildings in Mexico City considered a national treasure?

The student teacher noted in an evaluative reflection:

> I learned a lot about young children's learning by doing a lesson like this one with such young learners. Firstly, I learned new facts as the children were doing their "research" but more importantly, this made me think about how intelligent children are and how so many people underestimate children and their abilities.

Case Study Twenty-Two

A teacher of a dual language pre-K class led her preschoolers in a mini-study of the Chicana activist and author Sandra Cisneros. This teacher believes that four-year-olds can make the connection between identity, family loyalty, and activism on their developmental level of understanding when activities are appropriate.

Listening:

The teacher brought the preschoolers to the rug and explained what a memoir is—a personal/family story. Then she read *Hairs/Pelitos* by Sandra Cisneros (1997) in both English and Spanish.

Dialogue:

As they discussed the story, the students were able to tell her that *Pelitos/Hairs* was more than just about hair. It was about Sandra's love for her mother and her feeling of safety when with her. The teacher then showed them other works by Sandra Cisneros, *House on Mango Street* (1984) and *Caramelo: Or Pure Cuento: A Novel* (2002). She showed them that she was reading a book by an author that they could read too.

Action:

The teacher had arranged materials so that the students could break up into groups for writing, independent reading, sketching, or language. The language group was any of the students who wanted to read with her on the rug in Spanish. She had a group of five students and they took turns reading *Pelitos/Hairs* (1997) in Spanish and then paraphrasing the meaning. The following day the class did a Readers Theater using *Hairs/Pelitos*.

Case Study Twenty-Three

A student teacher of a preschool class in a diverse, inner-city public school planned her problem-posing around the developmentally appropriate content outlined by the National Association for the Education of Young Children (NAEYC) that she felt was deeply related to critical literacy as activism for young children. These points are as follows:

- The content and desired outcomes are meaningful and important to children's current well-being and later learning.
- Early learning standards are not merely scaled-back versions of standards for older children. Instead, the standards are based on research about the processes, sequences, and long-term outcomes of early learning and development.
- Standards recognize and accommodate variations in children's cultures, languages, communities, and individual characteristics, abilities, and disabilities. This flexibility supports positive outcomes for all children.

She reported:

In my observations I documented important details about the context of the classroom. First of all, language has a rich and accommodating presence. The wall displays, the charts, word walls, and interactive bulletin boards are prominent and carefully arranged at children's eye level. I found that my cooperating teacher refers to them everyday. Each display demonstrates a clear purpose and includes both illustration and written language. Other signs in the room offer directions for certain tasks. On the first day of school, the children received morning jobs that include signing in and answering the question of the day, among others. By the end of the first week, my cooperating teacher placed the Morning Jobs sign on the first table. The directions are numbered with a brief imperative sentence and an illustration. Another sign reminds the children of the steps for using the computer. It has fewer words and bigger pictures. Again, these signs challenge multiple domains.

As emergent readers and writers, the illustrations are the first symbols that the children understand. They give information and communicate messages to the children. With exposure and practice, letters and words will become more and more recognizable. The illustrations, therefore, lay a foundation for written language.

Based on what I have learned about the students in my classroom and developmentally appropriate guidelines, I have developed a series of problem-posing activities that will build on the children's knowledge and understanding of their surroundings. I want to explore with the children the role that signs play in their everyday lives. Through my observations, I know that the children recognize symbols to gather information, and that they use various tools, pencils, crayons, markers, fingers, and hands, to make images that give their information. My plans incorporate literacy, math, social studies, and art.

Day One

Listening:

She asked children to listen to *The Signs I See on the Way to K-108* by Jackie Brechbill.

This sign tells me where to go in. (Subway—*words*)
This sign tells me where to go out. (Exit—*words*)
This sign tells me when to walk. (Walking man—*picture*)
This sign tells me when to stop. (Red hand—*picture*)
This sign tells me the name of the park. (Washington Square Park—*words*)
This sign tells me the rules of the park. (No bikes, etc.—*pictures*)
This sign tells me my location. (Street sign, name of boy in class—*words*)
This sign tells me that I found my way. (*Welcome to K-108 words*)

The student teacher explained:

In constructing this book, my goal was to make the content more relevant for the children. First, they will recognize my name and realize that an author is not someone far away with no face. Anyone can be an author, including them. Second, I used real photographs in the book. The pictures were taken at the angle from which the children see, low to the ground. Finally, I was sure to use some pictures that the children were sure to recognize. For instance, the "Welcome to K-108" sign concludes the book by "telling me that I found my way." Authenticity will make the experience more meaningful. I also included page numbers.

Dialogue:

Then they discussed what they saw. They discussed what signs are, why they are used, and where they are seen. They talked about how some signs use pictures and some use words, how signs are used to give us information, give us directions, and keep us safe. The children added their own thoughts. It is possible to identify the different shapes and colors that are used for signs. They talked about the use of size in signs. Some signs are very big with big words and/or pictures because they have a very important message, like STOP. Other signs use smaller words because they need to give a lot of information, like parking signs.

Action:

They walked around the block to look for the signs used around the school. When they returned to the classroom, the children had the opportunity to draw what they saw and share their artwork with the class. They displayed the work and made some tally charts of how many children saw a stop sign and how many signs were made with a rectangle. Also, they made a Venn diagram of how many signs that they saw used pictures, how many used words, and how many used both.

Day Two

Listening:
They listened again to *The Signs I See on the Way to K-108* by Jackie Brechbill.

Dialogue:
They discussed what they remembered regarding the signs from the walk. Then the student teacher asked the children whether they recognized any signs from inside the school building. They discussed the purpose for signs in the school and in the classroom.

Action:
They explored the classroom to look for signs. When the children identified a sign, the student teacher asked for the purpose. Some children read the words on the signs and others read the pictures. The children were free to explore in groups, alone, or with adults in the room. After some time, they counted how many signs were in the classroom. They also noted and counted the places in the classroom where adding a sign might be helpful. Again, the children had time to create their own ideas about signs.

Day Three

Dialogue:
They talked about the book and how they saw different signs inside and out-side of the classroom and school. The student teacher asked the children whether they wanted to make books for the classroom about the signs they saw. She told them that each of them could add one sign to the book.

Action:
First, the student teacher asked the children to bring her the pictures from what they saw on the walk around the neighborhood. Meanwhile, she put together a Big Book that included the signs they saw around the school, in the school, and in the classroom. She called the children over to help her enter one of their drawings in the book. Each child had one entry and helped the student teacher figure out how to fit their sign in the right category and space.

Listening:
Together, they read their new book.

The student teacher reported about the series of problem-posing activities:

> I could see that it was good to build on the strengths of the students who I was planning by including using pictures as cues for gathering information, following directions, and making predictions. They recognize some symbols in language such as exclamation, question and quotation marks and know their purpose. They can identify simple patterns in colors and words. They express awareness of their surroundings, use social skills to articulate thoughts and feelings, and use art and their bodies to communicate early language and literacy skills.

This action became transformative for the children through their own developing literacy.

Case Study Twenty-Four

In a Montessori classroom consisting of learners of ages four to six years old, a problem-posing study of the rainforest was done.

Listening:

The teacher read Moira Butterfield's *Amazon Rainforest* (1992) to begin the study and give the children general information about this and an agenda of topics to be studied.

Dialogue:

Then she led a discussion about the book and focused on the Waorani Tribe as she showed photographs and asked children open-ended questions to give the study of the rainforest a human context.

Listening:

After a break of playing outdoors, the teacher read *Who Lives in the Rainforest* by Susan Canizares and Mary Reid (1999) to give the children more information about people living in the rainforest.

Action:

The teacher invited the children to participate in investigations at various child-centered learning stations. One was set up so that the children can create a "rainforest terrarium," another was a water table with rubber and plastic creatures that inhabit rivers and lakes in the rainforest, another was a "healthy" and "unhealthy" sorting activity that consists of pictures of environmentally safe activities and activities that cause pollution, another was a reading and drawing center with many nature magazines and drawing materials, and another was a center to study cocoons and butterflies. Finally, a writing center became the home for the photographs of the Waorani Tribe. The class had been discussing the fact that this tribe does not have a writing system, so this center was set up for children to imagine they were members

of the tribe and were creating their own writing system.
The teacher reported about part of her analysis of the lessons:

> The uniqueness of the multi-age community of the Montessori environment allows the children to help each other communicate and understand one another in the minority language; older children help younger children. Therefore, it is no surprise that there is a strong correlation between social skills and the ability to focus with language learning ability in early childhood. Emotional development and self-control are highly influential on language development. For example, if a child expresses frustration through crying and hitting, rather than using words, other children will be less likely to interact with a child who violates his/her comfort zone. Thus, the child loses potential social interactions that are valuable for his/her language development.

References

Ada, Alma Flor, & Campoy, F. Isabel. (2003). *Authors in the classroom: A transformative education process.* New York: Allyn & Bacon.

Berrigan, D. (1999, October). Address at the Commitment to Peace Conference, St. Paul, MN.

Brechbill, J. (2005). *The signs I see on the way to K-108.* Unpublished manuscript. New York.

Brown, M. (1998). *Arthur makes the team.* New York: Little Brown Young Readers.

Butterfield, M. (1992). *Amazon rainforest.* New York: Ideals Publications.

Canizares, S., & Reid, M. (1999). *Who lives in the rainforest?* Markham, ON: Scholastic.

Casey, K. (1993). *I answer with my life: Life histories of women teachers working for social change.* New York: Routledge.

Cisneros, S. (1984). *House on Mango Street.* New York: Vintage Books.

Cisneros, S. (1997). *Hairs/Pelitos.* New York: Dragonfly Books.

Cisneros, S. (2002). *Caramelo: Or Pure Cuento: A novel.* New York: Alfred A. Knopf.

Danneberg, J. (2000). *First day jitters.* New York: Charlesbridge Publishing.

Elbow, P. (1998). *Writing without teachers.* New York: Oxford University Press.

Freire, P. (1998). *Pedagogy of freedom: Ethics, democracy, and civic courage.* New York: Rowman & Littlefield.

Graves, D. (1994). *A fresh look at writing.* Portsmouth, NH: Heinemann.

Greene, M. (1992). Imagination and breakthroughs in the unexpected. Unpublished paper presented to the Association of Supervision and Curriculum Development. New Orleans.

Quintero, Elizabeth P. (2009). Young children and story: The path to transformative action. In S. Steinberg (Ed.), *Diversity: A reader.* New York: Peter Lang.

Quintero, Elizabeth P. (2004). *Problem-posing with multicultural children's literature: Developing critical early childhood curricula.* New York: Peter Lang.

Rosen, M. (2006). Lecture. Star School, Newham, England.

Rummel, M.K. & Quintero, E.P. (1997). Teachers' reading/teachers' lives. Albany, NY: SUNY Press.

Walsh, Ellen S. (1995). *Mouse count.* New York: Voyager Books.

Winter, J. (1994). *Diego.* New York: Alfred A. Knopf.

CHAPTER EIGHT
Artful Story: Context for Complex Harmony

I realized… that I am living in a time that has no driving social framework for a greater good. There are many, many disparate notions about how to make a better world, but theses are just so many voices singing a thousand songs in different keys, registers, and styles—a choir of Bedlam. (Mosley, 2006, p. 16)

Complicated Conversations—Artful Story Findings
Findings reveal the myriad of ways that critical literacy and artful story connect learning, teaching, integrated curriculum, and promote social justice. In the complicated contexts of 21st century histories, cultures, politics, and institutions—including schools—critical literacy has potential to provide the harmony for the thousand songs that Mosley (2006) mentions. There is potential for our learning from each other's songs.

Issues of early childhood literacy and learning, cultural and historical relevance, and the arts as curriculum facilitators and as manifestations of critical literacy were all addressed through the layers of story in this research study. Findings fell into categories identified from critical theory: (1) inclusion of participant personal historical and cultural frame, (2) multiple sources of knowledge through literacies, and (3) transformative action.

Does Participation by All Really Mean All?
If we believe this, how do we do it? Much research documents that preschool education is beneficial to all children across all economic backgrounds, although children whose parents have the least formal education and lowest incomes appear to benefit most (Barnett, 1995, 2001; Schweinhart, Barnes, Weikart, Barnett & Epstein, 1993). But this research seems to often be used to promote programs that try to push the schools' models of learning on families. Many dollars have been spent planning and implementing programs that push educators to design ways for parents to "help" the children do school work at home. This schoolwork is designed according to unending contributions of standards and guidelines, but rarely takes into account the knowledge and aspirations of the families. The subtle, or not-so-subtle, message is, if only those parents would speak like people in schools speak, and if only those families would think like people in schools think. If they would just value the same types of books and learning activities as people value in

the schools, and then spend an hour or so each night working on these things with their children, then we would have more successful students and fewer problems with the infernal "achievement gap!" But, if we honestly critically analyze those assumptions, it is clear that we are not really accepting of all participants' histories, cultures, and background knowledge. Are we tired of learning ourselves? Are we afraid of admitting that we educators have much to learn from people who have lived their lives in different ways in different places?

My contention and my intention for sharing some of the stories of hope has been to show committed and risk-taking early childhood teachers implementing practice that really does value where families and children come from and the knowledge they bring with them. And purposefully I present these glimpses in their "raw" form of student teacher lesson plans and reflections to show the importance of always revisiting all learning with a critical eye. In the words of educator and activist Bill Ayers, we have to have "hope" and we have to "doubt." He was talking about political leaders. I am talking about educators. I would like to believe these are important words for all of us.

A student teacher who has been working for many years as an assistant teacher in a state-funded preschool in Southern California read *Funds of Knowledge* (Moll, Gonzalez & Amanti, 2005) and was moved by the stories. She wrote some reflections about the book and made some connections to her own life and the lives of the children and families she works with:

> I thought that this book makes an excellent point about how we perceive our Latino families and culture. We are obviously interpreting things wrong. This comment, "the harder their lives, the more coping and survival skills they develop," really hit home for me because I grew up in a family of six with a single mother. I believe that my experiences growing up at times were extremely difficult and at the same time they have really taught me to strategize and be very resourceful.
>
> Why would it be any different for a Latino, African American, or Asian home? I strongly believe that we learn more in difficult challenges than we do when the answers are already supplied for us. This is not to say that all of us should suffer or struggle, but maybe it teaches us to be more accepting, charitable, and kind.
>
> One thing to keep in mind is that difficult socio-economic times can and most often do lead to devious behaviors. Take the example of a child growing up with parents and siblings who are very hungry, they may begin to steal food to feed themselves only later to learn that they can get away with just taking things as opposed to paying for them. I believe this to be an example for many poor families. My own brothers used to steal food when I was young…then one day after seeing the behavior, I tried my hand at it. Fortunately for me, my sister marched me back up to the store manager and made me return the item. I cried all the way home! But my point is that when people struggle financially they may understandably find it very difficult to remain honest and may even seek out ways to make life easier. I think this is why

many people of color take a bad rap. First they are suppressed, then forced into inner-city slums and fed the scraps, which only sends the message that that is all they are worth. They feel cheated and hunger for more, more of which they deserve—so, they rebel against society by taking what they feel they have a right to. Essentially, they take the easiest road they know in order to survive.

She then related the information about participants in the book *Funds of Knowledge* (Moll, Gonzalez & Amanti, 2005) to her home visits connected to her work responsibilities.

It is funny that I should read this after I had completed six home visits today. So many things were running through my head. My co-teacher speaking to the parents in Spanish was only one of the things I was trying to decipher. I sat there half paying attention to what was being said and the other half scoping out the environment and the interactions that were occurring. In the book, Gonzales reported that *educacion* is often explained in Spanish-speaking communities as a cultural concept that encompasses academic learning and nonacademic moral training such as learning the difference between right and wrong, respect for adults, and good manners. (p. 172)

If this is true then these families that I visited today have one heck of an education. I noticed in almost all of the homes we visited that the young children, of all ages present, were encouraged to shake our hand and they did without hesitation, regardless of their demeanor. The children were well behaved and greeted us with smiles and eye contact. The adults were all involved in the conversations taking place about the child whether it was a parent, an uncle, or grandmother; they all had some input. It was apparent that they all had close bonds with each other as well as with the children.

She then realized,

Imagine what message is sent if a teacher came to your home to teach you something—say, how to teach your children to behave. How insulting.

Then she mentioned the situation of another family, her first reaction, and then her epiphany after being with the family for a very few minutes.

Another home that we visited was actually a room behind another house. As I lay my eyes on the 12 x 12 room converted into a bedroom, kitchen, living room, and dining room I was heartbroken that anyone should live this way. However, upon reflection I can see that this family of four has much more than I do. You could see the bonds, adaptability, generosity, perseverance, and the eagerness of the parents to want more for their children and themselves. I think they have a wealth of funds of knowledge right inside their 12 x 12 walls.

There have been many examples throughout this book, but one more seems important to mention emphasizing the importance of this type of perspective taking about multiple sources of knowledge and authentic practice in our 21st century world. Once in a great while, I meet future teachers who say to me that it may be philosophically important for us to study people, knowledge bases, and histories from all over the world, but it isn't necessary in a practical sense because they will never move from their communities where they currently live and work. Well, not only does that belief sound almost unbelievable in our modern, mobile times, but I find myself pointing out how migrating people come to us, in the most unexpected places and ways, in our schools and communities. In Minnesota and Wisconsin, both urban and rural schools I worked with had many newcomers from Southeast Asia, the Balkans, and many different countries in Africa.

In communities in Southern California, there have been migrating families from Mexico and Central America for decades. The agricultural opportunities and the families of natives from those areas who came before have brought a continual group of newcomers. Within the group of people coming from Mexico, is a large, close-knit, indigenous group of families from Oaxaca, Mexico. The Mixtecs are indigenous inhabitants of southern Mexico whose language and culture pre-date the Spanish Conquest by hundreds of years. There are an estimated 500,000 Mixteco speakers today, almost one-fifth of whom live in the United States for at least part of their lives.

Today, soil erosion has left the Mixteca region in Mexico one of the most geographically devastated in the world. It is estimated that current Mixtec societies in Mexico are able to grow only 20% of the food they need to sustain their populations. The only option for thousands of Mixtecs is migration to other parts of Mexico and the United States. Money sent home from this out-migration sustains remaining Mixtec communities.

Mixtec language and culture are as different from Spanish/Mestizo Mexico as Navajo is from English. Beliefs about health, religion, and family include many traditional concepts, and are often at odds with "Western" concepts. Along with other indigenous cultures such as Trique, Amuzgo, Mixe, and P'urépecha, the Mixtec's unique language, art, and culture are in danger of being lost forever.

At the same time that Mixtecs were being forced to leave their land, the agricultural industry in the United States was searching for new cheap labor sources. The Bracero Program (started in 1942 to cover World War II labor shortages) brought the first significant number of indigenous Mexicans to the United States. Their numbers expanded greatly in the 1970s and 1980s, when many indigenous families were able to regularize their status through the 1986 Immigration and Reform Act. Mixtecs are concentrated in the most labor-intensive agricultural areas—areas that grow crops such as berries, tomatoes and grapes, stone fruit, citrus, and cut flowers.

Many of the immigrant families who arrived in the 1970s and 1980s raised their families here—with children now in college or successfully employed. Many have become U.S. citizens (Fox & Rivera-Salgado, 2004). Not only is the Mixtec community exemplary of an ancient culture with a rich history comparable to other indigenous groups in North America, but also their modern migrations on this continent in these complicated times illustrates the breadth and depth of our task as educators in valuing and learning from all participants.

However, there are stark barriers for many of the Mixtec people living in California. Many are illiterate, and most speak neither Spanish nor English, but only their native language, Mixteco. As a result, they face exploitation and discrimination in labor, housing, and everyday life. Most live in extreme poverty and lack basic provisions such as adequate housing, food, clothing, and other necessities of life. Central to their struggle is the fact that they cannot communicate with people beyond their own indigenous community, thus impeding their ability to obtain appropriate health care, educate themselves and their children, negotiate with their employers to improve their work situation, and exercise their basic civil rights (Wright, 2005).

Using Multiple Sources of Knowledge in Times of Accountability

Given the array of variation in histories, cultures, and languages represented by children in early childhood programs, there appears huge potential for multiple sources of knowledge and information. Many researchers (Cairney, 2002; Makin, 2003) have shown that early success with literacy learning depends on the degree of congruence between home and school reading and writing activities. And early literacy development is affected positively when the school literacy curriculum is aligned with children's reading and writing interests and out-of-school experiences (Alloway, 1997).

There are many resources describing how this can be achieved, including position statements from professional organizations such as the National Association for the Education of Young Children (NAEYC), the International Reading Association (IRA), the National Association for Bilingual Education, and others. There are position statements about the specific concept and content development and learning in mathematics, for example, from the National Council of Teachers of Mathematics, the arts, the sciences, for learners with special needs, and so on. And there are State and District Standards and Guidelines and Competencies in virtually every learning context. There are so many guidelines. What is a responsible educator to do? How is it possible to incorporate all these important guidelines and activities into the few hours we have with children in our programs? And more important, how is the critical educator able to connect these standards and recommendations for learning to the children's learning contexts in their homes?

We have seen teachers and student teachers developing, under a framework of critical theory and critical literacy, theoretically based content-learning experiences for children with the help of the professional standards from a variety of sources. And most importantly we have seen teachers and student teachers "tune in" to the children and their families and build upon their strengths, never lessening their responsibility to provide opportunities for building strong academic foundations for future educational success.

Years ago in a bilingual family literacy class in El Paso, Texas, participant teachers and I realized that several of the parents of the children had had years of experience working in cotton fields. We talked with them at length and convinced them that they would be the best teachers to come and demonstrate and explain the life cycle of the cotton plant, from seed to harvest. They taught and demonstrated and answered children's questions. We supported them with some literacy activities to extend the learning that they generated. The woman who led the section of learning about plants in our curriculum was a mother of two children who had never had the opportunity to go to school or become literate—ever. She told us at one point that this school building was the first she had ever entered. She and some of the other parents who had extensive knowledge about medicinal plants had become a treasured part of our curriculum. They had and were happy to share their multiple sources of knowledge.

I remember those knowledgeable participants when I observe the Mixtec participants. I listened to a man, one of the community organizers, talk about why so many of his people have had to leave their homeland. He explained that twenty thousand indigenous Oaxacan people from southern Mexico live and work in Southern California. He explained that the introduction by the Europeans of hoofed animals and the plow centuries ago disrupted the delicate environmental balance of the area of his homeland. Over decades, soil erosion of the ancestral farmlands of the Mixteca region had destroyed their ability to sustain themselves. Economic necessity has drawn Mixtecs to California in search of agricultural work. He spoke with such passion, information, and understanding of the connections among the science of sustainable agriculture and the way land is managed that I thought here is a man representing a community that really understands the consequences of mismanaging natural resources. What a teacher for us all.

A student teacher working in this part of California, in a program serving some families from the Mixtec community, wrote a reflection after discussing the *Funds of Knowledge* (Moll, Gonzalez & Amanti, 2005) book and the book by Fox and Rivera-Salgado (2004). She had been thinking about how to include multiple sources of knowledge in curricula and what she had been learning from the educators in the *Funds of Knowledge* book. She is a critical questioner:

> Something else just came to mind. I understand that we shouldn't present culture in a neat package and that we should promote individuality. In a previous chapter one boy sold candy and the mother would make it. The teacher did a thematic unit using the funds of knowledge of the individual. How is it then that you incorporate "all" of the individuals, without grouping, funds of knowledge? No child should be left out. Also, researchers are only interviewing a few children's families. How could it be possible to incorporate individuality based on a few families? Maybe, the questionnaires may help but then you miss out on all the information in each home.

She is thinking and doubting. This is good.

> For preschool at my program, we do a home visit (15–20) minutes for each family. I most certainly will be having more earthy conversations to see what I can learn about each family and will create a questionnaire to learn more about each family that we serve. I know that in order to learn more extensive information we would need many more visits, but you do what you can do. I feel that it is a good point that we should incorporate each family's "funds of knowledge" throughout the curricular year, not just in our multicultural month.

The student teacher went on:

> Of course, as Moll and his colleagues said, this process—of developing curricula based on knowledge—is the reverse of the typical Anglocentric curriculum developed by education specialists usually located far away spatially and conceptually, from the classroom.
>
> What comes to mind when I read this is one of the main reasons that I have chosen not to teach in elementary grades. Someone else is writing the curriculum that is especially distant from the children in your classroom. I think that for any teacher it might be the case that teaching to a standard that is not all inclusive and constructed with an illegitimate cultural basis is not the way children learn best.
>
> It is the freedom to explore curricula with no constraint on the human mind that gives way to new knowledge and the discoveries of enhanced creativity. If we teach to a standard that excludes a minority, how can we tap into the funds of knowledge? You can't! ... However, it is in our makeup to create and we are curious by nature and that leads to discovery. We cannot provide the answers to questions— children must go through a process of discovery to find answers in order for the information to be learned. Standards put the stamp on dittos, which stifle learning and replace the human spirit with conformed ideas that are implanted by rote memorization. Critical thinking is required on the children's part in all areas of learning.
>
> Furthermore, physical and cognitive development must match the required task through a process as well in order for the task to be obtained. The standards, many times, require children to complete certain tasks before they are physically and cognitively ready.

On a more positive note about how this teacher can use Moll and his colleagues' ideas about *Funds of Knowledge* comes from her reflections on the chapter about parent participation.

> I plan to share this chapter with my co-workers. I believe that if we choose just two or three families out of the twenty home visits, then we can interview in more depth with the intent of gaining some funds of knowledge to begin our year with. We do tap into these funds on occasion, but not like the book describes. We use their funds periodically and they are small parts as opposed to the whole picture of a family's culture, work, religion, and way of life.

Another one of the teacher participants in the study from this area of the country began to tell stories about one parent, or one elder, or one uncle, from the Mixtec people who had come into a classroom to tell children about cooking a certain form of masa (corn-based pastry) or specific flowers that have special meaning at certain seasons of the year.

Another participant, who works as a home-based Head Start teacher, spoke about the intergenerational linguistic strengths of children who had been in the United States for several years and learned to use Spanish and English while maintaining the native Mixtec language in the home. The examples she gave, and the opinions she'd developed, seemed to point to a cadre of family members/young adults who were not only linguistic experts, but also cultural brokers helping to bridge some of the differences in cultural practices and childrearing techniques.

Many Ways to Encourage Transformative Action
A teacher education student who had read the *Funds of Knowledge* (Moll, Gonzalez & Amanti, 2005) book wrote:

> The teacher in the book believed poverty was root of problems and was too big for her to change. My initial response: What is the problem? I remembered that many of these children were English Language Learners and their struggle was not within them, but with the "White man's social system"—it is really a form of oppression.

This led to a huge discussion in the university class about what she meant by "White man's social system," and to an even deeper discussion of what kinds of actions are currently being done both inside and outside the classrooms that can be transformative for families and children.

One example comes from an activist community working with the Mixtec people mentioned previously. They, the activists from the native community and the community at large, have formed a non-governmental organization called MICOP (Mixteco/Indigena Community Organizing Project). MICOP was founded in 2001 to address the pressing concerns of

Ventura County's most vulnerable and marginalized residents: indigenous farm workers from the southern Mexican state of Oaxaca.

MICOP's work is aiding Mixtecs to draw on their community strengths and overcome existing barriers. The communal tradition of "tequio," or community obligation, promotes a spirit of mutual assistance and community building.

MICOP is comprised of English-, Spanish-, and Mixteco-speaking people who have come together to empower and help improve the health and well-being of indigenous Oaxacans in the county. They mentor leaders, train promotores de salud, or health care outreach workers, and work to organize local Mixtecs to develop a collective voice for advocacy and action. Members of the Mixtec community serve on the Board of Directors and take an active role in all activities.

MICOP collaborates on celebrations of cultural traditions such as Día de los Muertos (Day of the Dead), Día del Niño (Children's Day), Guelaguetza (regional dance festival celebrating all indigenous groups), and Fiesta Navideña (Christmas) to build community strength and pride, and to add richness and diversity of all life in Southern California. The focal point of MICOP's work is monthly community meetings designed to build a sense of community and self-sufficiency among the county's Mixtec population, while helping Mixtecs access health care and educational and social services. Each meeting features an educational presentation, plus a traditional Oaxacan meal prepared by community members. In addition, food, clothing, disposable diapers, health care items, and other necessities are distributed free of charge to approximately 200 families per month.

Another form of important transformative action is the necessity of educators taking care of themselves in order to maintain both physical and emotional health for the struggles that are ongoing. In previous research (Rummel & Quintero, 1997) we documented the importance of nurturance of self for teachers. I have come to see this nurturance as necessary inspiration that becomes transformative in the professional and personal lives of teachers.

One student teacher in this current study, after reflecting on *Funds of Knowledge* and how it relates to her work, wrote:

> After reading and reflecting on Chapter 11 and my previous writings I realize that as an educator of children that it is sometimes easy to get excited or discouraged. Chapter 11 shares a series of interviews of the teachers that participated in the funds of knowledge project. They all learned something extraordinary either about the families or themselves. One teacher realized how she was prejudging her children in her classroom until her first home visit. The visit made her realize just how difficult life could be and that the mother, with her many tasks of taking care of her other

four children and her husband, really did not have time to read to her child. It was not that she didn't want to, but she was truly too busy.

I can associate with this teacher. I remember my initial thoughts when I first came to work with the children and their families in the community where I work. I can remember thinking, "Why do they keep having babies if they cannot care for the ones they have?" I have come to understand a great deal about the families, their religions, their values, and even some about their cultures through the years. When people around me make those kinds of comments I try to remember that it took me years to understand. As an educator of small children I have to say that I can see the importance of relationships and trust with the families. How can you help a family if they do not trust you? The funds of knowledge project taught me what I already knew deep inside. I think it just takes reminding so that I do not become complacent in my work. What I do is "Heart Work." I have an obligation as a teacher, an advocate for children and as a human being, to make the best effort I have to educate others about the importance of family in the educational system, how children need to be valued as individuals, how children learn best when there is meaning to what they are experiencing and that children are competent learners.

In my previous readings I felt more excited and when I read them again I became a little discouraged at my lack of action. I know it is because I just started back to school and I am trying to get in the groove of things, but that is only part of the reason. The other reason is fear. I fear my co-workers may not share in my vision. That is something that I will just have to face...now isn't it?

Implications of Study

The findings of this study could be explained in a more general way than by using the specific categories attributed to critical theory and critical literacy. We could say that this ongoing work by participating children, teachers, and families has given us documentation (1) that personal and cultural stories inform learning at the deepest and most meaningful levels, (2) that literacies, in multiple languages and of multiple forms, including intertextual and visual literacy, manifested particularly through the arts, were important pathways to learning, and (3) that participatory learning is multidimensional and has potential to lead to transformative action.

I have seen through the process and content of my research that, in the construction of narratives of experience, there was a relationship between living a life story and telling a life story. There are important implications about how we come to learn to listen to others' life stories. In other words, theory changes in light of different learners and different contexts. This approach to research uses experience as central to theorizing and to understanding practice and, as Clandinin and Connelly (1994) maintain, "For us, keeping experience in the foreground comes about by periodic returns to the works of Dewey (1916, 1936, 1938). For Dewey, education, experience, and life are inextricably intertwined" (p. 5).

The complexity, contradiction, ambiguity, and tension that the reader saw in each participant's contribution and story form the vitality of the information presented here. While the information falls into the educational themes addressed, the different learning experiences don't repeat themselves, but yield information about variations on the themes. As Lather (1994) suggests, I, the researcher, move beyond referential naiveté in a way that doesn't simply collapse the referent, that doesn't dismiss what Cornell West (1990) terms "a reality that one cannot not know" (p. 20). I believe, as Freire (1998) explains, we must consistently try to "diminish the distance between me and the perverse reality of the exploited" (p. 123). Freire goes on to say that we must be passionate about gaining "the knowledge of how to uncover hidden truths and how to demystify farcical ideologies, those seductive traps into which we easily fall" (p. 123).

So, curriculum, theory, and practice are never simple or straightforward. The National Early Literacy Panel (Strickland & Shanahan, 2004) identified that the characteristics of children from birth through age five that are most closely linked to later achievement in literacy are oral language development, phonological/phonemic awareness, alphabetic knowledge, print knowledge, and invented spelling. Researchers also have found that experiences with storybook reading, discussions about books, listening comprehension, and writing are crucial in early literacy development (Bus, Van Ijzendoorn & Pellegrini, 1995). Based on the best research evidence, access to appropriate, high-quality early language and literacy experiences enhances young children's development. The preschool curriculum, therefore, should emphasize a wide range of language and literacy experiences including, but not limited to, story reading, dramatic play, storytelling, and retelling.

However, what many early childhood educators will attest to is that teaching the "whole child" and addressing the complication conversation that is early learning and development are much more than the sum of the parts of the specific strategy recommendations. Considering our findings together, across cases, the potential of critical literacy and story based on learners' lives and interests is illustrated as dynamic, participatory curriculum. Through the process of critical literacy and the human layers of story that result, complex intellectual issues were addressed. The qualitative study has revealed findings of our using problem-posing activities with story and continues the dialogue about integrated curriculum for early childhood and childhood education. Critical literacy in forms of personal story combined with the arts does help children cross metaphorical and literal boundaries. What each child has to say was valued and became a point of departure for learning.

What do we learn from all of this? Humanity is in great flux. Millions of people are migrating by necessity and by choice. Histories are blending. Languages are mixing. Politics are as complicated as ever. Yet, there are some constants. Humans want and need to communicate. Humans do whatever they must to meet their basic needs for themselves and their loved ones. All parents want their children to be educated in ways that will ensure their success in life—whatever direction that life takes. Getting along in times of conflict is difficult, and small steps toward peace are as precious as ever. An important learning from this research into the realm of young children using critical literacy is that they are capable, creative, and passionate about making their world a better place.

I am a teacher educator. I have been doing this work for a long time and have seen the political pendulum swing back and forth several times in my country and in other countries where I have worked. Sometimes one philosophy and teaching method is in favor; then a few years pass, and that philosophy and corresponding teaching method goes out of favor and a new one takes its place. Sometimes politicians and policy makers make grand sweeping mandates that are not based upon research and are not well planned in terms of implementation (No Child Left Behind, for example). However, those of us in the trenches in the classrooms, in the teacher development programs, and in schools and colleges of education have been doing responsible research for years, many years, and we have learned some important constants regarding the learning and teaching of multilingual people who represent a multitude of histories. This requires rethinking the meaning of literacy and certainly the aspects of literacy that make literacy endeavors meaningful. Many literacy scholars today consider literacy events to be much more than decoding words, reading, and writing. Many even believe that the only way to delve into survival is through personal story as an important form of literacy.

Realizing that this stance could easily be seen as social romanticism, I must insist and reiterate what I have seen during my years of working with children and families. I have seen that in circumstances in which philosophies and methods such as those promoted in this book provide opportunities for small, but tangible, steps toward educators' learning to really use and build upon learners' past experiences and sources of knowledge. For example, in the United States, there is a blatant over-politicizing and at the same time grossly superficial treatment of immigration issues, legislation, and information about polity. Yet, when learners (children, youth, or adults) tell and write about their migration and settlement stories, the topic becomes layered with the complex issues that must be discussed and addressed in education, politics, and policy. The learners have very concrete suggestions for policy makers and educators, and many of these professionals are willing to listen and try to implement some ideas brought to the fore by the learners who have experienced upheaval and struggle.

The method of critical literacy encourages students to experience and make conscious the transformations that often occur through the reading of and reflection on literature, academic texts, and other forms of literacy including biographies. This natural outcome is not causal, but our thinking, our understanding of events, and consequently our behavior are influenced by the process. It is always important to keep an open mind regarding what we are all learning, and we must always ask what is really going on here. This is true in terms of policy and politics, and it is true in terms of the multicultural children's literature we use in our classrooms.

Critical literacy lends itself to ongoing scholarly research of teaching and learning. Teachers can and should join the culture of researchers if a new level of educational rigor and quality is ever to be achieved. In such a culture, teacher scholars will begin to understand the power implications of technical standards. In this context they gain heightened awareness of how they can contribute to the research on education. Perhaps learners and scholars can begin to put on the table the reality that all school textbooks are political (Schissler, 2006). As Schissler (2006) says, "A new knowledge frame that is more conducive to the ambiguities and the complexities of the world needs to be developed." Then we may be able to uncover more potential for all participants in the learning contexts, more acceptance of multiple sources of knowledge, and take transformative action in a variety of ways. Just a few suggestions have been presented here. We have a long way to go.

I hope the findings of this study give some concrete specificity to the importance of some very basic underlying tenets of effective learning opportunities and environments for young children. I hope that the philosophical and theoretical underpinnings of critical theory and critical literacy give even more substantive support to work with young children and their families that is based on true mutual respect for the knowledge and history that all learners bring with them throughout their lives. I hope that the documentation of the student teachers, teachers, and children in the examples proves in a variety of ways that authentic academic content can come from many sources and should be dealt with in a variety of ways, always considering the strengths as well as the challenges of the learners. And I hope we can continue to be inspired by the transformative action that all learners can effectively engage in, both in and out of school.

Finally, I would urge us all to follow the children. Even when we are with our children, caring for them day in and day out, sometimes the enormity of the learning that happens while they play escapes us. I maintain that by observing children's use of story (real or imaginary) we can see critical literacy in action.

Years ago, I visited a mother of a four-year-old child in the Head Start classroom where I was participating while I was studying literacy in graduate school. I had developed a nice relationship with the child and I knew she loved to draw and paint, but I had never seen her write any letters or her own name. I asked the mother about what Celi (not her real name) liked to do at home. "Oh, she plays with her older sisters all the time," the mother said. I asked whether they play one specific game or lots of different games. "Oh, almost always they play a pretend school. You know because Celi is the youngest, she likes to pretend that she is doing all the things her big sisters do at school. You know, because she is so little, she can't really do what they do at school, but she likes to pretend." I then turned to the child and asked whether she did writing or reading at this pretend school. "No," she said, "I'm too little." So, I said, "Okay, well … would you take this tablet (the one I had been taking notes on and just pretend to write like you do at 'school' while I finish talking to your mother?" "Okay," she said.

I continued to talk to the mother about family routines and the brothers and sisters for no more than three or four minutes. I looked over at Celi, and she had literally filled the page of the legal-sized tablet with writing. Most of the writing was recognizable as forms of letters of the alphabet. And, right in the exact center she had written CELI GONZALEZ.

Maybe she and her family thought she was "too little" for writing, but through story and transformative action involved in play, she had become a writer.

References
Alloway, N. (1997). Boys and literacy: A framework for working with Boys. In N. Alloway and P. Gilbert (Eds.), *Boys and literacy: Professional development units.* Carlton, Victoria: Curriculum Corporation.

Barnett, W. (1995). Long term effects of early education programs on cognitive and school outcomes, *The Future of Children, 5,* 25–50.

Barnett, W. S. (2001). Preschool education for economically disadvantaged children: Effects on reading achievement and related outcomes. In S. Neuman & D. Dickinson (Eds.), *Handbook of early literacy research,* pp. 421–443. New York: Guilford Press.

Bus, A. G., Van Ijzendoorn, M. H., & Pellegrini, A. D. (1995). Joint book reading makes for success in learning to read: A metanalysis on intergenerational transmission of literacy. *Review of Educational Research, 65*(1), 1–21

Cairney, T. H. (2002). Bridging home and school literacy: In search of transformative approaches to curriculum. *Early Child Development and Care, 172*, 153–172.

Clandinin, Jean D., and Connelly, F. M. (1994*). Handbook of qualitative research*. London: Sage.

Dewey, J. (1916). *Democracy and education*. New York: Macmillan.

Dewey, J. (1936). *Art as experience*. New York: Capricorn Books.

Dewey, J. (1938). *Experience and education*. New York: Collier Books.

Fox, J., & Rivera-Salgado, G. (Eds.) (2004). *Indigenous Mexican migrants in the United States*. Stanford, CA: Center for Comparative Immigration Studies.

Freire, P. (1998). *Pedagogy of freedom: Ethics, democracy, and civic courage*. New York: Rowman & Littlefield.

Lather, P. (1994). Gender issues in methodology: Data analysis in the crisis of representation. Unpublished paper. New Orleans, LA: AERA National Conference.

Makin, L. (2003). Creating Positive Literacy Learning Environments in Early Childhood. In N. Hall, J. Larson & J. March (Eds.), *Handbook of early childhood literacy*, pp. 327–337. London: Sage.

Moll, L. C., Gonzalez, N., & Amanti, C. (2005). *Funds of knowledge: Theorizing practices in households, communities, and classrooms*. Mahwah, NJ: Lawrence Erlbaum.

Mosley, W. (2006). *Life out of context*. New York: Nation Books.

Rummel, M. K., & Quintero, E. P. (1997). *Teachers' reading/teachers' lives*. Albany, NY: SUNY Press.

Schissler, H. (2006). Containing and regulating knowledge or tapping into the human potential? Some thoughts on standards, canonization, and the need to develop a global consciousness. Paper presented at the conference *National History Standards: The Problem of the Canon and the Future of History Teaching*. UCLA-Utrecht Exchange Program at the Netherlands Institute for Teaching and Learning History. Amsterdam, The Netherlands.

Schweinhart, L. J., Barnes, H. V., Weikart, D. P., Barnett, W. S., & Epstein, A. S. (1993). *Significant benefits: The High/Scope Perry Preschool Study through age 27*. Ypsilanti, MI: High/Scope Press.

Strickland, D. S., & Shanahan, T. (2004, March). What the research says about reading: Laying the groundwork for literacy. *Educational Leadership, 61*(6), 74–77.

West, C. (1990). The new cultural politics of difference. In R. Ferguson, M. Gever, T. T. Minh-ha, & C. West (Eds.), *Out there: Marginalization and contemporary cultures*, 19–38. Boston, MA: MIT Press.

Wright, A. (2005). *The death of Ramón González*. Austin, TX: University of Texas Press.

RETHINKING CHILDHOOD

JOE L. KINCHELOE & GAILE CANNELLA, *General Editors*

A revolution is occurring regarding the study of childhood. Traditional notions of child development are under attack, as are the methods by which children are studied. At the same time, the nature of childhood itself is changing as children gain access to information once reserved for adults only. Technological innovations, media, and electronic information have narrowed the distinction between adults and children, forcing educators to rethink the world of schooling in this new context.

This series of textbooks and monographs encourages scholarship in all of these areas, eliciting critical investigations in developmental psychology, early childhood education, multicultural education, and cultural studies of childhood.

Proposals and manuscripts may be sent to the general editors:

> Joe L. Kincheloe
> c/o Peter Lang Publishing, Inc.
> 29 Broadway, 18th floor
> New York, New York 10006

To order other books in this series, please contact our Customer Service Department at:

> (800) 770-LANG (within the U.S.)
> (212) 647-7706 (outside the U.S.)
> (212) 647-7707 FAX

Or browse online by series at:
> www.peterlang.com